CUMBRIA PAST

CUMBERLAND AND WESTMORLAND ANTIQUARIAN AND ARCHAEOLOGICAL SOCIETY

Founded in 1866, we exist to promote, encourage, foster and co-ordinate the study of archaeology, history, genealogy, customs and traditions of what is now the County of Cumbria - that is, the historic counties of Cumberland and Westmorland, together with Lancashire North of the Sands, and the Sedbergh district of Yorkshire.

Our journal ***Transactions*** is published annually in November, reporting on the latest archaeological and historical research in the county.

Our ***Newsletter*** is published three times a year, containing short articles, reports on the activities of the society, book reviews and news items.

Our website, **www.cumbriapast.com** has all the latest news and events, information about grants and bursaries, and on-line indexes for *Transactions* going back to 1866.

Membership is open to all who share our interest in the history and archaeology of Cumbria. Annual subscription is £21 a year for ordinary members, £25 for families, £6 for associates (in full time education). For further information, and to join on-line, see the membership page on the website, or write to
Dr Bill Shannon, Hon Membership Secretary, 12a Carleton Avenue,

Registered Charity No 227786

The Making of Carlisle
From Romans to Railways

Edited by

Mark Brennand and Keith J. Stringer

CUMBERLAND AND WESTMORLAND
ANTIQUARIAN AND ARCHAEOLOGICAL SOCIETY
2011

Cumberland and Westmorland
Antiquarian and Archaeological Society
Hon. General Editor
Dr Jean Turnbull

The Making of Carlisle
From Romans to Railways

EXTRA SERIES NO. XXXV

ISBN 978 1 873124 50 5

Printed by
Titus Wilson & Son, Kendal
2011

The Cumberland and Westmorland Antiquarian and Archaeological Society gratefully wishes to acknowledge the generous financial support provided by English Heritage towards the publication of this book.

Contents

Preface

On 13 October 2007 a conference was held at Tullie House Museum and Art Gallery to celebrate the heritage of Carlisle. More particularly, the conference provided the opportunity for experts in aspects of the city's archaeology and history to summarise developments in the understanding of its past resulting from intensive programmes of excavation and research over the previous 30 years. Whilst the results of much of this work have been published – for example, in the three volumes about the Millennium Project excavations – the enthusiastic response of the audience at the conference demonstrated that there was a real need for a book that would convey the accounts presented on the day in a more lasting medium.

In keeping with a long standing tradition, it was the Cumberland and Westmorland Antiquarian and Archaeological Society that came forward to take on this task. Some of the contributors to the conference agreed to write chapters, gaps were filled by encouraging others to set finger to key board, and the whole has been effectively pulled together by Mark Brennand and Professor Keith Stringer.

English Heritage has been delighted to provide some advice on the book, and financial assistance with its publication. Through the provision of specialist guidance and financial support, English Heritage has been closely associated with the investigation and analysis of Carlisle's archaeology and history throughout a period which has seen a very significant increase in our understanding of the city. It is thus fitting that English Heritage should offer its support for promoting this knowledge to a wider audience. The results published here speak for themselves, and all that remains for me to do is to invite you to read what is set before you, and to congratulate the CWAAS, the editors and the authors for producing such an excellent book.

Henry Owen-John
English Heritage Planning and Development Director, North West Region

List of Contributors

MARK BRENNAND
Senior Historic Environment Officer, Cumbria County Council

IAN CARUANA
Librarian of the Cumberland and Westmorland Antiquarian and Archaeological Society, and former Assistant Director of the Carlisle Archaeological Unit

FRANK GIECCO
Director, North Pennines Archaeology Ltd

JACQUI HUNTLEY
English Heritage Archaeological Science Adviser for North-East England

CARON NEWMAN
Archaeological Consultant

RACHEL NEWMAN
Senior Executive Officer: Research and Publications, Oxford Archaeology North, and a Vice-President of the Cumberland and Westmorland Antiquarian and Archaeological Society

RICHARD NEWMAN
Environmental Planning Manager, Cumbria County Council, and President of the Cumberland and Westmorland Antiquarian and Archaeological Society

TIM PADLEY
Keeper of Archaeology, Tullie House Museum and Art Gallery, Carlisle

PETER ROBINSON
President of the Cumbrian Railways Association

DAVID SHOTTER
Professor Emeritus, Lancaster University, and a former President of the Cumberland and Westmorland Antiquarian and Archaeological Society

SUE STALLIBRASS
English Heritage Archaeological Science Adviser for North-West England, and Honorary Research Fellow, University of Liverpool

KEITH STRINGER
Professor of Medieval British History, Lancaster University, and a Vice-President of the Cumberland and Westmorland Antiquarian and Archaeological Society

HENRY SUMMERSON
Author of *Medieval Carlisle: The City and the Borders from the Late Eleventh to the Mid-Sixteenth Century* (CWAAS, Extra Series, 25, 1993), and a former Research Editor for the Oxford Dictionary of National Biography

DAVID WESTON
Assistant Librarian of Carlisle Cathedral

JOHN ZANT
Project Officer: Post Excavation, Oxford Archaeology North

List of Figures

Editors' Notes

1. We are most grateful to all those who have kindly supplied figures for reproduction. The following organisations and individuals are owed special thanks: Carlisle City Council (for background detail in 3.1, 4.1, 5.1, 6.1, 7.1, 8.1, 9.1, A.1); Carlisle Library (1.3, 11.3, 11.7, 11.10); Corpus of Anglo-Saxon Stone Sculpture (5.8); Cumbria County Council (6.2); Cumbrian Railways Association Photo Library (11.11); Dean and Chapter of Carlisle Cathedral (7.3); North Pennines Archaeology Ltd (5.4, 8.4, 8.8–11); Ordnance Survey (1.5); Oxford Archaeology Ltd (2.1, 3.1–2, 3.4, 3.8, 3.10–11); The British Library Board (6.4, 8.7, 9.2); Timescape Surveys (4.2); Tullie House Museum and Art Gallery, Carlisle (front cover, 1.6–8, 3.3, 3.5–7, 3.9, 3.12, 4.4–6, 4.8–9, 4.11–13, 5.2–3, 5.5–7, 5.9–12, 6.6, 7.6–7, 7.9, 8.2, 8.5–6, 9.10, 11.1–2, 11.4); University of Manchester (4.9); University of Newcastle upon Tyne (4.7); Vindolanda Trust (4.3); James Armstrong (7.3); Robert Bewley (2.5); Peter Clack (1.5); Ben Edwards (4.10); Tim Gates (2.4); Robert Hogg (1.4); and Matthew Town (8.3). In addition, particular thanks are due to Carolyne Baines at Carlisle cathedral, Melanie Gardner at Tullie House and English Heritage staff at Carlisle castle for their assistance in obtaining images.

2. A short guide to suggested further reading is provided at the end of each chapter, and the following abbreviations are used:

   CWAAS Cumberland and Westmorland Antiquarian and Archaeological Society

   CW, 1, 2, 3 The Society's *Transactions*, Old, New and Third Series

Introduction

Mark Brennand and Keith Stringer

The city of Carlisle is located between the marshes at the head of the Solway Firth and the east–west corridor known as the Tyne Gap, and between the northern fringes of the Lakeland Massif and the Southern Uplands of Scotland. The city's historic nucleus occupies a gently rising promontory, defined on the north side by the River Eden and, on the west and east, by its tributaries the Caldew and the Petteril. As the subtitle of this book may serve to indicate, Carlisle's long history of some 2,000 years has seen many vicissitudes. By the same token, its development has experienced several formative eras, thanks especially to the colonising power of the Romans and then the Normans, the needs of national defence against the Scots during the later Middle Ages, and the remarkable Victorian transformation of the city.

Nevertheless, for all the changes over time, there are major themes of continuity. Not least, Carlisle has had a more or less continuous history as an important seat of regional administration, due partly to its remoteness from the main bases of governance in south-east England, for it lies about 313 miles (504km) by road from London. It thus played a focal role in the consolidation and expansion of Roman rule in the North, and it has served as a county town since the appointment of the first Norman sheriff of Cumberland around 1130. It was likewise the northernmost English cathedral city from 1133 until the bishopric of Newcastle upon Tyne was founded as late as 1882.

Yet, first and foremost, Carlisle's history was shaped by its status as a major fortress. As vital as Carlisle was in this respect to both the Romans and the Normans, its military significance was greatly enhanced by the protracted Anglo-Scottish hostilities from 1296 onwards, when it not only acted as the main bastion of the English Marches against the Scots, but often carried the war to them. After the Union of the Crowns of England and Scotland in 1603, Carlisle's military importance naturally declined, and it began to evolve in ways more akin to the pattern of development of most other centres of county and diocesan administration in England. It was sufficiently confident to petition (albeit unsuccessfully) for its own university in 1617; and, at least in the eighteenth century, there was significant suburban expansion outside the city walls. Yet Carlisle remained an important military depot, and it might still be called on to take an active fighting role. Most famously, during the

Jacobite Rebellion in 1745 it witnessed the last siege on English soil; and while the duke of Cumberland, in a show of bravado, likened the castle to 'an old hen-coop', he had to deploy 5,000 troops against it, and the castle and city capitulated only after a sustained two-day bombardment.

Such continuities owed much to the special nature of Carlisle's geopolitical setting. It lies close to the central point of the historic British Isles. This meant that its development and identity were routinely affected, politically and otherwise, by its proximity to the 'outer zones' of these islands. It does not surprise, for example, that Carlisle and its region continued to be regarded by the kings of Scots as rightfully part of their kingdom until such claims were abandoned by treaty in 1237. Nor is it any coincidence that the city's three medieval gates of Botchergate, Caldewgate and Rickergate continue to be known by their alternative names of English Gate, Irish Gate and Scotch Gate, respectively. Furthermore, major routeways converged on these gates from Shap, Stainmore and the Eden valley, from the Cumbrian coast and the Tyne Gap, and from Galloway and Annandale.

Carlisle was therefore a communications nerve-centre of the first order, and whoever controlled the town was also in a position to dominate a large tract of the North. More particularly, the implications of Carlisle's closeness to Scotland, only eight miles (12.9km) distant, can scarcely be exaggerated; for it was this factor – coupled with the ability to command the southernmost route of cross-Border traffic – that above all gave the city much of its distinctive status. As the English government put it in 1217, Carlisle was 'on the Border of Scotland' and basic to maintaining 'the king's peace and that of his kingdom'. These words were echoed by Daniel Defoe, writing almost exactly 500 years later, when he stated that Carlisle, being 'on the edge of Scotland, is the frontier place and key of England on the west sea, as Berwick upon Tweed is on the east'. Such observations are another way of saying that Carlisle's character was deeply influenced by its role as *the* Border city. And, moreover, the circumstances that made Carlisle a great fortress town also help to explain why it ultimately grew into a fully-fledged modern conurbation.

Thus Carlisle was already a major railway centre by the 1870s, and the coming of the railways was as great an event in its history as the arrival of the Romans or the Normans had been centuries before. Largely as a result, Carlisle's industrial base rapidly expanded, and it now offered market and service facilities to a more extensive hinterland. Its population also mushroomed, and it was characterised by contemporary observers as 'a city of considerable extent' and a 'thriving modern town'. While Carlisle never became a great metropolis to rival Newcastle or Glasgow, in the 1960s it was still a lively industrial centre, whose prosperity rested squarely on its nineteenth-century mainstays of textile-manufacture, food-processing, box-manufacture and engineering. And yet this experience of 'urban revolution' was based firmly on, and indeed reinforced, the city's traditional role as a major communications hub and gateway. Equally, there was a clear continuum from one age to another because the same strategic considerations that had once made Carlisle so vital to ancient colonisers – or former enemies – also attracted the Victorian railway entrepreneurs, who were themselves something of a colonising force in their own rights.

Nowadays Carlisle has lost much of its industrial vigour, but in important respects it remains true to its old-established role as the custodian of the western Borders. As an administrative headquarters, for instance, its authority was greatly increased by the creation in 1974 of the new county of Cumbria, currently the third largest territorial unit in English regional governance. It continues to function as a primary transport node, and it maintains its historic associations with south-west Scotland, so that for many Scots it exercises a stronger pull as a business and market centre than that of Glasgow or Edinburgh.

The modern cityscape also resonates with continuities. As was well said around 1870, Carlisle combined 'modern elegance with remains of antiquity', and it still reflects its historical origins to a greater extent than can be seen in many other urban centres. True, the physical integrity of the castle–town nucleus was undermined by the construction of Castle Way (a dual carriageway) in 1971. But, crucially, the railways skirted the castle and the old walled town, and in essence the layout of the core of the present city is largely determined by the main features of the layout of the medieval city. Moreover, while the castle and the cathedral remain the most imposing features today, there is all told an exciting variety of surviving local sites from which a remarkably full picture can be drawn of the fortunes of Carlisle and its inhabitants from the earliest times to the Victorian era and beyond.

It is partly for this reason that over the last few decades Carlisle has received increasing attention from archaeologists and historians alike, and it therefore seems timely to provide convenient access to their chief findings. More specifically, the idea for the present book emerged out of a conference on the archaeology and history of Carlisle, which was held in the city in October 2007 under the joint sponsorship of the Cumberland and Westmorland Antiquarian and Archaeological Society and English Heritage. It is also a pleasure to acknowledge that cooperation between these two bodies continued during the preparation of this volume, and that its publication has been facilitated by a generous award from English Heritage. The contributors to both the conference and the book were asked to reflect on the evolution of the city in the light of their own expertise in particular periods and fields. It was not the aim to produce a comprehensive narrative account of the dynamics of the city's development; yet, taken together, the chapters that follow not only set out the main results of recent research, but also span the whole spectrum of the city's experiences. Accordingly, and above all else, this book hopes to promote better understanding of Carlisle's rich heritage, and thereby to engage the interest of all who wish to learn more about Cumbria's past.

Chapter 1

The Growth of Archaeology in Carlisle

Ian Caruana

In the early twelfth century, the chronicler William of Malmesbury recorded a Roman inscription from the town reading MARII ET VICTORIAE. This is the first record of an archaeological observation in Carlisle. It is likely (but not provable) that what William saw was the Roman altar built into the gateway of the castle and used as a lintel above an internal doorway (Figure 1.1). This altar was discovered when the castle fabric was being recorded in 1987.

Figure 1.1. The Roman altar found in Carlisle castle in 1987; the fourth and fifth lines have dedications to Mars and the Victories (*photograph: author*)

The Antiquarians

For most ancient settlements, recognition of the importance of their antiquities begins with the work of the Tudor antiquarians John Leland and William Camden, and then bore fruit in major county histories at the end of the eighteenth century. This pattern is familiar in the Carlisle region because Hadrian's Wall and the existence of Roman inscriptions and sculpture attracted particular attention. However, Leland never visited Carlisle. Camden recognised the antiquity of the city based upon 'divers tokens of antiquity now and then digged up'. William of Malmesbury's reference is discussed by Camden, yet he has details of only two inscriptions in the gardens of Thomas Aglionby and Thomas Middleton, neither actually from Carlisle but 'imports' from Hadrian's Wall. Aglionby's inscription was a tombstone, later built into Drawdykes Castle at the time of Thackeray's rebuilding around 1678. The second is now lost.

For Carlisle, unlike Maryport or Birdoswald, antiquarian observations were very patchy. Although Roman remains were visible within the medieval town as late as the twelfth century, they had almost certainly disappeared by the sixteenth century. As late as 1746 the city walls, which judged by engravings were never spectacular, still served their defensive function but thereafter rapidly became a nuisance. The major monuments of antiquity were the cathedral, the castle and the citadel. What was so for the antiquarians was equally true for the ordinary visitor. Celia Fiennes in 1698 saw the walls and city gates ('in very good repaire'), the castle, the cathedral ('stately but nothing Curious'), and the town hall and cross, but was not much impressed by the few houses of quality or by her expensive lodgings. Daniel Defoe in 1726 wrote more favourably of the city, which was 'strong but small, the buildings old, but the streets fair', yet beyond a mention of the walls, castle, citadel and 'great church', it had nothing to excite the antiquarian.

Apart from William of Malmesbury's observation, the only Roman inscription recorded from Carlisle before 1787 is a now lost altar to Belatucadrus found before 1671. John Horsley, the best of the early antiquaries, although he recognised Carlisle's antiquity, barely mentions it, and then primarily in relation to the Roman road maps which were one of his major sources. Horsley states that Carlisle had produced two or three inscriptions, but these included those stones brought into the city from sites on Hadrian's Wall. While it is frustrating that so little is recorded from this time, the record of these 'imports' does at least demonstrate that there were observers who would have recognised antiquities had they been uncovered in the city.

Local Initiative and the County Society

By the end of the eighteenth century, economic changes in Carlisle were beginning to have an impact on the city in a variety of ways. The most important of these changes was the growth of the textile industry. Most of this was outside the old city, with the mills being situated mainly along the River Caldew or even farther away. These had little direct impact on areas of archaeological significance but they did alter the demand for housing. Although the new worker housing was often in the vicinity of the factories, pressure also built up for cheap housing within the walled city as prosperity expanded the range of services provided and of jobs created. Growing wealth in the city also encouraged the modernisation of older buildings, particularly on the main streets.

At the earliest stages of this process, the only measure of the impact on the archaeology is from the record of finds of inscriptions and stone sculpture. In 1787 work on the cellar of the Grapes Inn in Scotch Street led to the discovery of two altars and a statue of a mother-goddess. At a similar date a statue of the *genii cucullati* ('hooded spirits') was uncovered in the castle and a small dedication stone was built into a house in Castle Street. The next phase of recovery of Roman stones began in 1828 with the discovery of a Roman tombstone below West Walls and of other funerary remains, including a Corinthian capital, uncovered when the road through Gallows Hill was improved in 1830. A statue of Hercules was found when the News Room on the site now occupied by the Cumberland Building Society in English Street was built in 1830.

Archaeology occurs only when a proper record is made of observations and the discoveries of artefacts. In the eighteenth century, local finds were occasionally reported in the *Gentleman's Magazine* and in the scholarly journal *Archaeologia*, published by the Society of Antiquaries of London. The latter reported the altars from the Grapes Inn cellar. From 1774 there was regular local news reporting with the foundation of the *Cumberland Pacquet*, published in Whitehaven, but having a county-wide coverage. More purely Carlisle newspapers came with the creation of the *Carlisle Journal* in 1798 and the *Carlisle Patriot* in 1815. All the newspapers reported archaeological discoveries and the quality of their reporting was excellent. The information recorded in these early newspapers was known and used by Victorian archaeologists, and there is now further scope to exploit their records thanks to the systematic extraction of the archaeological reports by Tom Patten in the 1970s.

Another outlet for the dissemination of archaeological discoveries was William Hutchinson's *History of the County of Cumberland* (1794), which was the first county history to give serious coverage of archaeological finds. Nicholson and Burn's *The History and Antiquities of the Counties of Westmorland and Cumberland* (1777) had been a much more backward-looking work, with its emphasis being on the antiquarian study of family histories. For antiquities, the authors relied on Camden and Horsley and the manuscripts of Thomas Machell and Hugh Todd. Hutchinson, however, made far more use of his contemporaries to give him an up-to-date picture of the state of archaeological discoveries. His draughtsman, James Lowes, produced one plate of antiquities from Carlisle and Stanwix (Figure 1.2). Lowes's drawings have few artistic merits, but they remain a valuable source for modern students.

Throughout the nineteenth century, histories of Carlisle, directories and guidebooks continued to repeat and occasionally augmented the long-known facts. Collectors and antiquaries salvaged finds from construction workers as the city centre was modernised. In 1859, when the Royal Archaeological Institute visited the city, these finds were assembled in a temporary museum of curiosities. The catalogue of this exhibition also gives an important insight into the state of contemporary knowledge of Roman Carlisle. A small museum in Finkle Street became the nucleus of the newly built Tullie House Museum in 1893.

Figure 1.2. James Lowes's drawings of finds from Carlisle and Stanwix in Hutchinson's *History of the County of Cumberland* (1794)

Another significant development for archaeology was the foundation in 1866 of the Cumberland and Westmorland Antiquarian and Archaeological Society, whose *Transactions* provided information on various aspects of the past. In the North-East, the Society of Antiquaries of Newcastle upon Tyne had started a journal, *Archaeologia Aeliana,* as early as 1832 and some Cumbrian reports appear in its early volumes. The CWAAS belonged in the new wave of foundations which saw the creation of an archaeological society in most counties by the end of the nineteenth century.

At first, publication of the *Transactions* (1866–1900) was erratic, but by the 1870s they appeared regularly. The quality of the contents is inconsistent. Some of the material, such as folklore and customs, has fallen out of fashion and receives little coverage nowadays outside specialist journals. Other articles are little more than journalism and today would find their way into local magazines. From 1877 Richard Ferguson (Figure 1.3) produced a steady stream of reports on Carlisle's archaeology, many of which reflect the rebuilding of the city centre, including the laying out of new streets such as Bank Street. However, probably the most important publication from this time was not by Ferguson, but resulted from his encouragement. In 1879 H. U. McKie finally published his description of the observations he had made while supervising the construction of the city's sewers around the middle of the century. McKie's manuscript had been read at the visit of the Archaeological Institute in 1859, but it was Ferguson who arranged its publication. Although Ferguson's own publications dominate the *Transactions* at this period, this paper provides the most useful information to the modern student. McKie adopted a scientific approach and described what he had observed. By contrast, in Ferguson's reports the observations are intertwined with and distorted by dubious interpretations, which have lessened their importance in the longer run.

Figure 1.3. Richard Ferguson (d. 1900), President of the CWAAS, editor of its *Transactions*, and the main recorder of Carlisle's archaeology in the last quarter of the nineteenth century (*by courtesy of Carlisle Library*)

Twentieth-Century Doldrums

After Ferguson's death in 1900, archaeology in Carlisle went into a decline from which it only fitfully began to recover in the 1950s. The most immediate reason was the lack of archaeologists of the eminence of Ferguson, who combined academic credentials with eminence in local civic life. At Tullie House Museum, the curator Linnaeus Hope continued to collect and record finds until the mid-1920s, but did little outside his curatorial role, which included publishing catalogues of the archaeological collections, all edited by leading scholars of the day.

Another reason for the lack of interest in the city is that research in the region began to concentrate on other archaeological problems. Foremost of these was working out the definitive history of Hadrian's Wall. Some work had been done in 1886. Within the city, this linked up the known elements in Stanwix with those on Davidson's Bank, roughly behind the modern hospital. Significant progress was made in Willowholme and on Etterby Scaur, and the line was marked by a series of stone pillars which still survive.

The focus on Hadrian's Wall took attention away from Carlisle, but in the 1930s F. G. Simpson and the Cumberland Excavation Committee returned to problems connected with Stanwix. Following up work on the Vallum, traced on Stanwix Bank, and on the fort interior, Simpson and Ian Richmond eventually established the true extent of Stanwix fort, which had hitherto been wrongly located on all maps. Their final campaigns took place in 1939–40, just as the war started, and their work was never fully published.

The lack of focus on the city centre is particularly regrettable in retrospect because many shops were modernised during the 1920s and 1930s without any archaeological recording. For example, we can mention the extensions to Binn's Store (now House of Fraser) in 1924, the Clydesdale Bank in 1927, W. H. Smith in 1928, and Marks & Spencer in 1931. But after the Second World War, Robert Hogg – curator at Tullie House – began to be active in the field as well as at the museum. Hogg had been part of the team working with Simpson and Richmond in the 1930s, and he took into his archaeological work a problem-oriented approach that would have been familiar to his mentors. Hogg's first major paper arose out of discoveries made when the River Eden was dredged in 1951, but he expanded his work to study the whole question of how the Eden was bridged in Roman and later times. His next concern was to learn more about Carlisle's Roman fort, and for this purpose he made use of the museum's gardens, which he excavated over several seasons in the 1950s to uncover a series of levels, the earliest of which he took to be phases of the fort. In this he followed the report of discoveries made when the museum had been extended in 1892; but unfortunately he was misled by the too easy assumption that equated early Roman timber with military work. The same thinking was followed by Simpson, who examined the problem again in 1953 in an area of open ground beneath the demolished nave of the cathedral (Figure 1.4). Hogg also discovered two Roman roads, the position of one of which is laid out in Tullie House gardens, together with a stone-lined tank – interpreted as a shrine, but more likely a simple cistern.

Figure 1.4. F. G. Simpson's trench in the demolished nave of Carlisle cathedral in 1953 (*photograph: Robert Hogg*)

The last major piece of work carried out by Hogg prefigured the rescue activity of later decades. In 1953 Bulloughs store was extended towards St Mary's Gate, and excavations were conducted in advance of the construction. The work was on too small a scale to draw many conclusions about the layout of the city in earlier days, but it established a stratigraphic sequence of activity, which was dated by close examination of both the Roman and the medieval pottery by John Gillam and E. P. Jope. Moreover, the presence of misfired pottery sherds hinted at the presence nearby of medieval pottery kilns.

The Age of Rescue

The 1970s were a period of great expansion in rescue archaeology, but in Carlisle the pace of development was slower than in southern England. Thus city-centre buildings continued to be demolished piecemeal, and new structures erected, without any archaeological intervention. Examples include the site of Tesco's at the corner of Blackfriars Street and Victoria Viaduct, Stocklund House and Rufus House (DHSS) on Castle Street, and the YMCA and the Quaker Meeting House on Fisher Street. On English Street there were, among others, Littlewoods (now part of Marks & Spencer) in 1962, Boots and H. Samuel in 1965, Halfords (now Clinton Cards) in 1969, and Hepworths (now River Island and Millets) in 1974.

The construction of the Inner Ring Road (Castle Way) in 1971 cut a great slice through the space between the medieval castle and town, more or less following the ditch that had protected the castle garrison from an urban population of uncertain temperament. The road also crossed the medieval city walls on the west and east sides. Virtually no archaeological work was done in relation to this destruction, although Dorothy Charlesworth dug trenches east of Castle Green, which exposed the north edge of the ditch and some stone buildings. She thought that these buildings were Tudor in date, but they were probably fragments of the later Roman granaries within the fort. Unfortunately this work remains unpublished. Charlesworth did publish her observations in West Tower Street, which was widened at the same time to facilitate access to the new road system, and these established that the medieval city wall survived well below ground level and did not appear to have a Roman predecessor.

A few threatened city-centre sites were 'rescued' during the 1970s, notably the first phase of the Cumberland Building Society's premises on Castle Street excavated by David Neal, and the Vasey's site (formerly the old Blue Bell Inn whose façade was retained) on Scotch Street dug by Tom Clare. Manuscript reports exist for both these excavations, but they likewise remain unpublished.

Preliminary work also began in the Lanes, which figured prominently in 'modernising' the centre of Carlisle. The story of the planning battles surrounding the redevelopment, which go back to 1952, has been told in Mary Scott-Parker's *Memories of The Lanes* (2006). By the 1970s, the Lanes was blighted and some rebuilding was inevitable. In 1975 Paul Gosling, in Keays Lane, and Peter Clack, in Grapes Lane, did some trial excavations which uncovered elements of the medieval city. More importantly, Clack and Gosling were co-editors of *Archaeology in the North* (1976). The book gave a stark assessment of the threats to the surviving archaeology of Carlisle (Figure 1.5), and its publication not only alerted the city planners to the threats to the city's history, but prepared the way for the creation of the city's own archaeology unit.

The one bright spot in all the gloom was the presence of Dorothy Charlesworth, whose own work from 1973 to 1979 highlighted the potential of the archaeology of Roman Carlisle. She was an Inspector of Ancient Monuments for the Department of the Environment with responsibility for northern England. Although based in London, she also had a house in Cumbria and was President of the CWAAS. Her academic specialism was Roman glass, but she also had a strong interest in the Roman frontier. Following the destruction to Annetwell Street consequent on the building of Castle Way, the county Library service began explore the possibilities of expansion into the derelict land created to the north of its existing Tullie House site. In the event, the Library service found other premises and the

Figure 1.5. Map of Carlisle from Clack and Gosling's *Archaeology in the North* showing the extent of post-war demolition (in black) and areas under threat of potential damage in 1976 (in red) (*by courtesy of Peter Clack and reproduced by permission of Ordnance Survey on behalf of HMSO.*

land was ultimately used for BBC Radio Cumbria and for the expansion of Tullie House Museum.

In 1973 Charlesworth opened up a trench on the site of what is now the Radio Cumbria car park, and immediately exposed a first-century Roman turf-and-timber rampart. The excavations also revealed the exceptional preservation of organic remains such as wood and leather (Figure 1.6). Archaeological remains in this part of Annetwell Street had been truncated leaving little more than the primary fort remnants to be excavated. Nonetheless, the exposure of the Flavian rampart created something of a mystery. At the time, the conventional wisdom about Carlisle was that the Roman fort extended south from Tullie House and lay under the cathedral close. With hindsight, it is clear that the evidence for this belief was never very strong. Charlesworth continued to return annually to the site for short seasons moving eastwards from her 1973 trench. In 1978 she published a review of the archaeology of Roman Carlisle in the *Archaeological Journal* – a paper which forms the basis of all recent excavations in the city centre. It was not until 1979, in her final season at Annetwell Street, that the problem of the orientation of the Roman fort was resolved. A Roman gate was then partly exposed (Figure 3.3), and it was clear that the gate was facing south and that the rampart was the southern defence of a fort which extended northwards under the castle. The results were communicated to the Congress of Roman Frontier Studies in Stirling (1979), but it was also clear that the complexities of excavating such a site were too great for an Inspector with full-time professional responsibilities.

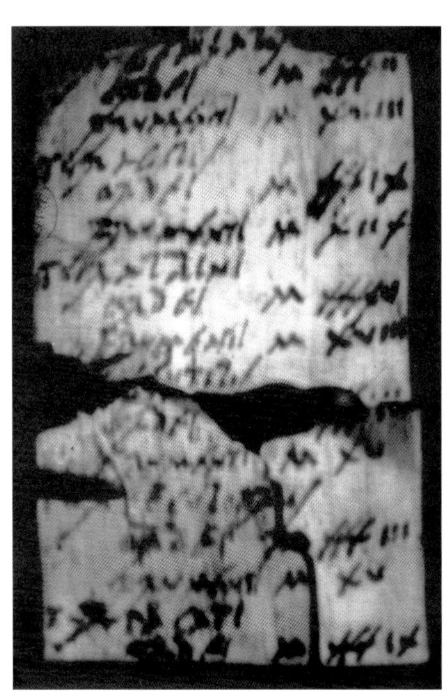

Figure 1.6. Writing-tablet from the Roman fort at Annetwell Street listing barley and wheat allocated to each troop of a cavalry regiment stationed there (*by courtesy of Tullie House Museum and Art Gallery, Carlisle*)

The Carlisle Archaeological Unit

In many ways, despite the threats posed by developments both large and small, the late 1970s were a period of great optimism for English archaeology. In her role as an Inspector for northern England, Dorothy Charlesworth responded by promoting local archaeological units with fixed bases and a remit dedicated to the rescue of sites within their own localities. These came to comprise the North-East Archaeological Unit, based in Newcastle University, the Cumbria and Lancashire Archaeological Unit, based in Lancaster University, and urban units in Newcastle and Carlisle, based within local authorities. Such units had advantages for archaeology in supporting stable work forces able to accumulate local knowledge and expertise. They were also capable of reacting quickly to local threats, and provided a watch on long-running projects that did not otherwise attract funding.

The Carlisle Archaeological Unit came into being to excavate in advance of the proposed Marks & Spencer's Food Hall, on Blackfriars Street, in 1977–8. The site was a classic example of urban archaeology with a deeply stratified sequence of Roman and medieval remains. There was comparatively little organic preservation, but in addition to the expected Roman and medieval structures there were bonuses. Below the Roman buildings was the first sign of prehistoric occupation in the form of ard-cultivation. Much more significant was the fact that careful excavation on a large open area was able to establish a stratigraphic sequence of occupation that went beyond the late Roman levels, as defined by artefacts such as coins, into the post-Roman and the Anglian periods. The discoveries made alerted archaeologists to the possibilities for new findings at this late Roman-early medieval interface. No other site in Carlisle has subsequently produced such significant results from the earliest post-Roman centuries, but Anglian coin finds are now commonplace in the city.

The work at Blackfriars Street was followed almost immediately by the first stages of work in the Lanes. Large open areas in Keays and Lawes Lanes were excavated from 1978 onwards. The potential of this area had already been shown by Paul Gosling's trial excavation in 1975, already mentioned. As the Lanes project developed, it became apparent that total excavation of the whole threatened area was not feasible. It was also apparent that the potential for all parts of the site was not the same. The Roman town was not as extensive as the walled medieval town, and the most valuable results came from the half of the site that lay behind the Scotch Street frontage. One of the fundamental aims of the project was to investigate the origins of the lanes, but it proved difficult to link any lane to a burgage on the Scotch Street frontage because of the extent of cellaring. Only one frontage, on Lewthwaite's Lane, was excavated. Efforts in the southern lanes were concentrated on an area where a major road from the east was seen to enter the Roman town (Grapes Lane). Elsewhere the cellars that had prevented investigation of the medieval town houses were exploited to give quick access to the earliest Roman levels that survived beneath their floors.

Analysis of the surviving buildings was undertaken as part of the overall project and a very extensive architectural survey was carried out by Judith Alfrey, who went on to complete an MA thesis on the domestic architecture of the Lanes. The drawings from the survey are now deposited in Tullie House Museum and Art Gallery. A copy of Alfrey's thesis is in the Cumbria Record Office (Carlisle), and an abbreviated synthesis of her research was published in Scott-Parker's book.

At the height of work on the Lanes, two other major projects came to fruition. Dorothy Charlesworth handed over to the Archaeological Unit responsibility for the completion of the Annetwell Street site. Under the direction of the author in 1981–4, the chronological complexity of Carlisle's Roman military past was finally exposed (Figure 1.7). At roughly the same time, demolition of two small properties on Castle Street, on land to the south of the fort, gave another opportunity for intensive archaeological excavation. Despite the restricted nature of this site, the richness of the surviving organic materials revealed much about activity within what is thought to have been an annexe to the fort proper.

Figure 1.7. The site of the Roman fort at Annetwell Street under open-area excavation in the 1980s (*by courtesy of Tullie House Museum and Art Gallery, Carlisle*)

The Age of Competition

Until the 1990s, the Carlisle Archaeological Unit monopolised work in the city. Recent changes have had much to do with archaeological politics, both nationally and locally, which are beyond the scope of this chapter. Two points

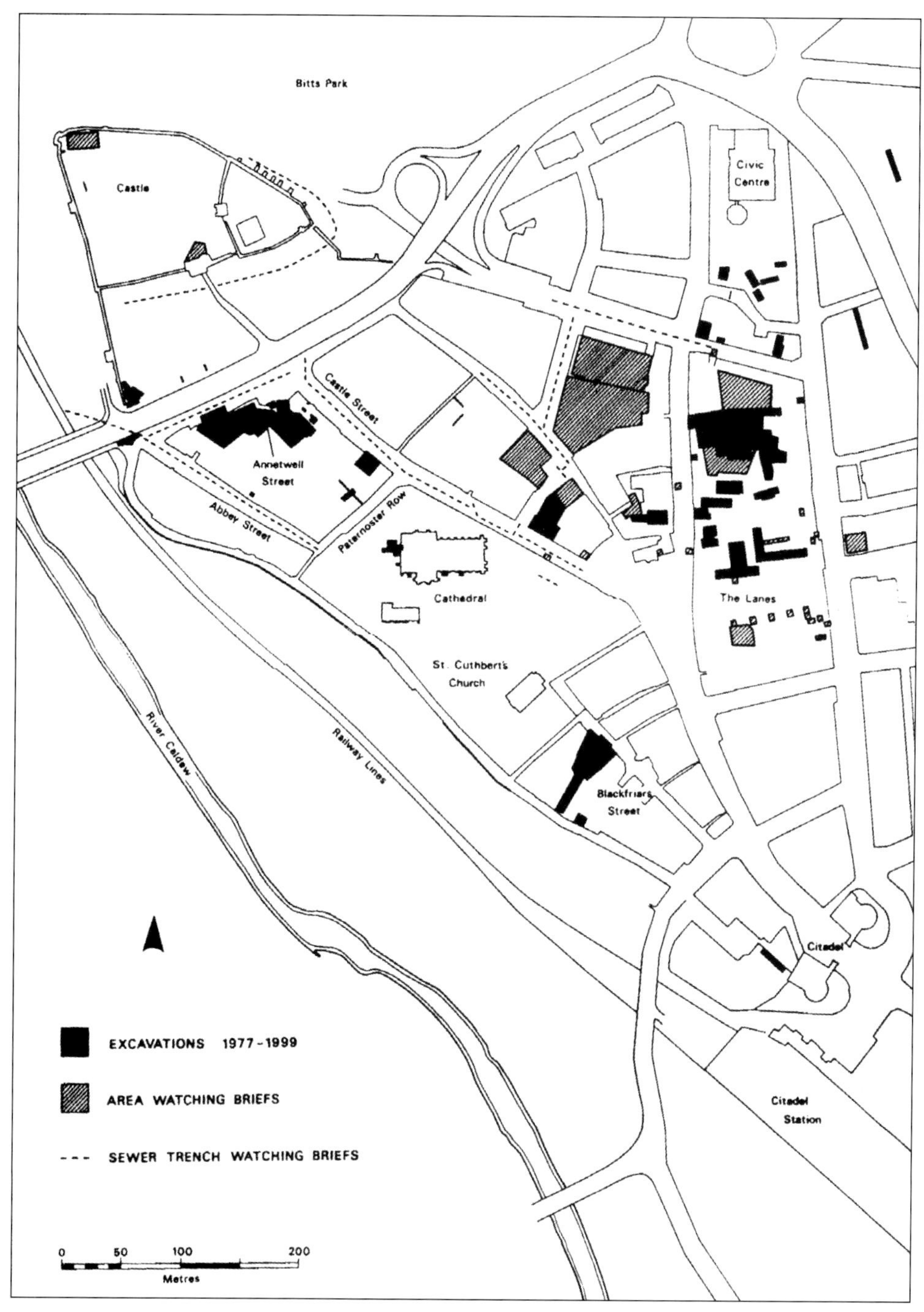

Figure 1.8. Map of Carlisle showing the extent of archaeological work from 1977 to 1999 *(by courtesy of Tullie House Museum and Art Gallery, Carlisle)*

are, however, relevant. Very large excavations like those at Annetwell Street and the Lanes have ceased to happen, although investigation of medium-sized sites, such as the Millennium sites in the late 1990s and work in the Roman cemeteries alongside Botchergate, continue to occur. As work in the city centre has diminished, attention has been devoted to a wider range of sites, including post-medieval industrial sites. Examples include the medieval St Nicholas hospital site which revealed an unknown Roman cemetery, a Romano-British farmstead discovered behind the Infirmary when suspected Civil War earthworks were investigated, and the mill at Harraby Green. The second point of note is that work is now won through competitive tendering, and a wide variety of organisations are thus conducting excavations within the city. The Carlisle Unit was disbanded in 2001. Some of the archaeological contractors who stepped into the vacuum have considerable local knowledge, but others have much more limited experience of the city and its archaeology.

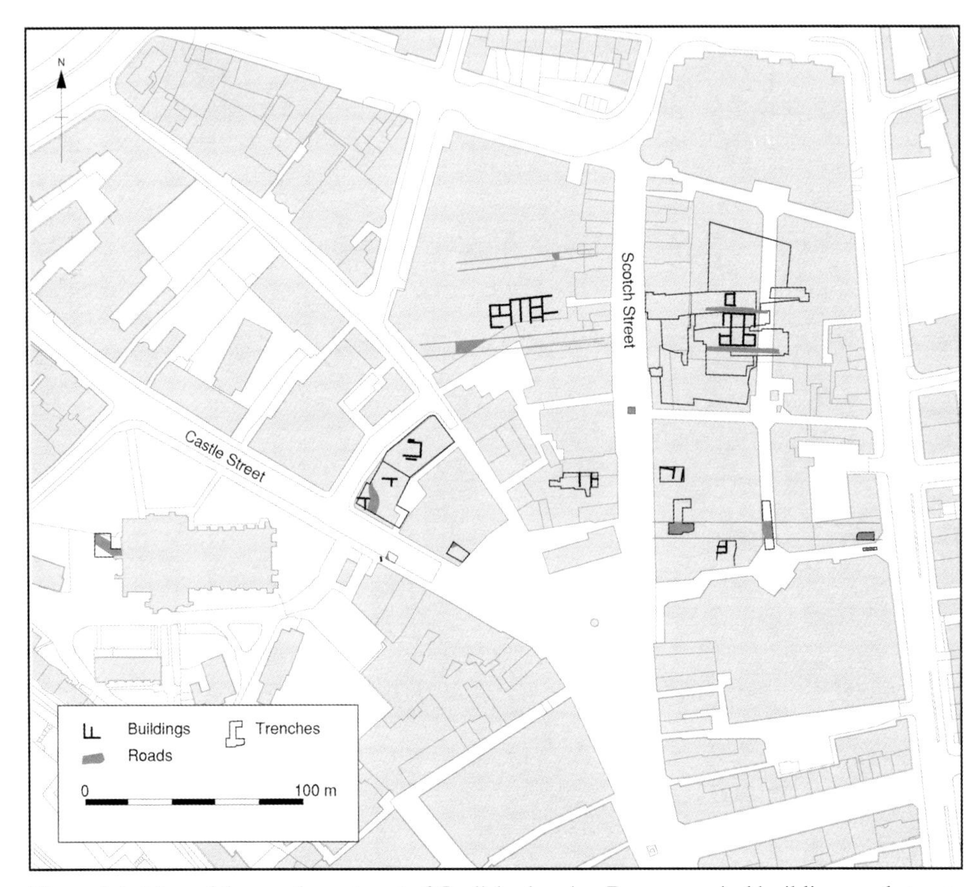

Figure 1.9. Map of the north-east part of Carlisle showing Roman period buildings and streets recorded by excavation since 1977

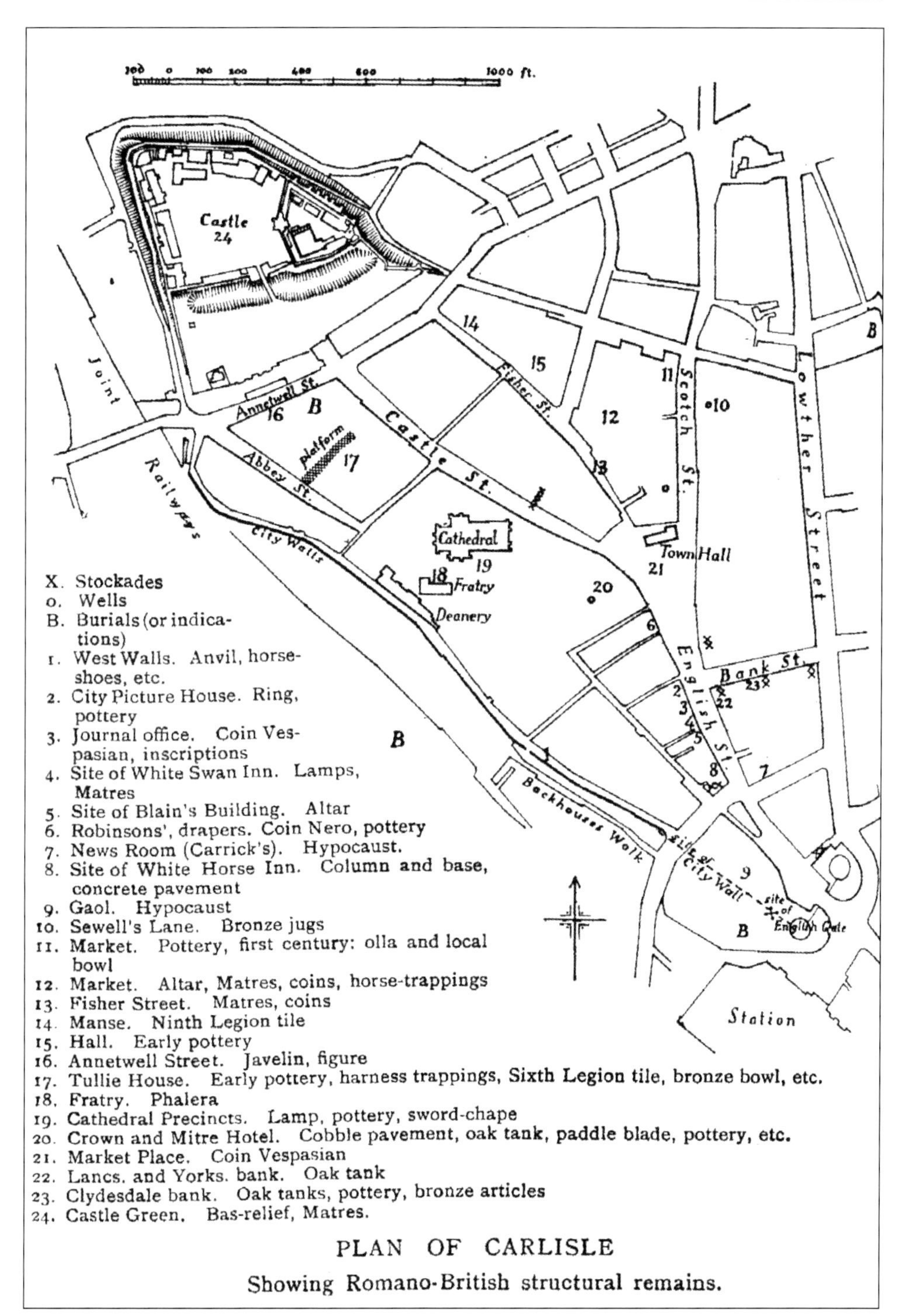

Figure 1.10. R. Cunliffe Shaw's map showing the extent of knowledge of Roman Carlisle in 1924, based entirely on find spots for artefacts

Conclusion

It is appropriate to conclude with some maps. The first (Figure 1.8) shows the extent of archaeological activity in the city in the period 1977–99. The second (Figure 1.9) is a composite plan of the results of a number of archaeological interventions, which shows how it has been possible to map out one part of the Roman town of *Luguvalium*. By contrast with Ronald Cunliffe Shaw's 1924 plan (Figure 1.10), excavation has given us street and building plans in place of find spots for artefacts. The following chapters expand on these discoveries.

★ ★ ★ ★ ★

Suggested Further Reading

D. Charlesworth, 'Roman Carlisle', *Archaeological Journal*, 135 (1978), pp. 115–37

P. A. Clack and P. F. Gosling (eds), *Archaeology in the North: Report of the Northern Archaeological Survey* (Durham, 1976)

Daniel Defoe, *A Tour through the Whole Island of Great Britain* (Penguin edition, London, 1971)

R. S. Ferguson, 'On a massive timber platform of early date uncovered at Carlisle, and on sundry relics found in connection therewith', *CW1*, 12 (1893), pp. 344–63

R. Hogg, 'Excavations in Carlisle, 1953', *CW2*, 55 (1955), pp. 59–107

R. Hogg, 'The historic crossings of the River Eden at Stanwix, and their associated road systems', *CW2*, 52 (1952), pp. 131–59

W. Hutchinson, *The History of the County of Cumberland* (Carlisle, 1794; reprinted Wakefield, 1974)

S. Jefferson, *The History and Antiquities of Carlisle* (Carlisle, 1838)

B. C. Jones, 'Joseph Nicolson and Richard Burn', in J. Simmons (ed.), *English County Historians* (Wakefield, 1978), pp. 160–86

H. U. McKie, 'Remarks and memoranda as to the subsoil, debris, and ancient remains discovered in cutting the sewers in the city of Carlisle', *CW1*, 4 (1879), pp. 337–43

M. Scott-Parker, *Memories of The Lanes* (Carlisle, 2006)

R. Cunliffe Shaw, 'Romano-British Carlisle: its structural remains', *CW2*, 24 (1924), pp. 95–109

Chapter 2
Carlisle's Early Environment and Setting

Sue Stallibrass and Jacqui Huntley

The Prehistoric Periods

During the last Ice Age, a huge Arctic ice sheet spread over Scotland and northern England, and Carlisle was buried by more than 1,000 metres of ice. After the coldest period about 20,000 years ago, there was a gradual trend towards warmer climate, but the Ice Age had a sting in its tail and there was a sudden cold period when the ice sheets and glaciers grew again and re-advanced across the landscape. Archaeological deposits within sheltered caves in the limestone of southern Cumbria indicate that people were living there in the Late Glacial period (between 12,000 and 10,000 years ago), using stone tools to hunt and butcher elk and reindeer, but we have no finds for this period from the Carlisle area. Here, the low-lying Solway Basin received a rich mixture of sedimentary deposits brought by ice moving across the Southern Uplands and Galloway mountains, the Lake District and the Irish Sea. Additional material was washed in by melt-waters flowing down the valleys, particularly the Eden valley. At times, the Solway was flooded by glacial lakes whose waters were dammed up by the ice sheet that lingered over the Irish Sea. Sudden and rapid warming of the earth's climate around 10,000 years ago finally melted this ice (and other ice sheets around the world) and the sea level rose by about 100 metres, submerging former low-lying coastal areas such as the Solway Firth. On land, the newly exposed surface revealed thick and varied deposits of sediments, which were rapidly colonised by opportunistic plants and insects.

By the Mesolithic period (*c.* 8000–*c.* 4000 BC), most of Cumbria was probably covered with broadleaved woodland inhabited by a range of wild mammals, birds and insects. People moved into the area following these new resources, although we have few archaeological traces of human activity at this time. One of the most recently recorded sites of this period is located at Stainton on the north bank of the River Eden just to the west of Carlisle. Here, thousands of distinctive tiny flint tools known as microliths were recorded on a terrace adjacent to a former channel of the river (which has shifted its channels periodically over the past few thousand years). There were only slight traces of structures and hearths associated with the material, but the flints are likely to represent many visits and camps by hunting and gathering groups, perhaps over many centuries. The tiny flints (Figure 2.1)

Figure 2.1. Mesolithic microlithic flintwork from Stainton (*by courtesy of Oxford Archaeology Ltd*)

would have been hafted in groups on wooden handles to form composite tools such as arrows and harpoons.

Similar assemblages of stone tools have been found at various sites along the Cumbrian coast, as well as in the Eden valley and on the limestone in eastern Cumbria, although in significantly smaller quantities. Much of the raw material for these stone tools came from small pebbles found in the glacial deposits or washed out in river gravels and beach deposits, but there is also evidence of some materials from outside the region, which are likely to have been traded over considerable distances. The waterside location at Stainton not only was adjacent to the onshore woodlands, but also gave access by boat or raft upstream via the River Eden to its tributaries, and downstream to its estuary and the sea. These varied habitats would have provided a rich variety of plants for food, medicines and fuel, as well as fish, birds and mammals for meat, eggs, feathers and skins. The presence of layers of charcoal in the peats of Solway Moss may indicate that Mesolithic people were controlling local vegetation by setting fire to it in small patches. The regenerating vegetation would have been young and lush, and would have tempted many browsing animals such as deer into the new clearings. There, the animals could be seen and hunted more easily than when they were in deep thickets of cover, and the greater levels of daylight would have encouraged young shrubs to produce more berries and nuts.

Cumbria and the lands around the Solway represent one of the best studied areas in Britain for evidence of past changes in climate and vegetation cover. The abundant large bogs and mosses provide excellent preservational conditions for long sequences of peat deposits (Figure 2.2).

The peats contain well-preserved pollen, larger plant remains (such as leaves and seeds), and the remains of micro-organisms – all of which tell us about the past landscape and environment (Figure 2.3). The plant remains not only reveal what trees, shrubs, mosses and flowers were growing in the area, but also provide 'proxy' indications of past climates, as most species have known tolerances and preferences for temperature ranges and rainfall distributions. Insects are also useful as proxy indicators, and even lower organisms such as testate amoebae can be used, as these are very sensitive to changes in surface water conditions.

Within the North of England, extensive wetland sites such as Bolton Fell Moss, Butterburn Flow, Coom Rigg Moss and Deer Dyke Moss have large catchment areas for pollen (some of which is windblown or brought in by streams), and these provide excellent evidence for what was happening at the regional scale. In the prehistoric periods, the numbers of people living in Britain were very low, and they are unlikely to have had major impacts on vegetation and insect populations. If several pollen sites indicate changes at the same time, then it is reasoned that these changes were widespread, and therefore more likely to be due to climate change than to local human

Figure 2.2. Taking a core for analysis of former environments *(photograph: authors)*

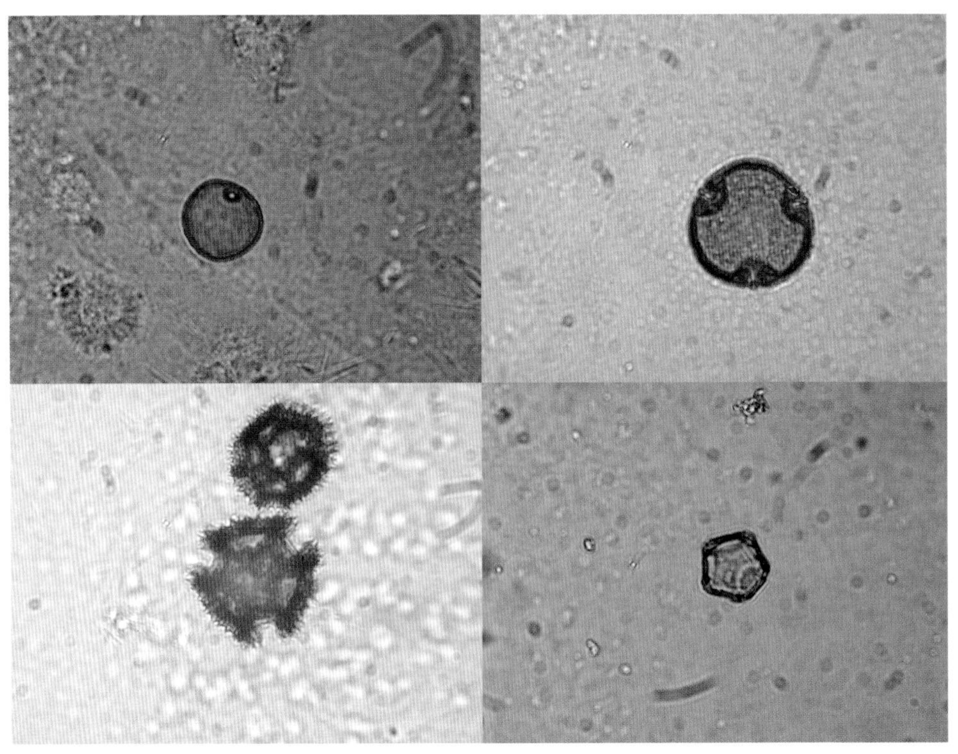

Figure 2.3. Pollen spores of, clockwise from top left, grass, lime, alder and dandelion (*photograph: authors*)

activities. There is evidence for major downturns in climate (known as 'wet shifts') during the later third millennium BC (Late Neolithic/Early Bronze Age) and several times during the mid-to-late first millennium BC (the Iron Age). In contrast, evidence for local human impact on the environment requires samples from sites with much smaller catchment areas, preferably adjacent to archaeological sites. The pollen of cereal crops, for instance, is produced in small quantities and does not travel far, because the plants tend to be self-pollinating. Finding cereal pollen, therefore, can be difficult, particularly if fields were small and located away from damp areas.

We have very little environmental evidence for human activity in Cumbria during the Neolithic Age, Bronze Age and early Iron Age. This is partly due to poor preservation conditions for organic remains away from the very wet areas, and partly due to the paucity of excavation of archaeological sites of these periods. Evidence from adjacent areas suggests that people in the Carlisle area may have become more settled during the Neolithic period (*c.* 4000–*c.* 2000 BC) by clearing areas of woodland to grow domesticated plants including cereals, and tending their livestock. Wild resources, such as hazelnuts, no doubt continued to be exploited. Evidence from the northern banks of the former course of the Eden has revealed Neolithic activity just beyond the modern city. Although there is no evidence of houses or settlement, people were clearly active in the area, leaving behind stone axe-heads, and wooden artefacts that were preserved in waterlogged conditions at the edge of the former river. This site at Stainton is very close to a large circular enclosure visible from the air, under the right conditions, as a cropmark. Although untested by excavation, the size and shape of the enclosure suggest that it was a prehistoric ceremonial centre (Figure 2.4). The styles of burial and ceremonial monuments in North-West England and south-west Scotland share similarities with those in other locations that border the Irish Sea, and it seems clear that maritime travel was important for prehistoric cultures around the Solway Firth.

Figure 2.4. The circular cropmark of a possible Neolithic hengiform monument (centre left) visible in fields near Stainton (© *Tim Gates*)

It is likely that numbers of people inhabiting the region continued to increase during the Bronze Age (*c.* 2000–*c.* 700 BC) and the early to middle Iron Age (*c.* 700–150 BC). Aerial photography surveys have been particularly informative, revealing the presence of hundreds of previously unknown small settlements dispersed throughout the region, with concentrations around the Solway and in the Eden valley (Figure 2.5). Some of the sites were unenclosed whilst others were surrounded by banks, fences or ditches. Since their sizes and shapes remained very similar for much of the Bronze Age and Iron Age, we cannot tell how many were occupied at any one time, how long each one was lived in, or even when they were lived in, except through excavation and the recovery of datable evidence. Few have been excavated, and not all of them produced datable material, although the palisaded enclosures at Scotby Road, Carlisle, and Burgh-by-Sands are both considered to be Iron Age structures.

Figure 2.5. Later prehistoric and Romano-British enclosures at Fingland on the Solway Plain (*photograph: Robert Bewley*)

Some of the enclosed settlements are associated with small field systems, and some of the fields contain cord rig, which has survived in the uplands to the east of Carlisle. This was a method of ploughing the soil up into parallel narrow ridges to maximise soil depth and warmth, whilst facilitating water drainage. It is associated with cereal cultivation and is similar to the more familiar but wider ridge and furrow of the medieval period. In tandem with the greater landscape evidence for later prehistoric settlements and field systems, we also have more evidence for such activities through finds of artefacts and from environmental evidence of land clearance, pasture and agriculture. Crops grown included cereals, particularly barley, found on a Bronze Age site excavated during the construction of the Crosby by-pass, and on the later prehistoric and Roman site at Ewanrigg, near Maryport. Pollen evidence shows that there was a notable increase in the areas of woodland cleared during the later Iron Age, before the Roman army invaded. This phenomenon was probably associated with population increase and the accompanying need to raise more animals and grow more crops.

Further evidence for agriculture can be found underneath the streets of Carlisle itself. Sealed beneath the earliest Roman levels within the city are a series of striated lines within the soil, representing scars from the ground being ploughed. These have been found on several sites throughout Carlisle, buried beneath deposits of the Roman period, even in areas where the ground has clearly been permanently or intermittently damp. The glacial deposits left behind by the melting ice sheet are highly variable, and well-drained sandy clay can change abruptly into sticky clay. Anyone with a garden in Carlisle will probably know exactly which type of land they live on! The plough marks, alongside the preserved plant remains, indicate that the area was used for a mixture of arable farming, pasture and rough ground before the Roman fort and civilian town were constructed, although we cannot tell whether this was immediately prior to the invasion or some years earlier. Insect remains in pre-Roman levels at Old Grapes Lane indicate the presence of refuse and dwellings, but there is a chance that these deposits were trampled downwards into underlying levels during the earliest Roman activities at the site. Despite this slight uncertainty, it is highly likely that people were living in this area before the Roman invasion, although we have not yet found definitive evidence of their houses.

The Setting of the City

The founders of the Roman fort at Carlisle, around which the town developed, chose a defensible location on a tongue of land between the rivers Caldew and Petteril, where they flow into the River Eden (Figure 3.1). It has been suggested that there might have been an Iron Age hillfort at this point, but if this was so, it now lies beneath the medieval castle. The situation is strategic, as it commands the river crossing from relatively high ground, while the north bank is considerably lower and prone to flooding. The siting of the Roman fort had sound military reasoning, but the consequences of the low-lying ground surrounding this point have been a bane to the residents of Carlisle ever since.

Carlisle is currently about eight miles (13km) upstream from the estuary of the Solway Firth. Estuaries are notoriously dynamic, with shifting channels, sand banks and saltmarshes, and we do not know whether or not the River Eden was navigable from the sea right up to Carlisle in the Roman period. Insect remains from Carlisle indicate that conditions were slightly warmer than now (the species found are similar to those living today in Kent) and the sea level was probably slightly higher. But navigability is affected by several other factors including the sediment load and water-flow of the river, as well as the draught of the boats. The main port for the western end of Hadrian's Wall may have been further west along the coast, bringing in troops, food and other commodities from distant parts of Britain and the Empire.

Before the canal to Port Carlisle was dug in the early 1820s, and before the construction of its flood-defence banks, the River Eden could flood the surrounding low-lying land to an even greater extent than it does now. We do not know where the ancient river crossings were located, but the location of the fort and the meeting of two important Roman roads at Carlisle imply that this was a good route through the local mosses to a point where the Eden could be crossed.

Although part of Carlisle's first fort lies on the sloping land that is now the Castle Green, the southerly portion (under Tullie House Museum and Art Gallery and the BBC building on Annetwell Street) reaches lower-lying land which appears to have suffered from dampness. This has been a boon to archaeologists as the soggy or waterlogged conditions have preserved organic remains unusually well, and explain why the important wooden writing-tablets have been preserved (Figure 1.6), besides other items of wood or leather, and the remains of insects and plants. Wild plants tolerant of wet ground such as blinks (*Montia fontana*) and aquatic buttercups (*Ranunculus* subgenus *Batrachium*) commonly occur across the peninsula, indicating damp ground and patches of standing water. This dampness was not so fortunate for the soldiers garrisoned in the south-east barrack blocks, as they probably had to squelch their way between the buildings. In fact, the control of clean water into the fort, and excess water out of it, seems to have been a major preoccupation throughout the fort's history.

Local Resources

Dendrochronology is the science of dating trees through their growth ring patterns, and oak is the most suitable tree for obtaining an indication of climatic conditions, as well as being a very durable and popular timber. With the sole exception of London, Carlisle has the best sequence of dendrochronological dates for the first two centuries AD in the whole of Britain. The earliest Roman fort was built of local timber and turf (Figure 3.2). Several of the oak trees used in this first fort were 350 to 400 years old when they were felled, suggesting the presence of substantial ancient woodlands nearby. The widespread use of alder and ash in the first build probably also indicates the exploitation of resources found in the immediate vicinity, and may have had the added benefit of clear-felling a *cordon sanitaire* around the military installation and river crossing. Alder is very tolerant of wet conditions and is likely to have been growing in large numbers on low-lying land and along the river banks (Figure 2.6). The disadvantage of using alder and ash for construction timber is that they are not very durable and tend to rot at ground level after five to ten years. This is probably why the subsequent builds made greater use of oak timbers.

There was increased felling of woodland within the Carlisle area through the Romano-British period (*c.* AD 70–410), but there is no evidence that the arrival of hundreds of Roman military personnel caused people to dash out and clear the forests. The influx of soldiers and associates certainly would have demanded a major increase in the amounts of cereals required to feed the population, but the jury is still out as to where exactly these cereals were grown. Good quality agricultural land is in short supply locally, and the best is mostly concentrated in the Eden valley, the Solway Plain and the low sandy ridges in western Cumbria. North of the Solway, the best soils are in the Dumfries coastal strip and the Annan valley. Topographically, the lands to the north of the Solway are similar to those towards the south, providing a mosaic of mosses, river valleys, and low-lying, relatively well-drained soils, with the Annan flowing through the centre and acting as a link rather than a barrier.

Figure 2.6. Alder carr woodland resembling that growing in the low-lying ground around Carlisle in the later prehistoric period (*photograph: authors*)

The Early Economy

Many archaeologists believe that by the time the Roman army had pushed northwards into modern-day Cumbria, the Roman authorities were already aware that there was an agricultural system in place that could provide for many of their needs, through taxing the native population. It might be assumed, therefore, that many basic foodstuffs were sourced locally. Nevertheless, Britain was part of an empire that stretched to eastern Europe, North Africa and the Middle East, and it is not always easy to tell where resources and commodities came from.

By the later Iron Age, the local people were growing spelt wheat and hulled six-row barley, and these continued as the main crops throughout the Roman period, with smaller quantities of bread wheat, oats and rye. Although there have been few excavations of rural Iron Age and Roman sites in northern Britain, they tend to produce more grains of barley than of wheat varieties, and the wheat tends to be spelt wheat rather than emmer (which was more common around Rome). The presence of spelt chaff also suggests that this wheat was grown locally, as threshing usually took place before grain was transported or stored. In contrast, grains of bread wheat are scarce at Carlisle and its chaff fragments even scarcer, and this crop may have been imported from outside the region. Some of the wooden writing-tablets found preserved in anaerobic ground conditions at Vindolanda refer to 'native barley' as well as to 'barley', which implies that the military made use of crops grown locally and crops brought in from elsewhere.

Almost all military sites in northern Britain have similarly yielded more barley than wheat remains, whereas Roman writings mention that soldiers were expected to eat wheat, whilst barley was food for their horses. It is still uncertain whether the auxiliary soldiers in northern Britain ate 'punishment rations' of barley, happily ate barley because that was what they were used to in their home countries, ate barley because it was what was available locally, used the barley to make beer, or kept tight control of their wheat but were more likely to be wasteful of their horses' barley.

The commonest animal bones at all the Roman sites in Carlisle, whether civilian, suburban, military or commercial, come from cattle. Livestock in the Iron Age and Roman period were rather smaller than modern breeds, standing to about one metre high at the shoulder, similar to modern Dexters (Figure 2.7). The size, shape and congenital markers of the cattle bones indicate that the civilians and soldiers at Carlisle obtained their cattle from related livestock, which might imply that the cattle were raised locally. It is possible, however, that some of the cattle were driven from distant pastures such as those in south-western Scotland, as was the case in the post-medieval droving system. In addition, the excavations in the fort indicate that 'extra' portions of cured beef were brought in. The evidence

Figure 2.7. A modern Dexter bull, similar in appearance to Iron Age and Romano-British breeds of cattle (*photograph: authors*)

consists of cattle shoulder-blades which were twice as common as any other part of the cow's anatomy. Holes through the blades may indicate where shoulders of meat on the bone were hung up to smoke or dry (Figure 2.8).

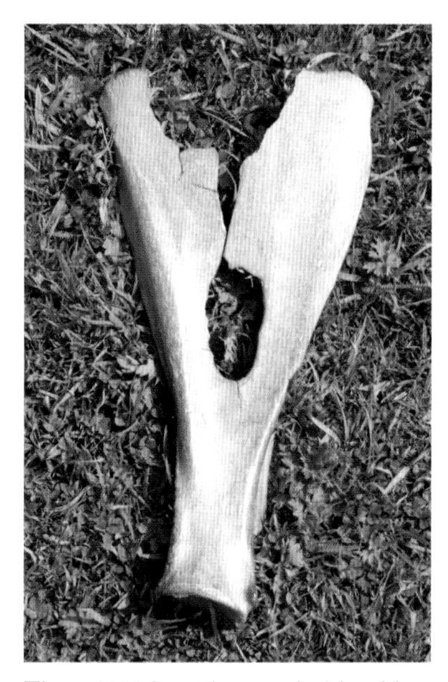

Figure 2.8. A cattle scapula (shoulder-blade) from Roman Carlisle with a hole where the joint may have been hung up to be smoked or cured (*photograph: authors*)

Sheep of the period were also small and light, while domestic pigs looked more like their wild ancestors with shoulders sloping down towards the hindquarters (hogbacks), straight noses and bristly hairs. The age-structure of animals recovered from excavations indicates that pigs and sheep were raised for meat, while the cattle were mostly kept on into relatively old age, which suggests that they were used for other purposes such as breeding stock, traction (for pulling carts and ploughs) and possibly for milk, before they were slaughtered.

Coastal resources appear to have been exploited on a very small scale, despite their presumed availability. There are a few bones from overwintering wildfowl (especially pink-footed geese), migratory fish including salmon and trout, and small inshore flatfish such as flounders and plaice. Shells from marine molluscs such as oysters are surprisingly scarce given that the Solway Firth is so close, and it must be presumed that these foodstuffs were simply not exploited to any significant degree, rather than being unobtainable due to environmental constraints.

The Landscape Legacy

The long, regional pollen sequences from Cumbria's large bogs indicate that there were no sudden changes in large-scale vegetation cover at either end of the Roman period. A tendency towards greater clearance had already begun in the later Iron Age and continued throughout the military occupation and into the post-Roman period, but changes were small scale and localised. There was still a significant amount of woodland in the landscape in the mid-sixth century, when the climate had become slightly cooler and wetter (very similar to how it had been in the Iron Age). Even during the Roman military phases, there had been some smallholdings within the urban area, and in the post-Roman period a soil built up that was well fertilised. It contains some evidence for cereal crops and weeds typical of damp ground, similar to the situation prior to the Roman invasion. It is notoriously difficult to date the development of these urban soils (since cultivation stirs everything up and mixes it all together), but radiocarbon dating shows that some 'fresh' animal bones were being deposited on this fertilised land, which also included materials dug up from the underlying Roman deposits. People must have been living near or in the former town, keeping their livestock there and cultivating the areas once occupied by the Roman military.

At the moment, there is so little environmental evidence for Carlisle between the end of the Roman period and the Norman Conquest (600 years later) that it is very difficult to assess whether or not there were any lasting changes. Many foods consumed by the military were similar or identical to those used by the civilian population, and it seems highly probable that local cereals and livestock provided a significant proportion of the soldiers' diet. There were some novel and non-local foodstuffs imported to Roman Carlisle, indicating a degree of administrative procurement of staples, coupled with the availability of some luxuries or comfort foods for soldiers a long way from home. But there was little lasting legacy in terms of irreversible changes to the vegetation and landscape, either in the region as a whole or at Carlisle itself. Despite the excellent efforts of the Roman military engineers, the problems of water control in Carlisle were never fully solved and continue to provide a challenge nearly 2,000 years later.

★ ★ ★ ★ ★

SUGGESTED FURTHER READING

H. Cool, *Eating and Drinking in Roman Britain* (Cambridge, 2006)

P. Coombes, R. C. Chiverrell and K. E. Barber, 'A high-resolution pollen and geochemical analysis of late Holocene human impact and vegetation history in southern Cumbria, England', *Journal of Quaternary Science*, 24 (2009), pp. 224–36

P. Dark, *The Environment of Britain in the First Millennium AD* (London, 2000)

A. Grant, 'Domestic animals and their uses', in M. Todd (ed.), *A Companion to Roman Britain* (Oxford, 2007), pp. 371–92

J. P. Huntley, 'Late Roman transition in the North: the palynological evidence', in T. Wilmott and P. R. Wilson (eds), *The Late Roman Transition in the North: Papers from the Roman Archaeology Conference, Durham 1999* (Oxford, 2000), pp. 67–72

M. R. McCarthy, *Roman Carlisle and the Lands of the Solway* (Stroud, 2002)

Ordnance Survey, *Map of Roman Britain*, 5th edn (Southampton, 2001)

S. Stallibrass and R. Thomas (eds), *Feeding the Roman Army: The Archaeology of Production and Supply in North-West Europe* (Oxford, 2008)

C. Wells, 'Environmental changes in Roman North-West England: a synoptic view of events north of the Ribble', *CW3*, 3 (2003), pp. 66–84

Chapter 3
The Roman Army in Carlisle

John Zant

For scholars of the Roman army in Britain, Carlisle is of exceptional interest. This is due partly to the strategic importance of the site, which resulted in a long and complex history of military activity, but more especially to the fact that the city has not one but two internationally significant Roman forts within its modern boundaries – that at Carlisle itself, which occupied the prominent bluff dominated today by the medieval castle, and the Hadrian's Wall fort at Stanwix, on the north bank of the River Eden (Figure 3.1). Although situated less than one kilometre apart, the two forts had quite distinct histories, and almost certainly fulfilled different operational roles. Carlisle has seen a considerable amount of modern excavation, albeit largely in the southern part of the fort, and is remarkable for exceptional waterlogged preservation of organic materials in the lower levels, which relate to two superimposed timber forts of the late first to mid-second century AD. Evidence relating to occupation during the second half of the second century, when the military status of the site is unclear, and to the stone fort of the third to fourth century, is also plentiful, although little organic preservation occurs in these levels. By contrast, archaeological work at Stanwix has been piecemeal, and few organic remains have been recovered. The fort is, however, notable for being the largest on Hadrian's Wall, and the base, from the mid-second century AD, of the largest cavalry regiment in Roman Britain.

The First Fort at Carlisle (*Luguvalium*)

At the time of the Roman invasion of southern Britain in AD 43, the North-West probably lay within the tribal territory of the Brigantes, whose queen, Cartimandua, seems to have entered into a treaty with Rome. Northern Cumbria may have been home to the Carvetii, a people who are generally regarded as a sub-group of the Brigantes. Friendly relations between Cartimandua and Rome would probably have kept the region free from military occupation for a generation, although the Roman historian Tacitus implies that factional tensions within the tribe may have necessitated military intervention on one or more occasions.

According to Tacitus, the *status quo* was shattered in or about AD 69, when the Roman world was plunged into civil war following the death of

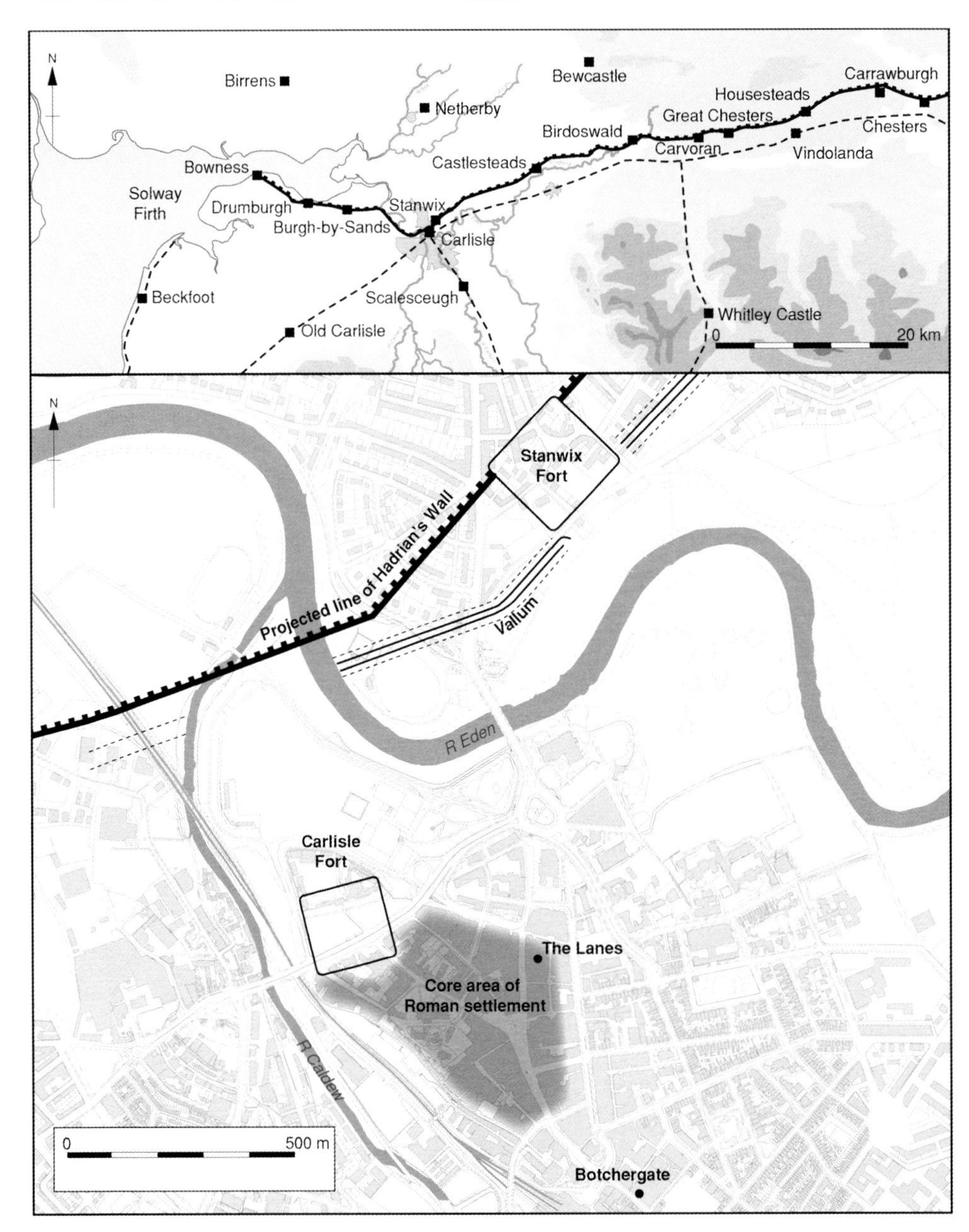

Figure 3.1. Map of Roman Carlisle and its position on the northern frontier (*by courtesy of Oxford Archaeology Ltd*)

the emperor Nero. The army in Britain, distracted and probably weakened by troop withdrawals, was taken by surprise when Cartimandua's former consort Venutius, who was by this time actively hostile towards Rome, took advantage of the situation to oust the queen, who had to be rescued by

Roman troops. In the war which followed, Venutius was eventually defeated and the whole region was occupied. It was towards the end of this period, as the Roman army consolidated its position, that the first permanent fort was established at Carlisle (Figure 3.2), as part of an extensive network of forts and roads designed to hold down the newly conquered territories.

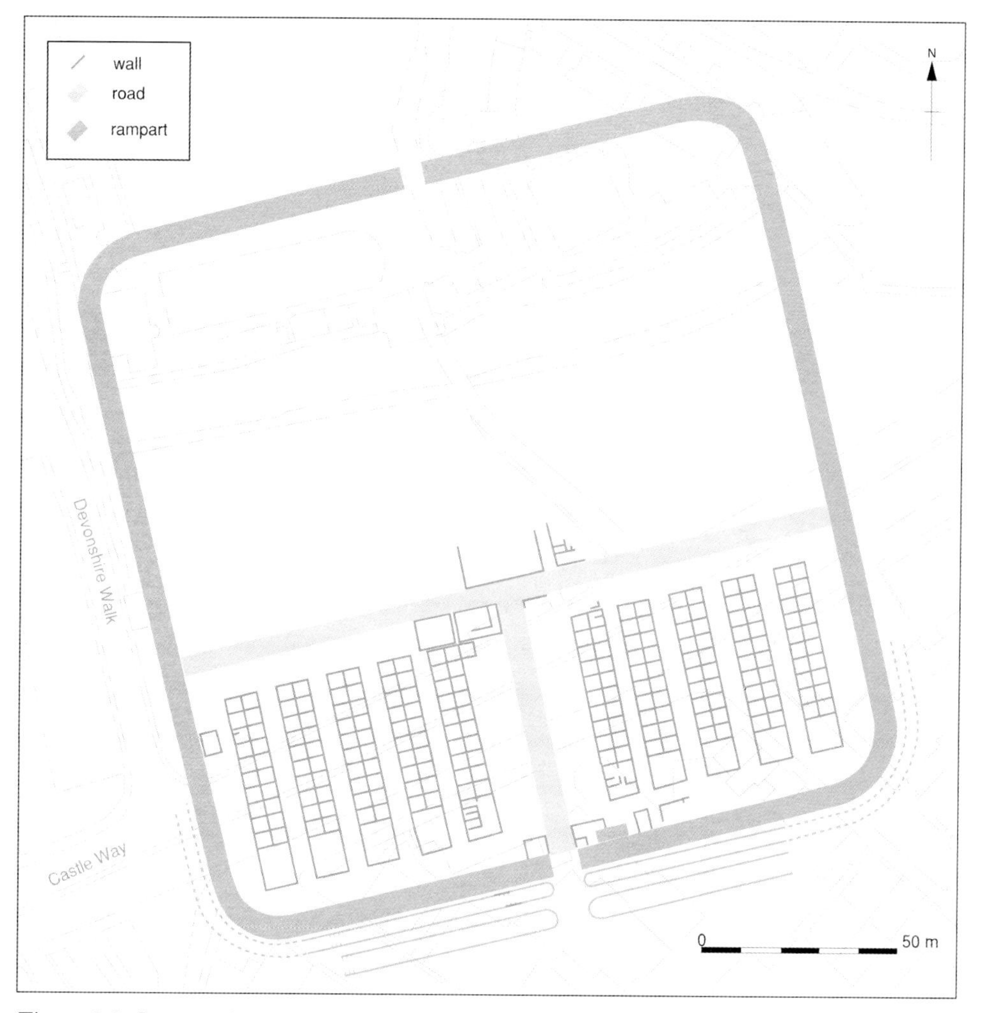

Figure 3.2. Suggested reconstruction of the first fort at Carlisle, built AD 72–3 (*by courtesy of Oxford Archaeology Ltd*)

Tree-ring dating of timbers built into the south rampart indicates that the fort was founded in the autumn or winter of AD 72–3. Some care seems to have been taken to secure oak for the defences, but the internal buildings incorporated a lot of alder and some ash. Since this is likely to have rotted quickly at ground level, it may indicate either that Carlisle was viewed as a comparatively temporary installation, to be given up when the conquest of the whole island was completed (as seems to have been the strategic goal during this period), or that the fort builders were more concerned with the rapid construction of winter quarters, using any timber that came readily to hand, than with the long-term structural integrity of the buildings.

The fort was almost certainly 600 Roman feet (*c.* 178m) square, covering an area of approximately 3.2 hectares (7.9 acres). Its defensive perimeter comprised an earth-and-timber rampart fronted, on the south at least, by a pair of ditches. The south rampart and south gate (Figure 3.3) are situated south of Annetwell Street, whilst the west rampart lies beneath the medieval city wall on the western edge of the grassed area in front of the castle. The north and east ramparts have never been seen, but their likely positions can be estimated. The main road south followed the line of Blackfriars Street and Botchergate (Figure 3.1), and a defended annexe may have existed on this side.

Figure 3.3. The timber threshold of the south gate of the first fort at Carlisle (*by courtesy of Tullie House Museum and Art Gallery, Carlisle*)

In the autumn/winter of AD 83–4, the interior of the fort was reconstructed. The defences do not seem to have been altered, but the putative annexe may have been enlarged and new buildings were constructed within it. In contrast to the original structures, all the new fort buildings were constructed of good-quality oak. The use of this very durable material might have been due to a change in the perceived function of the fort, from (perhaps) a comparatively temporary installation to a base with a long-term role in the military dispositions of the region. Conversely, rebuilding may have occurred for very practical reasons, since the employment of inferior timber 11 years earlier may have meant that the original buildings were now structurally unsound. With the exception of a few comparatively minor internal changes, the fort does not seem to have been substantially altered between AD 83–4 and its abandonment in the early years of the second century.

The southern part of the fort contained long, narrow barrack blocks aligned north to south (Figure 3.4). Each would have accommodated either a cavalry

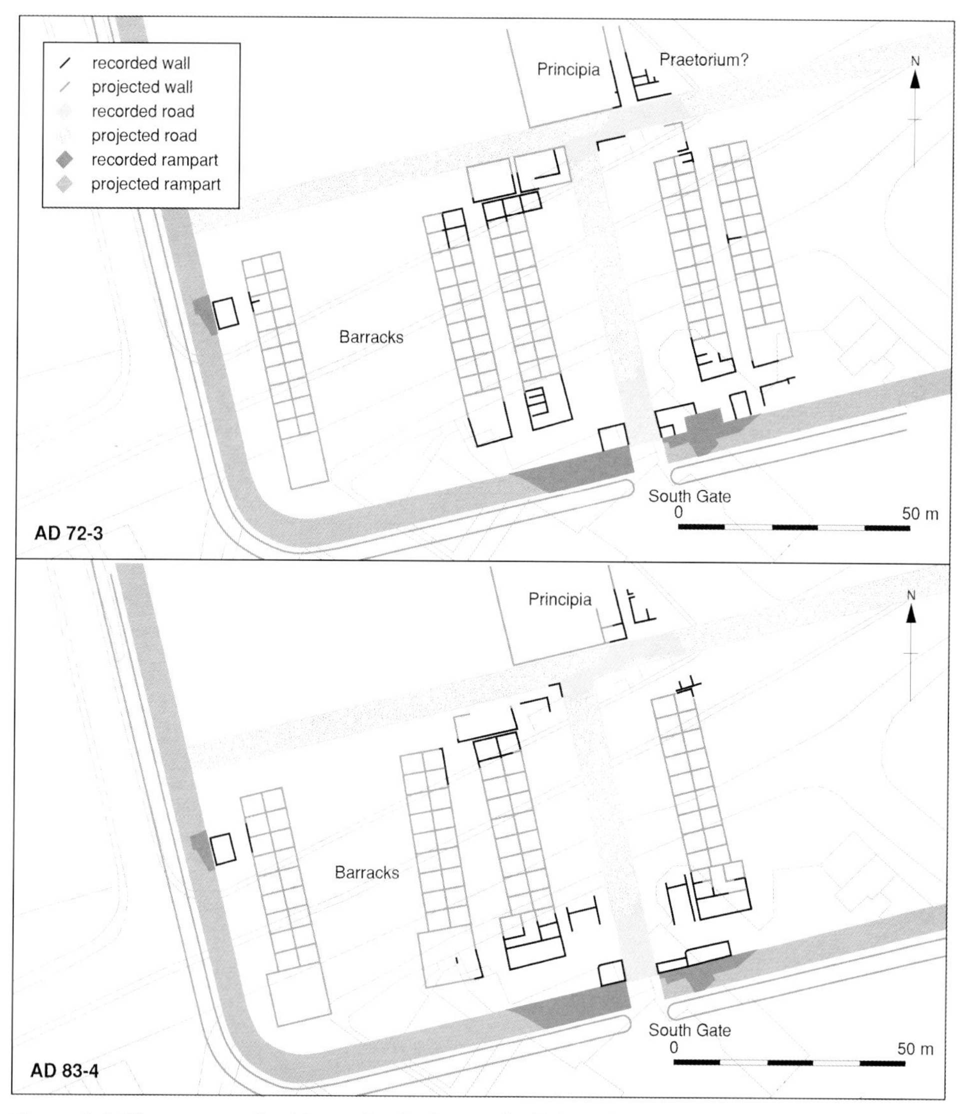

Figure 3.4. The excavated evidence for the fort at Carlisle as first built (AD 72–3) and following internal reconstruction (AD 83–4) (*by courtesy of Oxford Archaeology Ltd*)

troop of approximately 30 troopers (and probably also their horses) or an infantry century of 80 men. In the first phase (AD 72–3 to AD 83–4), space seems to have been available for up to ten barracks (though fragments of only five have been excavated) and there were presumably more in the unexcavated northern area, but the actual number is not known. The barracks constructed in AD 83–4 were slightly more spacious, and consequently there was room for only eight to the south (five of which have been partially excavated) and (potentially) eight more to the north. Also in the southern part of the fort, several small timber structures were erected immediately inside the south and west ramparts, and further detached buildings were squeezed in between the northern ends of the barracks and the main east to west road. Some of these were workshops, whilst others may have been used for storage or even as extra accommodation. The fact that buildings were seemingly crammed into almost every available space suggests that the fort, though of above-average size for its type, was filled to capacity.

Figure 3.5. A storage vessel fragment from Carlisle with a label describing the contents, a tunny-fish relish from southern Spain *(by courtesy of Tullie House Museum and Art Gallery, Carlisle)*

A small part of the fort's central range has been investigated, exposing fragments of what are believed to be the headquarters building (*principia*) and the commanding officer's house (*praetorium*). The excavated area of the latter yielded evidence for leather-working and the small-scale production and repair of copper-alloy objects, suggesting that it may have been a workshop serving the commander's household. Rubbish deposited between the *principia* and the *praetorium* included a storage vessel fragment with a rare, ink-written label describing the contents, a tunny-fish relish imported from the Cadiz region of southern Spain (Figure 3.5). In view of the vessel's findspot, and the likelihood that its exotic contents were beyond the pocket of the rank-and-file soldiers, there is a strong possibility that it derived from the commander's kitchen.

With few exceptions, the main load-bearing walls of the principal buildings were of post-in-trench construction, with flat-bottomed wall-posts set at regular intervals in foundation trenches. However, two buildings erected in the southern part of the fort during the early AD 90s were unusual in having posts mortised into large oak beams laid directly on the ground (Figure 3.6). In all cases, wall-panels, composed of withies woven vertically around horizontal staves and plastered with clay, were used as infill between the wall-posts. These were retained in position by means of slots cut into the adjacent posts, into which the ends of the staves were fitted. In some cases, traces of off-white plaster were found adhering to interior and exterior wall-faces, proving that at least some (perhaps all?) of the fort buildings had been plastered. Evidence for roofing is sparse, though neither ceramic tiles nor stone slates were employed in any of the excavated structures. Thatch, turf, or heather may have been used for some of the more utilitarian buildings, and the use of wooden roof shingles seems likely, though only one or two definite examples are known from Carlisle. Another possible scenario is that roofs were plank-boarded.

Figure 3.6. The foundations for a timber building erected in the fort at Carlisle around AD 93–4, with wall-posts mortised into large oak beams (*by courtesy of Tullie House Museum and Art Gallery, Carlisle*)

Early Roman forts were normally constructed by legionaries, since the legions contained the necessary specialists and craftsmen. At Carlisle, pottery from construction levels suggests that the first fort may have been built by men of *Legio II Adiutrix*. This legion came to Britain from Germany around AD 71, and is known to have been stationed at Chester by the mid–70s. That the reconstruction of AD 83–4 may have been the work of *Legio XX Valeria Victrix* is suggested by a writing-tablet from the fort annexe, dated 7 November 83, which records a loan between two soldiers of the Twentieth.

Over the 30 years or so of its existence, the first fort is likely to have held a number of different regiments, either in whole or in part, but there is very little evidence for named units at this time. In the early Roman period, forts such as Carlisle served as bases for auxiliary regiments of cavalry (*alae*) and infantry (*cohortes*), or for a combination of both (*cohortes equitatae*). These were nominally of 500 or 1,000 men, and were recruited from native peoples who had been assimilated into the Empire. There is, however, increasing evidence that some forts might have served for a time as 'brigade headquarters' for strike forces put together for a particular campaign. Details remain sketchy, but these forces may have comprised elements from several regiments, both cavalry and infantry (in some cases including legionary troops), or perhaps one full-strength unit supported by detachments.

In view of Carlisle's size and strategic position, a cavalry presence might be anticipated. A number of strands of excavated evidence, including harness fittings (Figure 3.7), horse bones, and environmental evidence for horse parasites and hay, do suggest the presence of horses in the fort, but these could conceivably have been officers' mounts or even pack animals However, that the primary garrison may indeed have included a cavalry contingent is suggested by another piece of evidence. This is a writing-tablet addressed to a trooper of a 500-strong cavalry regiment, the *Ala Gallorum Sebosiana*, who was seconded to the mounted guard of the provincial governor Gnaeus Julius Agricola. Whether the tablet can be taken as proof that this unit was in garrison at Carlisle during Agricola's tenure as governor (AD 77–83), or merely indicates the presence of a single trooper, is open to question. It is noteworthy, however, that the regiment was probably transferred from Germany to Britain at the same time as *Legio II Adiutrix*, which, as we have seen, may have built the first fort at Carlisle.

Figure 3.7. An ornate bronze harness mount from an early level within the fort at Carlisle, *c.* AD 72–3 (*by courtesy of Tullie House Museum and Art Gallery, Carlisle*)

Other writing-tablets indicate that a cavalry unit, probably (but not definitely) the *Ala Gallorum Sebosiana*, was certainly present at some time in the late first to early second century. One of the tablets records the issue of three days' barley and wheat rations to the 16 troops of a 500-strong cavalry regiment (Figure 1.6). The document is of particular interest because it preserves the names of most of the troop commanders (*decuriones*), and provides detailed information on the precise quantities of grain issued, the larger amounts of barley presumably representing fodder for the horses, the wheat being for the troopers themselves. Another tablet from the same context is a report from one of the regiment's decurions, Docilis, to his commanding officer, the prefect Augurinus, concerning missing lances.

The strategic importance of Carlisle makes it likely that other military units were accommodated in the area on a more or less temporary basis, either on their way north into Scotland or during phases of withdrawal. The possible existence of a number of temporary camps is suggested by the discovery of military-style ditches at several sites in the city, for example, on Botchergate and at the Lanes (Figure 3.1). That a more substantive pseudo-military or 'official' enclave may have been located on the northern part of the Lanes, some 300 metres east of the fort, is suggested by the excavation of a series of extremely large timber buildings in this area. The earliest, probably dating to the early second century, has been interpreted as a *mansio*, a kind of travel-lodge providing accommodation for military and civilian officials.

The Second Fort at Carlisle

During the early AD 80s, the Roman army's intention seems to have been to consolidate its hold on Scotland, but by the early second century a complete withdrawal south to the Tyne–Solway line had taken place. The principal reason for this is likely to have been the inability of the army to hold all of the territory acquired over the previous 20 years in the face of extensive troop withdrawals for service in the emperor Trajan's wars on the Rhine and Danube. The reduction in troops also resulted in the abandonment of some forts in northern England, although most were rebuilt after only a short break. At Carlisle, the fort buildings were demolished and the defences dismantled around AD 103–5. Interestingly, at approximately the same time as the fort was abandoned, a writing-tablet from Vindolanda attests the presence of a senior military officer, the *centurio regionarius* or 'centurion in charge of the region', at Carlisle. The duties and powers of this officer are not clear, although it is possible that his responsibilities included control of the local native population.

Precisely how much time passed before the fort was rebuilt (again in timber) is not known, though it is unlikely to have been more than two years, and may have been as little as a few months. Thereafter, it continued in use without any obvious rebuilding into the AD 120s. The size of the new fort is not clear, though it was built on the same site as the first fort, and its layout appears to have been similar to that of its predecessor (Figure 3.8). In the central range, a new *principia* was erected and another building occupied the site of the earlier commanding officer's residence. This was probably a workshop, but as only the south-west corner has been seen, it is not clear if it was a free-standing building or, as was the case in the primary fort, formed part of the commander's house. In the *principia*, both internal and external walls were plastered, and at least part of the structure was weather boarded. Barracks aligned north to south were placed in the southern part of the fort, of which three have been partly excavated. These were of similar width to the earlier barracks but were seemingly shorter.

Approximately six kilometres south-east of Carlisle was the legionary pottery and tilery at Scalesceugh. Although poorly understood, this installation appears to have been established during the early second century and

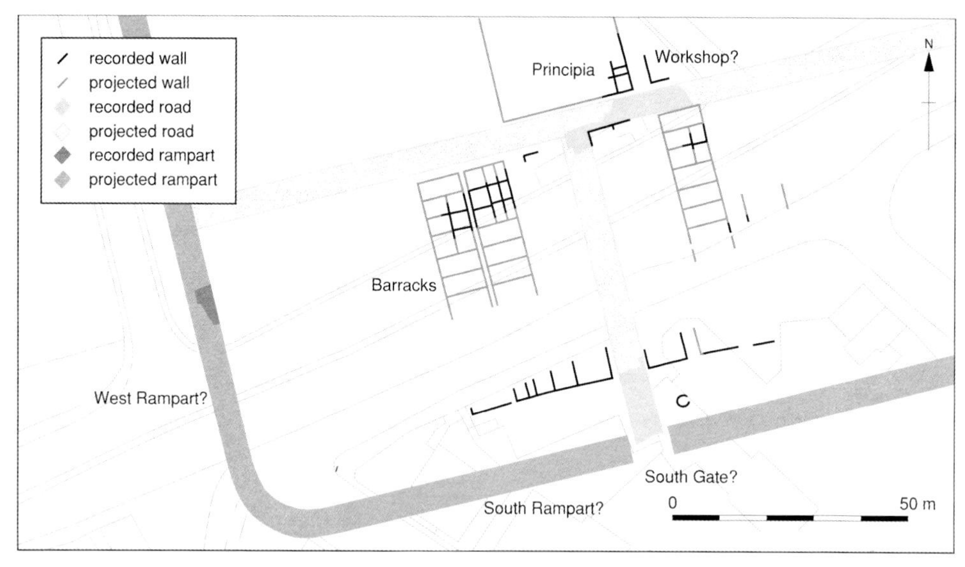

Figure 3.8. The excavated evidence for the second fort at Carlisle, built *c.* AD 105 (*by courtesy of Oxford Archaeology Ltd*)

continued in use, perhaps intermittently, into the third century. Amongst its earliest products were stamped tiles of *Legio IX Hispana*, examples of which are known from the fort and civil settlement at Carlisle. A recent re-examination of the stamps has demonstrated that all come from the same die, and may therefore represent a single episode of production that occurred before *c.* AD 110, when the Ninth is known to have left Britain. It has been suggested that the tiles were produced specifically for the reconstruction, by *Legio IX*, of the Carlisle fort around AD 105.

The garrison of the second fort is not known, although the reduced length of the barracks suggests a change in the type of unit and/or a reduction in size. Similarly, the absence of rampart-back buildings or other ancillary structures in the southern part of the fort suggests that there was plenty of available space at this time. Several cavalry regiments are recorded on inscriptions from Carlisle during the second century, but there is no compelling reason to see any of them as forming the garrison. A strong Gallic influence is, however, indicated by certain types of pottery that have been excavated from early second-century levels in the fort.

The idea that the fort at Carlisle may have been part of an early second-century frontier system pre-dating the construction of Hadrian's Wall in the AD 120s has been, and continues to be, a matter for debate. It is generally acknowledged that, following the Roman army's withdrawal from Scotland, the Tyne–Solway corridor was held by a slightly greater concentration of military units than elsewhere in the North, stationed in a series of forts placed at reasonably regular intervals and connected by an east–west road.

Until recently, this disposition was seen by most scholars as marking the establishment of a frontier system (the so-called Stanegate frontier) extending from Corbridge in the east to Carlisle in the west. In some quarters, however, the concept of this frontier has been challenged, although the most recent re-evaluation suggests that the Stanegate sites could have performed a frontier-control function.

Sometime during Hadrian's reign (AD 117–38), a marked change in the character of occupation at Carlisle occurred. In the central range, though the *principia* and the possible workshop continued in use, the nature of the activity within both seems to have changed. In the headquarters, this was reflected by the deposition of numerous weapon-heads (arrows, spears and artillery bolts), 22 of which were recovered from a small part of the building, together with what may have been part of a wooden rack for storing projectiles. In the workshop, a build-up of dark soils occurred, within which a great deal of rubbish had been dumped. This included a cache of articulated armour fragments – perhaps destined to be broken up for recycling – containing scale shoulder-guards and several laminated limb defences (Figure 3.9). In the southern part of the fort, all the known buildings were demolished and replaced with new structures, some of which had an industrial function, or with cobbled surfaces. Deposition of metal-working debris, particularly that generated by iron smithing, also greatly increased at this time.

The significance of these developments is difficult to assess, though they imply a change, at least in part, in the function of the fort. The catalyst for this remains unclear, but since it almost certainly occurred during the AD 120s it would be logical to associate it with the construction of Hadrian's Wall, which probably began in AD 122–3, and in particular with the establishment of the Wall-fort at Stanwix, less than one kilometre to the north (Figure 3.1). On the face of things, it would be reasonable to expect this to have marked the end of Carlisle as a military base, but this did not happen. Instead, the fort may have become less a base for a regular military unit than a works depot manned by a relatively small number of specialist personnel. It was eventually demolished around the middle of the second century AD, perhaps as a consequence of the Roman reoccupation of southern Scotland in the early AD 140s, when many forts in the North were given up and a new frontier, defined by the Antonine Wall, was established on the Forth–Clyde isthmus.

The Establishment of the Fort at Stanwix (*Uxelodunum*, later *Petriana*)

Whilst the possibility of a pre-Hadrianic military presence at Stanwix cannot be completely ruled out, it seems likely that the first fort was built during the AD 120s, as part of the Hadrian's Wall frontier. West of the River Irthing, the Wall was initially constructed of turf, as were its forts and milecastles, though

Figure 3.9. A scale shoulder-guard and a laminated limb defence from a possible workshop in the central range of the second fort at Carlisle, *c.* AD 125–40 (*by courtesy of Tullie House Museum and Art Gallery, Carlisle*)

the turrets were stone-built from the beginning. It was subsequently rebuilt in stone, but in some sectors this may not have occurred until the late AD 150s or after. The Turf Wall has not been certainly observed at Stanwix, although what may have been part of the ditch that fronted it has twice been seen (but not excavated). The Stone Wall ran diagonally, north-east to south-west, across the modern suburb, and sections across its ditch have been excavated at Tarraby Lane and Knowefield. In this area, the Vallum, the enigmatic earthwork that lies behind the Wall along its entire length, runs parallel to it, approximately 140 metres to the rear. Further south, its position and spatial relationship with the stone fort remain problematic, though it seemingly turned sharply to the south just beyond its south-west angle. The Wall is presumed to have been carried over the River Eden on a bridge situated close to the river's present-day confluence with the River Caldew. Many bridge stones were dredged from the Eden close to this point in 1951 and some are still to be seen on the riverbank.

As originally planned, the Wall was to be garrisoned by troops stationed in the milecastles and turrets set at regular intervals along its length. The men were to be drawn from pre-existing forts, of which Carlisle was one, situated a short distance to the rear. However, at an early stage in the construction process, a decision was made to place full-sized forts on the line of the Wall. On the Turf Wall these were of turf and timber, although, like the Wall itself, they were subsequently rebuilt in stone. At Stanwix, the existence of a primary fort seems virtually certain, although direct archaeological evidence is extremely sparse. In the playgrounds of Stanwix Primary School, a spread of turf incorporating the possible remains of a turf stack or revetment was observed beneath deposits relating to the stone fort. The precise significance of this could not be determined but it may be either the denuded remains of a Hadrianic fort rampart or a spread of debris from the turf phase of Hadrian's Wall itself. Perhaps the best evidence for an early fort is provided by the alignment of the Vallum, which appears to have been laid out in relation to a smaller fort than the large stone installation. Dating of the earliest levels within the civil settlement on the west side of the stone fort is also suggestive of a Hadrianic presence. The identity of the regiment in garrison at this time is not known, but there is sufficient evidence to indicate that it was a 500-strong cavalry unit.

Excavation has proved that the Stanwix sector of Hadrian's Wall was rebuilt in stone before the stone fort itself was erected in the AD 160s, since a stretch of the Wall had to be demolished to facilitate its construction. Whilst the outline of the fort's defensive perimeter has been established (Figure 3.10), and a few small-scale investigations have been conducted within the interior, it remains one of the least known of all the Wall forts. However, its size (3.96ha or 9.79 acres) leaves no doubt that it was the base for the *Ala Petriana*, the only 1,000-strong cavalry unit in Roman Britain. From the

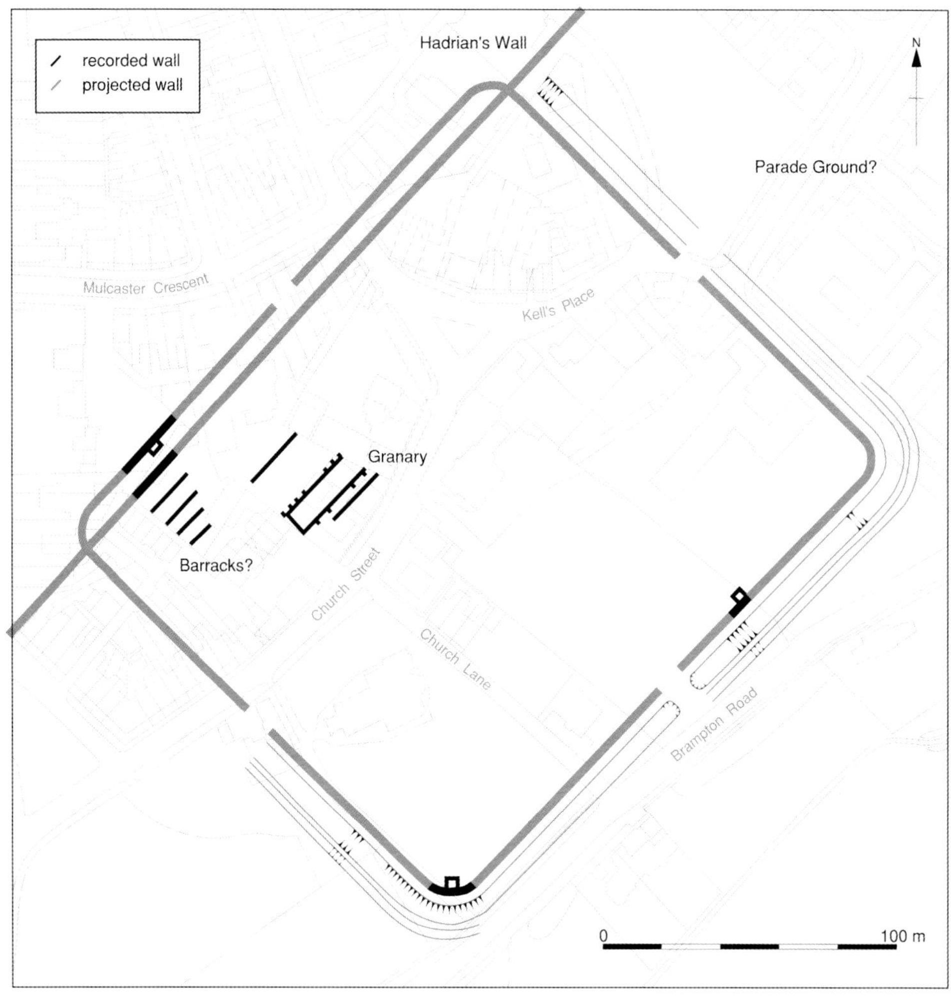

Figure 3.10. The excavated evidence for the late second-century stone fort at Stanwix (*by courtesy of Oxford Archaeology Ltd*)

limited evidence available, it would appear that the fort was continuously occupied from the mid-second century to the end of the fourth century at least. Fragments of various internal buildings have been located, including a granary and probable barrack blocks, but the layout remains poorly understood.

East of the fort is an extensive spread of compacted clay and cobbles. The exact significance of this is not known, although one interpretation is that it represents the remains of a parade ground. Parade grounds were a standard feature of Roman forts and were used for training purposes as well as for parades and displays on ceremonial occasions. Beyond the fort's west gate, evidence of a civil settlement has been found, and possible settlement remains have also been noted south of the putative parade ground, close to the Brampton road. The existence of a cemetery, approximately 400m north-east of the fort, is suggested by the discovery of urns containing cremated bones at Croft Road, Whiteclosegate.

Carlisle in the Mid-to-Late Second Century

The second half of the second century is one of the most obscure periods in the history of the fort at Carlisle. Excavation has revealed quite complex sequences of archaeological deposits, but the nature of the occupation they represent remains poorly understood. It is not even clear if the site was occupied by a conventional fort at this time, although this is looking increasingly unlikely. Initially, a build-up of dark soils occurred, suggesting complete or near-complete abandonment of the site. This was followed by several phases of activity, including the construction of a few small timber buildings, some of which were associated with cobbled roads and gravelled surfaces. In the south-east quadrant of the former fort, a large, stone-footed courtyard building was erected sometime after AD 165. This was associated with a road to the west, roughly on the line of the main north to south road of the earlier forts, and a turf-and-clay rampart to the south. A large ceramic waterpipe found some distance to the north might have been associated with this building, but this is not certain. More soil accumulated in the area of the former central range immediately prior to the construction of a new stone fort in the early third century, but to the south, occupation seems to have continued up to the time that work on the stone fort began.

The presence at Stanwix, probably from the AD 160s, of the *Ala Petriana* may explain the comparative lack of military activity south of the river during this period, although it did not prevent the Carlisle fort from being reoccupied in the early third century. That the fort site was not absorbed into the expanding civil settlement seems certain, however – unlike the putative southern annexe, which does appear to have been given over to civilian occupation by the mid-second century, a development presumably coincident with the abandonment of the second timber fort. What evidence there is suggests that the fort site continued to serve as a military enclave during the second half of the second century, but the precise nature of the occupation is not known. The large courtyard building on the south was presumably the residence of a high-ranking military officer, although on present evidence it appears to have existed more or less in splendid isolation, surrounded, perhaps, by a few small timber structures.

THE STONE FORT AT CARLISLE

In the early third century, the soldier-emperor Septimius Severus personally conducted a major military campaign in northern Britain, and succeeded in penetrating as far as north-east Scotland. However, following Severus's death at York in AD 211, his sons, we are told, abandoned their father's conquests and concluded a peace in order to return to Rome. It was at some point during this period that the fort at Carlisle was rebuilt in stone, probably as part of a very extensive refurbishment and reorganisation of the frontier zone that is attested archaeologically at many sites in northern England.

Unfortunately, the character of the Severan installation is currently far from clear, due to the conflicting nature of some of the available information. On the one hand, what is known of the internal layout suggests a fort of more or less conventional type (Figure 3.11). Key elements, including both of the major roads and the *principia*, occupied the same positions as those of the earlier forts, whilst to the south were barracks, now aligned east to west. In so far as it is possible to tell, therefore, the new base had a similar layout to that of the earlier forts and could conceivably have been of similar size.

Whilst the interior may have had the appearance of a 'normal' fort, however, there are problems with this hypothesis when the defences are considered. On the west, a stone wall 1.1 metres wide was constructed inside the earlier west rampart. To the south, though, the turf-and-clay rampart

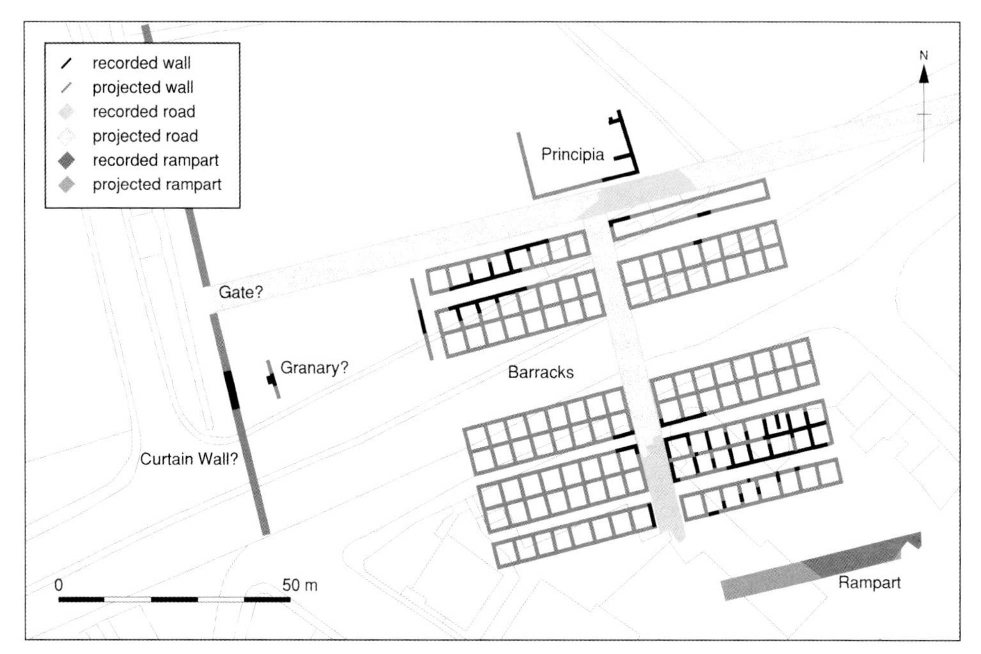

Figure 3.11. The excavated evidence for the third-century stone fort at Carlisle (*by courtesy of Oxford Archaeology Ltd*)

associated with the later second-century courtyard building was heightened and faced with clay blocks set on a stone foundation. Further south still, a stone wall that *may* have been the southern equivalent of the western wall has been observed on Abbey Street and Castle Street. Even if this feature could be proved to be contemporary with the western wall, however (which it cannot), the clay-faced rampart would remain problematic, as no similar feature appears to have existed on the west.

The fort buildings were probably stone-built to roof height, externally at least, though some internal partitions may have been largely timber-framed on stone sleeper walls. Only the south-east corner of the *principia* has been excavated, but it yielded a building stone of *Legio VI Victrix*, demonstrating that the fort was built by men from this unit, which came to Britain in the AD 120s and was based thereafter at York. It seems there were at least eight barracks in the southern part of the fort, four on either side of the main north to south road, though only two have seen any substantive excavation. They were separated by cobbled roads approximately three metres wide. Additionally, four other buildings, identical to the barracks but half the width, have also been recorded, two on the north, fronting the main east to west road, and two on the south, adjacent to the clay-fronted rampart. The significance of these structures remains uncertain, though it is possible that they served as officers' accommodation. In the south-west quadrant, adjacent to the west wall of the fort, a small fragment of a possible granary has been observed.

That the fort was occupied by legionaries in the first half of the third century is demonstrated by several inscriptions found in Carlisle. However, whilst a construction detail from *Legio VI* seemingly built the fort, it appears to have been garrisoned by detachments from the other two British legions, *Legio II Augusta* and *Legio XX Valeria Victrix*, which were perhaps brigaded together for at least part of the time. The size of the garrison cannot presently be estimated, since not only is the total number of barrack blocks within the fort unknown, but it is also unclear how many men each barrack was supposed to accommodate.

There remains the broader question of why a military presence should have been required in Carlisle at all during the third century, in view of the proximity of the large cavalry fort at Stanwix. Whilst it is possible that the legionaries performed administrative and/or policing duties in the frontier zone, there may be more to it than this. Indeed, it is even possible that the re-establishment of a garrison at Carlisle was directly linked to the presence of the elite cavalry unit across the river. On the Roman frontiers in Germany and on the Danube, several sites are known where two forts, often situated only a few hundred metres apart, were in use at the same time. The rationale behind such an arrangement, it has been suggested, was to allow the highly mobile cavalry garrison of one of the forts to be redeployed rapidly without compromising the security of the frontier, which would continue to be watched over by the infantry in the other fort. Following this argument, the garrison at Carlisle may have been intended to maintain watch on the frontier during periods when the *Ala Petriana* at Stanwix was required for service elsewhere. It is also possible that the legionaries were there to provide a degree of protection for the expanding Roman town which, though situated in a comparatively exposed position right on the northern frontier, does not seem to have been enclosed by walls or other defences.

Carlisle and Stanwix in the Fourth Century and Later

Archaeological evidence suggests that the third century was a period of stability at Carlisle, at least in terms of the fort layout. The excavated buildings were occupied throughout this period but few modifications were made. Practically nothing is known of Stanwix at this time, though the limited coin evidence might point to a reduced level of occupation for at least part of the century. The military base at Carlisle certainly continued to be occupied throughout the fourth century and almost certainly beyond, although the precise nature of some of the activity remains unclear. Sometime during the fourth century, a heated room was inserted into the east range of the *principia* (Figure 3.12), and a latrine-pit, served from within the building, was built against the east

Figure 3.12. The *principia* of the stone fort at Carlisle during the late fourth century, and contemporary rubble surfaces outside the building (*by courtesy of Tullie House Museum and Art Gallery, Carlisle*)

wall. The fills of this feature yielded seeds from a range of medicinal plants, suggesting that this part of the headquarters may for a time have taken on some kind of medical function. In the second half of the fourth century, the *principia*'s colonnaded portico was remodelled using large, socketed foundation slabs reminiscent of those known from late Roman contexts in the Hadrian's Wall forts at Haltonchesters and Rudchester, some 60–70 kilometres east of Carlisle. In the external area east of the *principia*, a timber 'lean-to' was erected, on coin evidence, after AD 388. Following the demolition of this structure, the area, and also the main east to west road directly in front of the *principia*, were surfaced with sandstone rubble and cobbles. This surface was in turn cut by a few shallow pits prior to the accumulation of a thick deposit of dark soil that sealed almost all the latest Roman levels. Precisely what time-scale is represented by this sequence cannot be determined, but it seems likely that occupation continued in this part of the fort well into the fifth century.

During the period when the rubble surfaces were in use, approximately 250 late Roman coins, including a few minted after AD 378, and almost 150kg of animal bones, mostly butchery waste, were deposited in this part of the fort. In contrast, no coins and only a few fragments of bone came from inside the *principia*. It is not clear if the bones derived from on-site butchery or were brought from elsewhere for use as hardcore in the late surfaces, though such material is unlikely to have been transported far. A very similar pattern of coin loss is known from the fort at Newcastle, at the eastern end of Hadrian's Wall. There, the excavators suggested that it could best be explained by envisioning the development of a cash-based market within the fort during the late fourth century, and it seems highly probable that Carlisle provides another example of this phenomenon.

In the southern part of the fort, at least one of the third-century barracks was partially reconstructed during the fourth century. The other excavated barracks in this area all underwent a variety of internal modifications before being demolished. For the most part, the levelled fort buildings were sealed by a build-up of dark soils that mark the end of intensive occupation on the site until the establishment of the medieval castle in the late eleventh or early twelfth century. Part of the east wall of the *principia* probably stood into the twelfth century, however, and elements of the barracks remained upstanding for centuries, with some walls being robbed to ground level only in the medieval period.

Evidence for late Roman occupation at Stanwix is extremely limited, though traces of timber buildings and other occupation deposits, dated by pottery to the second half of the fourth century or later, are known from the fort interior. Stanwix presumably continued to serve as the base for the *Ala Petriana* until the end of the Roman period, since the unit is named as the garrison in the *Notitia Dignitatum*, a late fourth-century listing of military and civil commands in the Roman Empire.

Whether or not a garrison was maintained at Carlisle remains uncertain. The scarcity of obviously military objects in the latest excavated levels within the fort could point to a lack of soldiers in the later fourth century, but this cannot be regarded as a reliable indicator, since very little military equipment has been recovered from third-century deposits on the site, when the fort was unquestionably occupied by the army. However, the ultimate fate of the fort, and of its garrison, remains obscure. Historical sources suggest that Britain was progressively depleted of troops during the first decade of the fifth century. Some soldiers were doubtless withdrawn from the frontier garrisons, but most were probably taken from Britain's mobile field army, which would have been stationed further south. That at least part of the fort at Carlisle remained in use into the fifth century can no longer be doubted, but developments thereafter are unclear. All that can be said for certain is that no firm evidence for continuity of occupation beyond the fifth century has yet been found, though it has been suggested that the road which entered the fort from the south may have remained in use as late as the twelfth century.

★ ★ ★ ★ ★

SUGGESTED FURTHER READING

P. Bidwell and M. Snape, 'The history and setting of the Roman fort at Newcastle', *Archaeologia Aeliana*, 5th ser., 31 (extra volume, 2002), pp. 251–83

D. J. Breeze, *J. Collingwood Bruce's Handbook to the Roman Wall*, 14th edn (Newcastle upon Tyne, 2006)

I. D. Caruana, 'Observations in the *vicus* of Stanwix Roman fort on the site of the Miles MacInnes Hall, 1986', *CW2*, 100 (2000), pp. 55–78

J. A. Dacre 'An excavation on the Roman fort at Stanwix, Carlisle', *CW2*, 85 (1985), pp. 53–69

P. A. Holder, *The Roman Army in Britain* (London, 1982)

C. Howard-Davis (ed.), *The Carlisle Millennium Project: Excavations in Carlisle 1998–2001. Volume 2: The Finds and Environmental Evidence* (Lancaster, 2009)

A. Johnson, *Roman Forts of the 1st and 2nd Centuries AD in Britain and the German Provinces* (London, 1983)

M. R. McCarthy, *Roman Carlisle and the Lands of the Solway* (Stroud, 2002)

M. R. McCarthy, *The Roman Waterlogged Remains and Later Features at Castle Street, Carlisle: Excavations 1981–2* (CWAAS, Research Series, 5, 1991)

D. C. A. Shotter, *Romans and Britons in North-West England*, 3rd edn (Lancaster, 2004)

R. S. O. Tomlin, 'Documenting the Roman army at Carlisle', in J. J. Wilkes (ed.), *Documenting the Roman Army* (British Institute of Classical Studies, Supplement, 81, 2003), pp. 175–86

G. Webster, *The Roman Imperial Army*, 3rd edn (London, 1985)

J. Zant, *The Carlisle Millennium Project: Excavations in Carlisle 1998–2001. Volume 1: The Stratigraphy* (Lancaster, 2009)

Chapter 4
Roman Carlisle: Its People and Their Lives

David Shotter

Outside almost every Roman fort in North-West England, a small urban development (extramural settlement) of civilians became established, usually known as a *vicus* (Figure 4.1). The only known exception to this was at the fort at Hardknott, above the Furness Fells, where presumably environmental conditions and the apparently intermittent nature of its garrison-pattern did not encourage this kind of permanent commitment on the part of civilians.

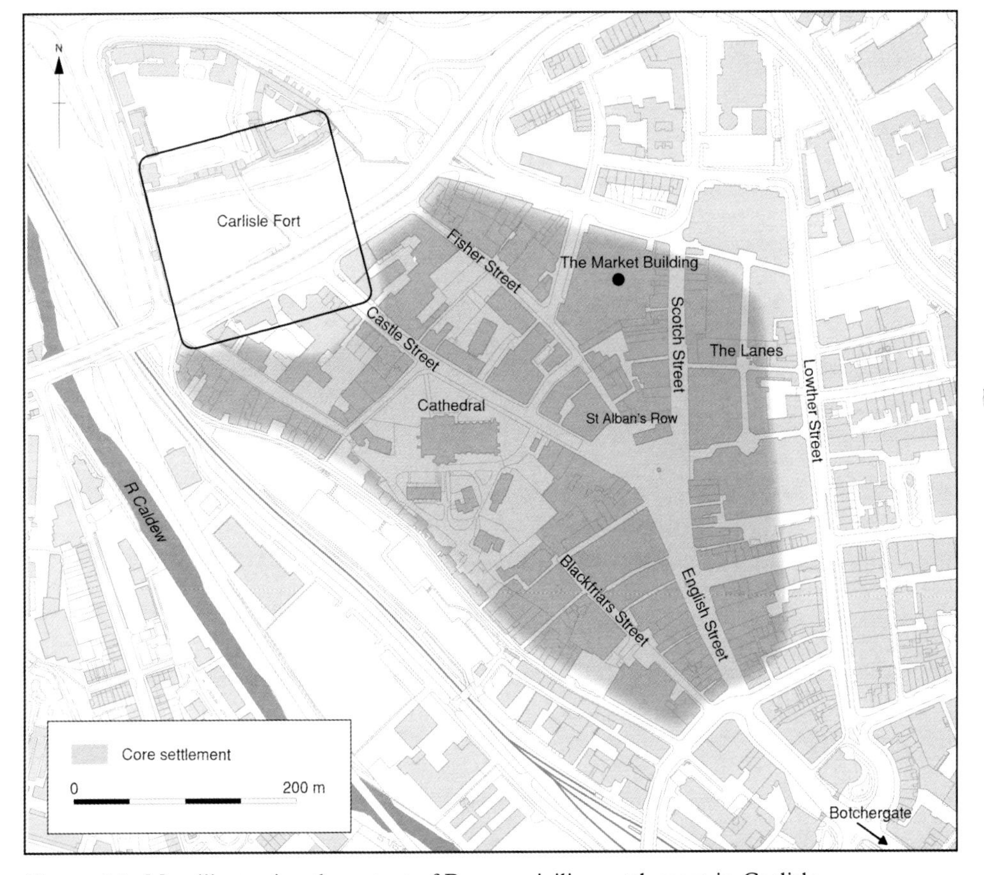

Figure 4.1. Map illustrating the extent of Roman civilian settlement in Carlisle

Urban Origins

Present evidence, from aerial photography, geophysical survey and some excavation, suggests that such towns were not strictly planned, but grew (and, presumably, on occasion shrank) according to need and circumstance (Figure 4.2). In some cases, building appears to have taken place on land previously unused, whilst, in others, the *vicus* developed over areas formerly under military control and, as at Vindolanda, some of the surviving military buildings were re-used: barrack-buildings were readily convertible into the 'strip-houses', which represented the most common type of accommodation found in the extramural developments outside forts (Figure 4.3). On the other hand, the amphitheatre at Chester has been shown to have been constructed on land which had been farmed over the previous two centuries. Recent excavations have shown that the first Roman fort at Carlisle, too, had been built on land previously under the plough. This, of course, raises the question of what happened to the previous inhabitants: were they simply ejected? Alternatively, were they relocated or compensated in some way? We do not know if the Roman military authorities were 'user-friendly' in their handling of such matters.

The inhabitants of these towns, or *vici*, provided a range of goods and

Figure 4.2. The fort at Maryport and the extensive civilian settlement to its north as revealed by geophysical survey (*by courtesy of Timescape Surveys*)

Figure 4.3. An aerial photograph of the fourth-century fort at Vindolanda and the excavated portion of the civilian settlement to the west (*by courtesy of the Vindolanda Trust*)

services for the soldiers in the adjacent forts and, of course, for themselves also. Such developments probably represented the introduction of a 'market-economy' into the Roman North-West. Although the forts had their own workshops (*fabricae*) for the repair of equipment, some repairs were probably carried out on a commercial basis in the *vici*. The residents of the extramural settlements also engaged in a range of manufacturing processes, the 'end-products' of many of which were aimed at the soldiers in the forts. Common amongst these were pottery-utensils, religious objects and clothes-fasteners ('brooches'), which were made of metal – predominantly bronze – and frequently decorated with enamel-work. The products of such skills, therefore, did not need to be imported into Britain, but were well within the scope of local manufacturers. Pots and pans of various kinds were made (for example, on Fisher Street in Carlisle), although some of these – particularly the 'classier' items – were probably brought in by travelling merchants from other parts of Britain, as well as from further afield, and sold on by local entrepreneurs through shops in the civilian settlements (Figure 4.4). It is

Figure 4.4. The remains of a timber wagon-wheel recovered from a timber-lined well of second-century date in the Lanes (*by courtesy of Tullie House Museum and Art Gallery, Carlisle*)

clear now, however, that the proposition that Roman Britain was heavily dependent on other parts of the Empire for foodstuffs and for consumer-durables was, at the least, an exaggeration, although there was – and, indeed, had been for some time – a market in Britain for more exotic items of food and drink from other provinces.

The civilian settlements also acted as market-places for those who lived and worked in the wider hinterlands of the forts. Farmers probably drove their livestock into town on the hoof, and sold them for slaughter to local butchers, who then sold on the parts that they could not use. Hooves, for example, might be sold for processing into glue, horns perhaps for 'craft-items', or occasionally picks, whilst hides could be sold to tanners for eventual manufacture into such items as tents and shoes. Whilst some grain was taken by the authorities by way of taxation, that which was surplus to the farmers' requirements might be sold for baking or brewing. In their turn, local farmers presumably sank the profits that they made from such transactions into the purchase of items that they required. The Vindolanda writing-tablets provide some insight into such activities, and it was in this way that the inhabitants of the settlements became significant economic, as well as social, links between the men in the forts and those who lived and worked within the forts' *territoria* (designated territory).

Beyond this, both soldiers and inhabitants of the civilian settlements had broader needs – for entertainment and for places to eat, drink and gamble.

Brothels, too, would inevitably have found a place in the life of the town. At the other end of the scale were religious needs, and such settlements evidently contained temples dedicated to a range of gods and goddesses, who may have had a special connection with the soldiers' homelands, or who exercised a protective guardianship over the needs and interests of soldiers and civilians. From Carlisle, for example, we find dedications to Cautes (a Mithraic figure), and to the *Matres Parcae* (Mother-goddesses who were guardians of Fate), as well as a tombstone to a Greek who appears to have been a Christian. As was commonly the case in Roman Britain, temples were probably mostly of the Romano-Celtic type, which indicates a process of assimilation with the local population, as does the practice of providing some deities with a 'double' Romano-Celtic nomenclature (for example, Mars Cocidius, where Cocidius was a local deity at nearby Bewcastle, with properties similar to those of the Roman god, Mars). Carlisle has itself produced an example of this, with a dedication to Mars Barrex. Another 'doublet' is the god, Mars Ocelus, who was coupled on a fragmentary dedication with an invocation of the 'godhead' (*numen*) of the emperor (Figure 4.5). Although few emperors thought of themselves as living deities, 'emperor-worship' was a required act on the part of Romanised communities, as a demonstration of their political loyalty.

Figure 4.5. The dedication-slab invoking the Romano-British deity, Mars Ocelus, and the 'guardian-spirit' of an emperor whose name was later erased (*by courtesy of Tullie House Museum and Art Gallery, Carlisle*)

The Public and Private Buildings

One of the most important (and imposing) of any town's buildings was the main bath-house, which in Carlisle evidently stood on the site now occupied by the market hall. This would have been used by both soldiers and civilians, although probably at different times, with decisions on such matters as this being left in the hands of the fort-commander. Besides facilities for bathing and cleansing, the bath-house provided the opportunity for social intercourse and a range of activities which we today would probably associate with a leisure-centre.

Many of the buildings that lined the streets of Roman Carlisle would have conformed to the 'strip' type – long, narrow, structures with their gable-ends facing onto the streets, thus emphasising the fact that street-frontage space (and thus proximity to potential customers) was at a premium. As can be seen at Vindolanda, such 'strip-houses' tended to have a shop (or a 'factory-shop') on the street-frontage itself, with living-accommodation behind, and perhaps workshops at the rear for whatever was sold in the shop. At Vindolanda, as already noted, some former military barracks were 'reinvented' as 'strip-houses'. The street-side shops would have been engaged in such businesses as selling 'take-away' food and drink, and a variety of manufactured items. There would also have been larger houses, probably of the courtyard or 'winged corridor' type, perhaps for wealthier civilians or as residences for certain officials. A good example of the latter type, to which underfloor central heating was added in the fourth century, was excavated in the early 1980s at Keays Lane, on Carlisle's Lanes.

The combination of all such activities within a relatively small area, and along narrow streets and alleyways, would have produced an environment that was lively and perhaps a little claustrophobic, noisy (probably with a variety of languages being spoken), and inevitably dirty and smelly as well. As we watch the development of Roman Carlisle, it becomes easy to appreciate the relevance of the comment made by the third-century historian, Dio Cassius, about the arrival of Roman garrisons along the Rhine: assessing the impact of the new culture on the German tribespeople, Dio wrote in his *History of Rome* that, whilst the Germans did not forget their ancestral habits, 'they were adapting themselves to Roman ways, were becoming accustomed to hold markets ... and were becoming different without knowing it'. The large volume of Roman coins found over the years in Carlisle – many of them in the non-military areas – certainly suggests that the inhabitants of the civilian settlement readily took to coined money as a means of exchange in their everyday lives.

The People

The populations of such towns were probably noticeably cosmopolitan, including retired soldiers and their families, traders from various parts of the Empire, and locals amongst whom might be the girl-friends, and perhaps children, of serving soldiers. It should be noted that soldiers were not permitted to enter into legal marriages whilst still on active service – until this law was rescinded by the emperor, Septimius Severus, early in the third century AD. After retirement, however, as we see from military discharge-diplomas, the legitimacy of soldiers' pre-existing relationships and of any children whom they may have had within those relationships was officially recognised. Thus, many people, from home and abroad, were drawn into these settlements by the opportunities for making a living. A good example of this is provided by Barates, a sculptor from Palmyra (in Syria), who had married Regina, a lady from the southern British tribe of the Catuvellauni, and who lived and worked at South Shields. Carlisle itself was evidently home to a Greek, Flavius Antigonus Papias (Figure 4.6), and more people of eastern origin – many 'doctors', for example – may lie concealed behind fully Romanised personal names.

Figure 4.6.The tombstone of Flavius Antigonus Papias (*by courtesy of Tullie House Museum and Art Gallery, Carlisle*)

Another group from whom settlement residents might have come consisted of military veterans, who had decided to take their pensions and gratuities and settle in retirement close to where they had served, utilising the opportunities for opening up new business-ventures. At times, serving soldiers may also have been billeted in the towns, when they had been drafted in on a temporary basis, which may have happened in the late first century AD to legionary soldiers in Carlisle.

Such towns, then, grew as need dictated, not evidently following any regular pattern of development, but presenting on a small scale what might be termed 'urban sprawl'. Generally, they were not walled, although there is some evidence of an earth-and-turf bank and ditch arrangement at Ribchester (Lancashire). This may, however, have been a special case, as is possibly suggested by the name of the site – *Bremetennacum Veteranorum* (The Veterans' Town of Bremetennacum).

Whether or not the Roman town of Carlisle was walled remains unclear. Although Bede, in his *Life of St Cuthbert*, writes of Cuthbert's being shown the walls in the later seventh century AD, there is no firm archaeological evidence as yet to support the existence of town-walls in the Roman period. It is, in any case, very unlikely that Carlisle would have been permitted to have walls earlier than the third century. In the absence of walls, the built-up areas of Roman towns no doubt gradually gave way to a kind of rural suburbia. The only sign of formal limits would have been the tombs that lined the main roads running out of the *vici*, as for reasons of health and the risk of accidental defilement of graves, Roman law enacted that the dead (except for infants) should not be buried within settlements. Of course, towns might grow to a point where they overlapped earlier cemetery areas, and in Carlisle's case there is evidence that this may have happened along Botchergate (the main road out of Roman Carlisle to the south). Cemeteries, too, can tell us a great deal, not just about individuals, but also about the level of prosperity in a settlement. Graves unearthed in the nineteenth century along London Road (the modern A6) provided, through the wide variety of burial practices revealed, clear evidence of wealth on a scale more substantial than has been evident at most north-western Roman cemeteries that have been excavated (Figures 4.7 and 4.8).

Figure 4.7. The tombstone of Aurelia Aureliana (*by courtesy of the University of Newcastle upon Tyne*)

It remains unclear how far, if at all, inhabitants of such settlements were permitted to organise or elect leaders. It is probably safest, on present evidence, to assume that 'gatherings' may have been limited to religious or ceremonial occasions, and perhaps to meetings of trades guilds. Dio Cassius, for example, writes of the Germans in the age of the emperor Augustus 'coming together in peaceful assemblages'. Certainly, the appearance on a number of inscriptions in the North of England of the collective word *vicani* ('townspeople') leaves open a fruitful area for further research. It might also be noted that crime was not absent from Roman Carlisle: a skeleton found in a sandstone-lined well on the Lanes was certainly that of a murder victim, as were two skeletons found beneath the floor of a *vicus*-building at Housesteads, near Haydon Bridge. The murder victim from Carlisle, who was male and probably in his forties, had been beaten about the head with a blunt instrument, and his body thrown down the well and covered with rubbish. A facial reconstruction of this man can be seen in Tullie House Museum and Art Gallery (Figure 4.9).

Figure 4.8. The tombstone of Vacia: the representation is of an adult female, though the deceased was only three years old (*by courtesy of Tullie House Museum and Art Gallery, Carlisle*)

It has to be emphasised at the outset that two special considerations applied to Carlisle: first, it was for most of its life in the Roman period a fort with an adjacent 'frontier-town', where the opportunities for business-profit – as well, of course, as the risks – would have been greater than at most civilian settlements in the North-West. The volume of Roman artefacts and coinage found in lowland Scotland serves to emphasise the reality of the commercial opportunities across the frontier. In this respect, Carlisle provides an obvious parallel with Corbridge in the North-East. This would probably have ensured both continuity and stability of activity at Carlisle, whereas the fortunes of some extramural settlements – perhaps most – fluctuated according to the state of the fort-garrisons. Perhaps if a garrison (or part of it) was moved on, then the residents of the adjacent town – or some of them, at least – moved with it.

Second, at some point – probably in the early third century, although

Figure 4.9. Facial reconstruction by Caroline Wilkinson of the Roman murder victim found in the Lanes (*by courtesy of the University of Manchester and Tullie House Museum and Art Gallery, Carlisle*)

there is no evidence for the precise date – Carlisle appears to have been made the principal town of the Carvetii, a tribal group (*civitas*) which was possibly formed by the Roman administrators out of a section of the Brigantes, the chief northern tribe at the time of the conquest. It appears from a milestone recently discovered at Langwathby near Penrith, and which had been set up on the authority of the *Civitas Carvetiorum*, that Carlisle, which was known as

Luguvalium, enjoyed this status by at least AD 223 (Figure 4.10). With such a 'promotion', Carlisle's role would have extended beyond the mere servicing of its local garrison. Wealthier Carvetians would have been expected to take on regional administrative responsibilities to be exercised from Carlisle, and there would have been a group of suitably 'dignified' buildings in which to conduct such activities. Although the sites of such buildings remain largely elusive, a variety of recent excavations have pointed to the later second and early third centuries as a time of change and transition in Carlisle and, in particular, there are suggestions that the remains of monumental buildings may lie beneath the area of Abbey Street, the cathedral and Tullie House Museum and Art Gallery. There are also signs of a new road-layout, and of land-reclamation. In addition, the discovery over the years in the city area of at least seven substantial hoards (disposable savings) of Roman silver coins – including one which contained gold coins as well – serves to highlight the likely wealth of some of Carlisle's Romano-British residents.

Figure 4.10. A milestone from Langwathby giving a date (AD 223), the abbreviated Roman name for Carlisle (LVG[uvalium]), and the identity of the 'local authority' (C[ivitas] CAR[vetiorum]) (*photograph: Ben Edwards*)

The Development of Roman Carlisle

The development of Roman Carlisle can thus be briefly summarised. A Roman fort – perhaps for a 500-strong auxiliary cavalry garrison known as the *Ala Gallorum Sebosiana*, probably together with some legionary detachments – was established no later than AD 72–3 on a site, already under cultivation, which is now largely occupied by the castle. It is evident from the Vindolanda writing-tablets that, within a few years of this, Carlisle had come to exercise a role of regional responsibility through the agency of a man named Annius Quester, a 'regional overseer' (*centurio regionarius*). Early on, extramural activity has been found to have developed at a number of separate sites – Blackfriars Street, Botchergate and Castle Street, although the last appears to have been at first an annexe to the fort, and thus under direct military control, but not required beyond the 130s or 140s, as more services became available in the *vicus*.

At Blackfriars Street, excavations in the late 1970s showed that timber 'strip-houses' were constructed in the late 70s AD, with their gable-ends facing onto the street. Despite building-modifications and evident changes of use, these remained in place throughout the Roman period, perhaps surviving until the sixth, or even the seventh, century. It has been suggested that they may have been in use by wealthy merchants as storage-buildings. In common with the fort beneath the castle, these buildings also appear to have been constructed on land which, when the Romans arrived, was already in use for agricultural purposes, and this again prompts the question of how such confiscations were managed. Although obviously tough, the Roman authorities, particularly in the aftermath of the events which had precipitated the rebellion of Boudica in AD 60, were not likely to have been gratuitously heavy-handed.

The developments along Botchergate, which like its modern successor (the A6) probably represented the main road into Carlisle from the south, were different both in chronology and in character. The earliest use was apparently as a cemetery area, which in the early second century was replaced by 'strip-houses' aligned at 90 degrees to the road. Some of these showed signs of industrial use, including one which was evidently involved in lead-smelting. The use of lead for such items as water-pipes and for clamping the building-blocks of large-scale stone structures prompts the suggestion that these developments on Botchergate were connected with major building-developments elsewhere in Carlisle, such as we might expect in connection with the town's elevation of status. However, during the first half of the third century, the Botchergate site appears to have returned to use once again as a cemetery area.

The frequent changes noted at these sites (and, indeed, at the fort itself) suggest that it may have taken some time for the shape of the Roman town of Carlisle and the pattern of its settlement to become firm. A similar observation also applies to the results of excavation work in the 1980s in the area dominated by the series of medieval lanes running between Scotch Street and English Street in the west and Lowther Street in the east. At first, the characters of the buildings at the northern and southern ends of the Lanes were very different, although by the mid-second century the Lanes area as a whole had become far more homogeneous. Initially, the southern areas – for example, on Old Grapes Lane – exhibited none of the pressures on space evident at Blackfriars Street; instead buildings, one of which was a round house of pre-Roman style, were mostly contained within hedged or ditched enclosures. Their chief purposes appear to have been domestic and agricultural – perhaps denoting the rural suburbia encountered on the fringes of a number of civilian settlements.

On the northern areas of the Lanes, however – for example, on Keays Lane and Laws Lane – the remains of more spacious and impressive accommodation were found. One structure was particularly well built, especially in the matter of its joinery, and its general condition was reminiscent of the type of house (*praetorium*) provided in forts for garrison-commanders. This has prompted the suggestion that it may have been intended for an official, such as the 'regional overseer' already mentioned. This building appears to have had a short life, before it was replaced – perhaps following a fire – by long rectangular timber structures. As elsewhere, the signs are of a town that was developing and changing rather than settled and static.

Urban Prosperity and the *Civitas Carvetiorum*

By the later years of the second century, as we have seen, building on the Lanes appears to have become more homogeneous in quality. One later building was evidently of a complex type and eventually contained at least one room with underfloor central heating. This building, because of its overall quality and because of the frequent modifications to which it was subject, certainly suggests residents of substance and/or importance. Similarly, another building of quality – evidently a house – was partly excavated on Scotch Street. This was equipped with its own bath-house, which showed signs of continued use well into the fifth century, and perhaps later. Both these buildings are strongly suggestive of growing prosperity in Carlisle, and a small female head with a 'gated crown', symbolic of the guardian of urban life, which was found on the Lanes, provides a glimpse of at least one citizen's sense of pride at Roman Carlisle's development (Figure 4.11).

Figure 4.11. Personification representing the female deity protecting Roman Carlisle (*by courtesy of Tullie House Museum and Art Gallery, Carlisle*)

Such signs of prosperity and success clearly fit well with Carlisle's new status, for it is unlikely that such a 'promotion' would have been considered unless a reasonable-sized body of wealthy men, with a capacity for continued wealth-generation, were to hand. Such men would not have come simply from Carlisle itself, but would have been drawn from the whole of Carvetian territory. To illustrate this, the only named elder that we have is Flavius Martius, described as a 'senator' of the *Civitas Carvetiorum*, whose tombstone was found at Old Penrith. Men like Flavius Martius accepted the privilege of local administrative power, despite the fact that the privilege was balanced by the duty (*munus*) of having to pay for it. Nothing could give a clearer view of the Roman 'urban ethos' than this indication that it was those who undertook burdens who should also win the privileges. Some of these wealthy men perhaps lived in Carlisle, but many will probably have made their wealth by farming in areas such as the Solway Plain and the Eden valley. It is clear that, with a large frontier-army to feed, the volume of arable and pastoral land in Carvetian territory would have needed to be substantially expanded.

Figure 4.12. The tombstone of the 'lady with a fan' (*by courtesy of Tullie House Museum and Art Gallery, Carlisle*)

The names of some of those who lived in Roman Carlisle are known from inscriptions and graffiti, and, indeed, the quality of some of the surviving tombstones, such as that of the 'lady with a fan' (Figure 4.12), provides further indication of the prosperity of some of Carlisle's citizens. Of the names that are known, a number are of women, whose tombstones were erected by their grieving husbands: Ulpius Apolinaris and Julius Fortunatus could well have been Carvetian senators. Only Flavius Antigonus Papias (Figure 4.6) provides us with an indication of his origins: he was a Greek (perhaps a doctor) and very likely a Christian who, on his death, had his memorial erected in Carlisle.

The Fourth Century and Later

One indication of the success of Romanisation in Carlisle is provided by the signs of long-term survival there of aspects of the Romano-British town and its culture, for although we have little direct evidence of the nature of activity in Carlisle in the later years, the few pieces that we do have are significant. As we have seen, evidence for continued activity in the late fourth century and beyond has come from a number of sites. In particular, the gold *solidus* of the emperor Valentinian II (AD 375–92), found in the bath-house of the residence on Scotch Street, because it was sealed within a stratified deposit between phases of rebuilding work, indicates that the building must have remained in use well into the fifth century (Figure 4.13). In its turn, this of course means that some in the town were trying to hold onto the old certainties of the Romanised way of life long after Britain had ceased formally to be part of the Roman Empire and subject to Roman administration. A similar story of very late rebuilding comes from the site of the 'strip-house' on Blackfriars Street.

Figure 4.13. A gold *solidus* of Emperor Valentinian II (AD 375–92) from Scotch Street, which was probably not lost until some date in the fifth century (*by courtesy of Tullie House Museum and Art Gallery, Carlisle*)

Excavations in 1998–2001 in the centre of the fort added significantly to this picture. It was found that large numbers of Roman coins of the third and fourth centuries lay scattered outside the fort's headquarters building (*principia*) on the surfaces of adjacent streets. Such lost coins may have derived from commercial activities in the second half of the fourth century, and perhaps from streetside gambling – a popular pastime amongst Romanised populations. This phenomenon, which has also been recognised in recent years in the forts at Vindolanda and Newcastle, suggests the possibility that, in the later years of the fourth century, the centre of the Roman fort came to be used as a kind of emporium or market.

In conclusion, it has become increasingly clear that what we have traditionally called 'the end of Roman Britain', even to the point of assigning a date to it (AD 410), was not so much an event as a process continuing throughout the fourth century and beyond. Eventually, money to pay the army's wages and the collection of taxes faltered and failed as the administration of Roman Britain lost its coherence. Change was in the air, although we should not imagine that people in Carlisle or elsewhere in Roman Britain viewed this as a 'release from servitude'. They had come to accept Britain's place in the Roman Empire, had profited from it and had helped to uphold it. For many, as the fourth century gave way to the fifth, Romano-British remained their lifestyle and their culture.

★ ★ ★ ★ ★

Suggested Further Reading

A. R. Birley, *The Roman Government of Britain* (Oxford, 2005)
D. Charlesworth, 'Roman Carlisle', *Archaeological Journal*, 135 (1978), pp. 115–37
B. J. N. Edwards and D. C. A. Shotter, 'Two Roman milestones from the Penrith area', *CW3*, 5 (2005), pp. 65–77
N. J. Higham and G. D. B. Jones, *The Carvetii* (Gloucester, 1985)
M. R. McCarthy, *A Roman, Anglian and Medieval Site at Blackfriars Street* (CWAAS, Research Series, 4, 1990)
M. R. McCarthy, *Roman and Medieval Carlisle: The Southern Lanes* (Carlisle Archaeology Ltd, Research Report, 1, 2000)
M. R. McCarthy, *Roman Carlisle and the Lands of the Solway* (Stroud, 2002)
T. Patten, 'The Roman cemetery on London Road, Carlisle', *CW2,* 74 (1974), pp. 8–13
C. S. Sommer, *The Military Vici in Roman Britain* (Oxford, 1984)
T. Wilmott, *Birdoswald Roman Fort: 1800 Years on Hadrian's Wall* (Stroud, 2001)
J. Zant, *The Carlisle Millennium Project: Excavations in Carlisle 1998–2001. Volume 1: The Stratigraphy* (Lancaster, 2009)

Chapter 5
The Early Medieval Period

Rachel Newman

The period after the end of Roman governance in Britain is one of the most elusive, in both the historical and the archaeological record: not for nothing has it been termed the Dark Ages! It is little more than 20 years since Nick Higham, in *The North to AD 1000*, wrote that

> the end of the artificial, Roman, economy has deprived the archaeologist of diagnostic, artefactual evidence on all but a small minority of sites, and has left us dangerously dependent on documentary sources, the interpretation of which is unusually difficult ... To set beside these [few] sources are a handful of inscriptions and a very limited amount of archaeological evidence, much of which is of questionable value if only because of chronological imprecision.

Ten years before that, Clack and Gosling, in *Archaeology in the North*, and in associated comments, suggested, only slightly tongue in cheek, that the logical conclusion to be drawn from the almost complete lack of archaeological sites that could be dated to between AD 400 and 1100 was that the region had been largely depopulated, as a substantial population could not possibly be quite so invisible. Since then, however, the picture regionally, and in Carlisle (Figure 5.1), has begun to become clearer, and at last we can start to put a little flesh on the bare bones of the historical sources. Caution must be at the front of our minds, however, as in a Roman settlement such as Carlisle, issues of cultural conservatism and residuality must also be considered.

It is clear, from the growing corpus of information, that the traditional historical division of the early medieval period into three sub-periods, which may be called 'sub-Roman', 'Anglo-Saxon' and 'Viking Age', each spanning approximately 200 years, is much harder to identify on the ground than might have been expected from a reading of the historical sources. Before the campaign of modern excavations in the city, from the late 1970s onwards, evidence for early medieval activity was based to a great extent on largely unstratified finds, often recorded only in antiquarian literature. Indeed, it is only really in the last 30 years that sites, other than burials, that can be firmly associated with the early medieval period in the North-West in general have begun to be excavated, sometimes unintentionally, as is mostly the case in

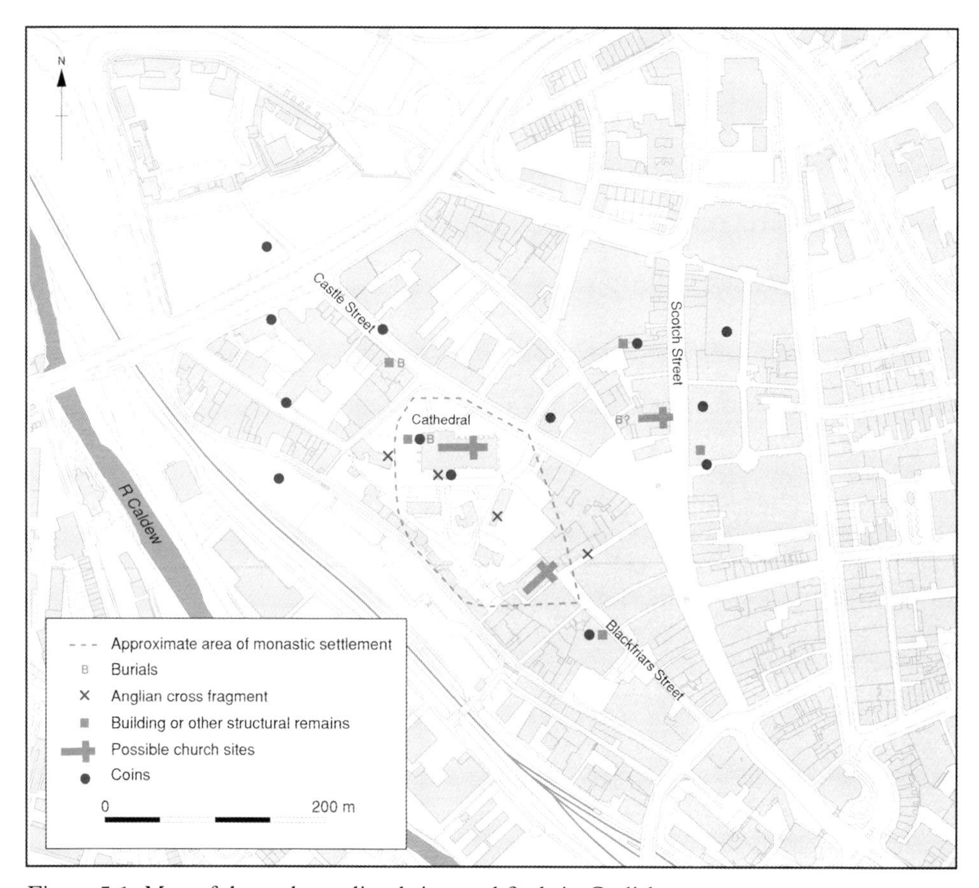

Figure 5.1. Map of the early medieval sites and finds in Carlisle

Carlisle, when the main aim of the excavation has been to examine evidence for other periods.

Although the evidence is still slender, and in Carlisle the number of excavated sites providing information about the period can be counted on the fingers of one hand, it can honestly be said that archaeological thinking has been revolutionised as a result. In addition, the linking of palaeoecological studies to archaeology has proved that our understanding of the past can be expanded exponentially, particularly since it has started to remove our dependence on the scanty cultural indicators in favour of absolute dating, primarily through radiocarbon assay, and if fortunate, in Carlisle, by dendrochronological analysis. Unsurprisingly, this has demonstrated that there was quite extensive early medieval activity in Carlisle, which had previously not been recognised as such.

The Ending of Roman Traditions

The end of Roman governance in Britain has traditionally been placed in AD 410. Increasingly, however, archaeological evidence indicates that, culturally, Roman sites were changing from at least the early to mid-fourth century, suggesting, perhaps, that it would be more accurate to talk of the 'ending' of Roman Britain, rather than 'the end'. It is also questionable whether on clearly Roman sites, such as forts, and civil settlements as at Carlisle, the occupants thought of themselves as something other than Romano-Britons until well into the fifth century, if not later. In this, historical sources may be telling, since the anonymous *Life of St Cuthbert* reports that in Carlisle in 685 the saint met a 'reeve' (*praepositus*) called Waga, a British name for a man with a title that was clearly Roman in origin. It is also recorded that Cuthbert was shown a functioning 'fountain', surely part of the municipal water-management system, similar to (or even part of) that found in the fort during the Millennium Project excavations.

The area in the centre of the Roman fort at Carlisle was clearly a focus of activity in the later fourth century, and this activity would appear, from the amount of coinage dropped, the numbers of animal bones left scattered about, and the type of pottery discarded, to have had market aspects, especially since the pottery included large storage vessels from which smaller quantities could have been decanted. The vessels also clearly demonstrated continued trade with the Mediterranean, apparently into the fifth century. This activity centred on the headquarters building (*principia*) and a lean-to structure against its eastern side, as well as on the main road through the fort, to the south. Animal bone from a floor of the lean-to building, selected for its 'fresh' state, was dated by radiocarbon assay to AD 210–440, not perhaps surprising, but given that the surface also produced a coin of AD 388/92, it can be suggested that this phase of Roman activity may have begun in the last decades of the fourth century, and extended well into the fifth. The demolition of the fort did not take place until after this, again suggesting that it had some formal function until at least the middle of the fifth century. It is of interest to note that similar activity has also been recognised in the fort at Newcastle.

At Stanwix, the fort has also provided evidence for late activity, with seemingly large timber buildings constructed over the stone structures of the Hadrianic and later stone fort (Figure 5.2). These were seen in the playground of Stanwix Primary School, but have not been subject to formal excavation, so their dating must remain speculative.

When the evidence for late activity is examined in conjunction with that from other forts on Hadrian's Wall, and particularly at Birdoswald, the traditional view of a sudden and possibly dramatic change from the Roman period into a Dark Age of chaos is challenged. At Birdoswald, the fort

Figure 5.2. The faint traces of a building overlying the demolition levels in the Roman fort at Stanwix (*by courtesy of Tullie House Museum and Art Gallery, Carlisle*)

granaries were reused as a meeting-place and possibly as accommodation, having been partially reconstructed, from the late fourth century onwards, with a complete rebuild, some time later, partly over the main road through the fort, although still respecting the open portal of the west gate. Of note is the fact that the material used changed from stone to timber at this time, and the latest building resembled what we would recognise as an early medieval hall. There was, though, no evidence of any break in occupation during these changes. It may be that, here at any rate, we are witnessing the genesis of the society mentioned by early writers such as Gildas, who wrote that Britain splintered into a mass of small kingdoms, with war-bands (the remnant garrisons?) attached to them. It could therefore be suggested that the end of Roman Britain was not accompanied by marching feet, or flags flying, except, perhaps, when the field army was withdrawn around the year AD 406, resulting in the frontier garrisons becoming increasingly isolated, until at last the system of overall command disintegrated, leaving the fort commanders to shift for themselves. They would have continued to do what they knew best: running the garrison as a military unit and controlling the surrounding area. In other words, it could be said that the real end of Roman rule in Britain was when the pay chests failed to arrive.

In the civil settlement of Carlisle, a similar picture of continuity well into the fifth century is beginning to emerge. A rebuilt Roman building of some substance on Scotch Street contained a gold *solidus* of Emperor Valentinian II (AD 375–92) (Figure 4.13) in the hypocaust (underfloor heating) system (Figure 5.3). Given that this was sealed by three phases of flooring, it is clear that the building continued to be used well after this date, and its occupants must have maintained an urbanised, Roman lifestyle well into the fifth century, if not beyond. In addition, it seems that craftsmen capable of maintaining such systems were also still living in the area. More recently, potential evidence of continuity into the fifth century has been found elsewhere on Scotch Street, in the form of two phases of late activity overlying better dated late Roman levels. The earlier of the two consisted of a timber building on shallow cobble foundations, which had been constructed on a markedly different alignment from the late Roman structure on the site. It had also encroached over an adjacent road. Following its demolition, this was cut by a series of small pits containing substantial post pads, on the same alignment, although extending over a larger area, denoting a building at least 10 by 14 metres (Figure 5.4). This building method differs markedly from the traditional Roman techniques, and is reminiscent of the latest building in the granary sequence at Birdoswald. In addition, a ninth-century coin and other metalwork would suggest early medieval activity at or near the site, although most of these seem to have been found in contexts where they were clearly residual.

Figure 5.3. The rebuilt hypocaust in a building on Scotch Street (*by courtesy of Tullie House Museum and Art Gallery, Carlisle*)

Figure 5.4. Post pads forming the corner of a timber building on Scotch Street, which post-dated a late Roman building (*by courtesy of North Pennines Archaeology Ltd*)

Further south, a potentially 'sub-Roman' building was recognised west of the cathedral, stratigraphically above Roman levels yet sealed by the ubiquitous dark soils that cover Roman Carlisle. In Blackfriars Street, a period of abandonment was noticed, when the Roman buildings were demolished and the site appeared to revert to open land, but this seems to have occurred in the third century, and to have continued throughout much of the fourth century. Later, though, a new stone building was constructed, following the earlier layout on the plot and respecting the Roman road. This building mirrored the 'standard' Roman pattern, being rectangular, and built gable-end on to the road; in other words, it was 'Roman' in every way. Later, the building fell out of use, and an oven or kiln was built across its north-western corner, with a stokepit beyond the ruined building. Even after this had fallen out of use, the road continued to be maintained and repaired, and another structure, this time of timber, with evidence for large, earth-fast posts, was constructed on the site of the former stone building. This seemed to use masonry from demolished structures as packing for the posts, which might suggest demolition in the surrounding town, and it seems to have been repaired at least once, as is implied by the close setting of some of the posts in the gable adjacent to the street, although these could also be interpreted as evidence for a porch. All these phases of activity followed the Roman layout, and contained Roman material. It was not until sometime later that a change occurred, and another timber building, this time of post-in-slot construction, was built on a completely different alignment (almost at right-angles), not respecting the Roman building-lines or the road. Activity pre-dating the medieval city continued even beyond this, with evidence for a pit and a well on the site, both clearly later than the last building. The well had been timber-lined, and oak fragments pitched on end were found in the lower fill, one of which produced a felling date of after 655. It thus seems that the largest period of abandonment was within the Roman period, and that there was relatively unbroken occupation on the site until well into the seventh century, if not beyond.

The Kingdom of Northumbria

It is therefore becoming increasingly apparent that the Roman way of life did not end at the beginning of the fifth century, or perhaps even in the middle of that century, but continued for a considerable period, even though there was no longer a 'centralised' government. The scanty documentary sources imply that the war-bands and 'petty kingdoms' mentioned by Gildas slowly started to coalesce, and by the sixth century a kingdom apparently known as Rheged held sway over much of Cumbria. Welsh poetry looked back to this time as a golden age, which, it is suggested, ended when Rheged's king, Urien, was killed at the siege of Bamburgh, the centre of a nascent Anglo-Saxon kingdom known as Bernicia. Its king, Aethelfrith, united Bernicia with its Anglo-Saxon neighbour to the south, Deira, to create the kingdom of Northumbria, and then turned his attention to the west, defeating the Welsh in a great battle at or near Chester in 615. By the middle of the seventh century, it seems that all of Cumbria had been incorporated into Northumbria, just possibly by dynastic marriage rather than by conquest, as there are hints that Aethelfrith's younger son, Oswy, who became king of Northumbria in 642, had been married to a British princess, who was subsequently 'thrown over' for an Anglo-Saxon wife. What all this meant in terms of population movement is unknown and, archaeologically, sites of this period are infrequent in the region as a whole; those known could also all be described as atypical, in other words, not containing evidence of 'normal' domestic accommodation.

In Carlisle, the latest 'Roman' activity is almost always sealed by a build-up of dark soils (Figure 5.5), seen over almost every Roman town in Britain. Exactly what these 'dark earths' represent – or even how they formed – is still hotly debated. In some towns, there is evidence for large-scale dumping, whilst in others the soils seem to result from the demolition or natural collapse of Roman buildings. In Carlisle, however, there is no good evidence for either, and, indeed, in the fort there is very little recognisable demolition debris, as though anything that was useful had been scavenged, and little rubbish was left from the process. Yet across the fort and Roman settlement,

Figure 5.5. The considerable build-up of 'dark earth' over the Roman stone fort at Carlisle (*by courtesy of Tullie House Museum and Art Gallery, Carlisle*)

up to 600 millimetres of material had accumulated over the last 'Roman' buildings before the first recognisably medieval buildings were constructed. If one allows that the maximum period in which these soils could accumulate was no more than 650–700 years, then this is the same sort of growth rate as an average peat bog, which is fed by the decay of organic matter growing on it. Studies of Second World War bomb-sites in Germany and Britain have, however, demonstrated the same, or an even faster, growth rate for soils, presumably as a result of the rampant vegetation that colonised such sites. Many believe that the 'dark earths' must contain large amounts of charcoal or other organic matter to produce their rich, dark colouring, and that the growth rate must be stimulated by the turning over of the soils, perhaps by horticulture. Whilst this is extremely plausible, there is no stratigraphic evidence within the fort at Carlisle for the disturbance of the uppermost Roman levels by anything other than deliberate robbing, which might have been expected if deep digging had taken place. Yet the amounts of residual material in the lower levels of the soils are marked, and these must have come from disturbance somewhere.

It is notable that the amount of artefactual material lessens dramatically from the base of the dark soils, where there are substantial quantities of pottery and animal bone, as well as Roman coins and other artefacts, to the top, where there are very few artefacts at all. One of the few recognisably 'sub-Roman' finds, a brooch that can be dated to the fifth to seventh centuries, was found in such material at the cathedral, but it is rare to be able to recognise activity within these soils. At the Lanes, however, a timber-lined pit found beneath Crown and Anchor Lane produced a dendrochronological date of 771–816, and also a Trewhiddle-style strap-end of the ninth century. A timber-lined well found during the Castle Street excavations produced another dendrochronological date of 770–803 (Figure 5.6), and the site also contained

Figure 5.6. A timber-lined well on Castle Street providing a dendrochronological date of 770–803 (*by courtesy of Tullie House Museum and Art Gallery, Carlisle*)

the grave of a middle-aged female (Figure 5.7). This grave demonstrates some of the challenges of balancing stratigraphical information and absolute dating of different types, as one of her bones was radiocarbon-dated to AD 640–1000, but stratigraphically the grave seemed to post-date the infilling of a well which contained timber producing a dendrochronological date of *c.* 1150. Other features can be almost impossible to recognise, particularly if their fills are similar to the surrounding soils. For instance, an early medieval radiocarbon date was gained from a piece of animal bone from a shallow pit at the base of the dark soils in the Roman fort, which would suggest an intrusion, but none could be seen within the stratigraphy. Not everything Roman was demolished, either, as the east wall of the fort's headquarters building (the *principia*) remained standing throughout the accumulation of these soils, as did some of the walls of barracks to the south, and they appear to have been visible features when the castle was being constructed, since they seem to have dictated the layout of apparently twelfth-century structures in its outer ward. In addition, the main road from the south gate of the fort to the headquarters building may have remained in use as late as the twelfth century, although the main road running east–west across the centre of the fort had certainly fallen out of use when the fort was demolished.

Figure 5.7. The grave of an adult female on Castle Street, possibly early medieval in date (*by courtesy of Tullie House Museum and Art Gallery, Carlisle*)

According to historical sources, Carlisle in the later seventh century had become a royal estate, some 15 miles (24km) in circumference. Whether this was a direct transfer of the *territorium* of the Roman fort, and the rule of its commander, however, must remain pure speculation. The Northumbrian king, Ecgfrith, gave this estate to St Cuthbert shortly before 685, and the saint is said to have visited a nunnery there, as well as establishing a monastery 'nearby'. Whilst there is some evidence from both the Continent and Kent to suggest that nunneries were frequently established in Roman forts, the excavations to date in Carlisle have provided no evidence for such activity, although one might speculate that the prime site within the fort would have been beneath the present keep, since this was the highest, driest point within the walls. Potential evidence that the fort's walls survived for some time can also be deduced from the comment in Bede's *Life* that St Cuthbert perambulated the walls of the 'town', although the excavated portion of the western wall was sealed by 'dark earths', so it did not remain standing throughout the period. Absolutely no evidence has been found yet that the civil settlement was walled at any time in its history. Instead, there is growing evidence for a substantial religious site in the area of the present cathedral (Figure 5.1). The church to the south, St Cuthbert's, is dedicated to the saint who had visited Carlisle and had influence within the settlement. The position and alignment of this church, close to the cathedral, yet on a Roman street and aligned to it, so that it is far from the approved true east–west orientation, would indicate an early foundation. In addition, there is an antiquarian reference to the remains of an earlier building being seen below the medieval church when it was demolished in the eighteenth century.

The fact that all the pre-Norman stone sculpture from Carlisle comes from this general area is also suggestive that this was the centre of early Christian activity.

It is the quality and scale of the early medieval Christian stone sculpture that marks Northumbria out from the other Anglo-Saxon kingdoms; indeed, this era was, like the time of the kingdom of Rheged, looked back on by later Anglo-Saxons as a golden age for Christian teaching, when Northumbria, as the dominant kingdom in the seventh and eighth centuries, set the standard for European kingship. The stone sculpture also gives a firm indicator of the broad pattern of churches in the landscape, even though this cannot be said to be complete. These sculptures are not, however, equally spread across time and space, their distribution in part at least being dictated by the underlying geology. There are 36 sites in Cumbria that have produced early medieval stone sculpture, of which 20 contain material from the eighth and ninth centuries, which can be linked to the kingdom of Northumbria, some 28 pieces in all. It is generally believed that this Northumbrian sculpture was related to monastic activity, and that it reflects an elaborate network of national and international contacts within the early Christian world, with many Mediterranean motifs being expressed within the carving.

Carlisle has three such pieces, all from the vicinity of the cathedral (Figure 5.8). All are fine, well-executed sculpture, parts of the heads of free-standing crosses of the type that still stands in the churchyard at Bewcastle. Unusually, however, two contain elements of inscriptions on them. This is an extremely rare phenomenon, although Cumbria does contain a larger percentage of inscriptions than the rest of Northumbria. The motifs on these cross-heads display both elements of vinescroll, indicative of the tree of life and a

Figure 5.8. A fragment of a Northumbrian cross-head found near the cathedral (© *Corpus of Anglo-Saxon Stone Sculpture*)

'trademark' of Northumbrian sculpture, and small panels of interlace, again a typical early medieval design.

Figure 5.9. A ninth-century coin from Castle Street (*by courtesy of Tullie House Museum and Art Gallery, Carlisle*)

There are also increasing numbers of the early to mid-ninth-century coins known as stycas, minted by the Northumbrian kings, found within Carlisle (Figure 5.9). Their pattern of distribution, however, has a clear bias towards the centre and west of the medieval city, seemingly reflecting the centre of commercial, political, and religious power in the settlement (Figure 5.1). It is notable that this does not include the area of the Roman fort, suggesting that, by this time, this was not a focus, at least for commercial activity.

The 'Viking Age' in Carlisle

Politically, the collapse of royal power within Northumbria in the ninth century led to instability, which continued relatively unabated until the imposition of Norman rule more than 200 years later. The documentary evidence, as well as that of place-names in Cumbria, and the North more generally, suggests that one of the factors for this destabilisation was influence from peoples of Scandinavian descent, firstly as raiders and then seemingly as settlers. In addition, in northern Cumbria there seems to have been a resurgence of political influence from British speakers, probably from the kingdom of Strathclyde (around present-day Glasgow). Both of these groups, however, have proved notoriously difficult to discern in the archaeological record, and there is considerable doubt, as there is with the extent of settlement of Anglian speakers, as to what this political influence meant in terms of population movement. Whilst there is some evidence for a Scandinavian presence in the area, as has been demonstrated by the group of six graves at Cumwhitton, some seven miles (11km) to the east of Carlisle, and also some diagnostic artefacts, the influence of Strathclyde is archaeologically invisible at the moment. A dispute that arose in the early twelfth century between the churches of England and Scotland, when the bishopric of Glasgow claimed authority over Cumbria as far south as the Rey Cross on Stainmore, is perhaps a legacy of secular political influence.

The earliest recorded direct Viking influence in the area comes from the Anglo-Saxon Chronicle, which records that a Viking army over-wintered on the Tyne in 866/7. A twelfth-century source claimed that a slightly later Viking raid on Carlisle, presumably associated with this army, laid waste the city, and that it remained deserted for the next 200 years. This claim can be challenged archaeologically, at least to some extent, as in no excavations has any evidence of destruction been found either within or at the top of the ubiquitous 'dark earths'. Furthermore, excavations immediately to the west of the cathedral have produced evidence of an orderly cemetery of more than 40 graves, seemingly of the ninth or tenth century, associated with a wealth of artefacts of the period (Figures 5.10 and 5.11). Graves that can be dated to the tenth or eleventh century are extremely rare in Britain, which has been taken as evidence of the rapid conversion of the pagan Vikings to Christianity, possibly within a single generation, as Christian graves usually contain no datable artefacts, and the baptised would have been buried in churchyards, which are rarely subject to archaeological investigation. It is therefore telling that these graves appear to be in a Christian context, adding weight to the hypothesis that the cathedral area was the focus of religious activity in Carlisle from at least the seventh century onwards. In contrast to this physical evidence of continuity of Christian practices, documentary sources would suggest some dislocation, as Eadred, called the former abbot of Carlisle, was prominent in the party which carried St Cuthbert's remains on their travels through the fragmenting kingdom of Northumbria in the later ninth century. This has generally been taken as evidence that he, like the community of St Cuthbert on Lindisfarne, had been forced to flee from the onset of anarchy.

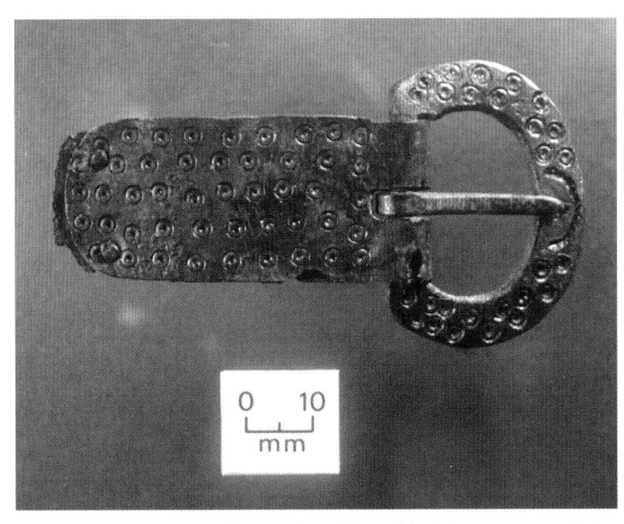

Figure 5.10. An early medieval buckle from west of the cathedral showing the ring-and-dot motif so characteristic of Hiberno-Norse objects (*by courtesy of Tullie House Museum and Art Gallery, Carlisle*)

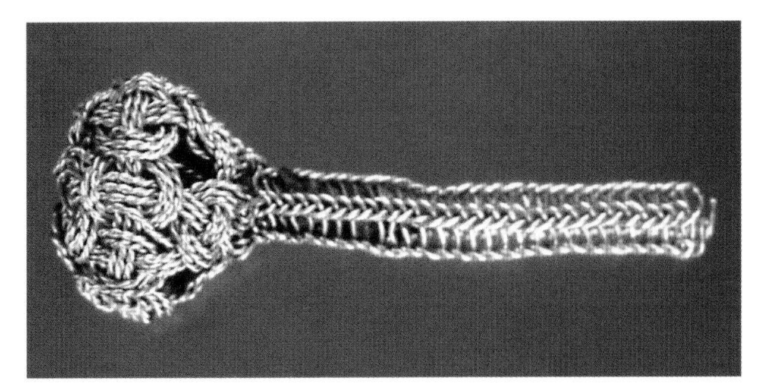

Figure 5.11. A gold toggle from west of the cathedral (*by courtesy of Tullie House Museum and Art Gallery, Carlisle*)

The area of the Roman fort, adjacent to the medieval castle, has also produced a small but rich collection of material dating from the tenth and eleventh centuries. Whilst there is no evidence for any structures in the areas excavated to date, animal bone in a shallow pit produced a radiocarbon date of AD 890–1160. This suggests that at least some features may have cut through the 'dark earths', although they proved impossible to recognise in the stratigraphy. Certainly, the early medieval assemblage from the area was sufficient to suggest activity somewhere in the vicinity.

As for the kingdom of Northumbria in the eighth and ninth centuries, by far the most visible evidence for Scandinavian influence in Cumbria, with the exception of the wealth of place-names, is the presence of stone sculpture with distinctive cultural motifs. Within Cumbria, the 36 sites have produced 111 fragments dating to these two centuries, yet Carlisle is one of the few places where there is little evidence of its influence. In contrast to the fragments of the three Northumbrian crosses, only one piece of sculpture that can be dated to this late period has been found, again in the vicinity of the cathedral. This is a rather crude cross head, and in contrast to the fine Northumbrian carving, it has badly executed designs.

The Coming of the Normans

In 1092, the Anglo-Saxon Chronicle records that King William II (Rufus) marched north, ejected one Dolfin from Carlisle, and built a castle there, populating the surrounding area with his supporters. Evidence for the latter can be seen in the surrounding place-names: Botcherby, Rickerby, Aglionby, and so on. Perhaps tellingly, these tend to have Norman prefixes, representing people's names, yet Scandinavian suffixes, the *by* ending, perhaps reflecting the dialect or even language spoken in Carlisle at the time. This was, in effect, the Norman Conquest of Cumbria. Exactly who Dolfin was is a matter for debate, although he may well have been a scion of the family of Gospatric, who had held the earldom of Northumbria earlier in the eleventh century. This major incident in Carlisle's history, marking the end of the early medieval period, is again almost invisible archaeologically, apart from a single coin of William II, found trampled into the top of the 'dark earths' close to the future access route into Carlisle castle (Figure 5.12).

Conclusions

In comparison with some other periods in our past, the archaeological record for the early medieval period is highly incomplete, and we are only just beginning to move from a situation where there is a complete dependence on a few scattered documentary references on which to peg the odd isolated pieces of archaeological evidence, to a point at which the archaeological record

Figure 5.12. A silver penny of King William II (1087–1100) found on the surface of the 'dark earth' outside the castle *(by courtesy of Tullie House Museum and Art Gallery, Carlisle)*

can start to create a framework of its own. This has largely been the result of meticulous excavation over the last 30 years or so, coupled with the use of scientific techniques, particularly those for dating. It is clear, though, that even now only limited types of site – largely associated with religious beliefs, Christian or otherwise – are unequivocally recognisable in the archaeological record, and the vast majority of the early medieval population remains archaeologically invisible. Techniques such as radiocarbon dating, DNA analysis and, where possible, stable isotope analysis need to be used at every opportunity, therefore, to test the assumptions that are often made about the date of a site, particularly late in the Roman sequence, and those about the ethnic origins of individuals, particularly when these bodies are associated with cultural material. Carlisle is especially fortunate in that much of the city has a high water-table, creating waterlogged archaeological stratigraphy, resulting in the survival of ancient timber. This means that dendrochronological analysis can be used to date sites, sometimes with remarkable accuracy. Whilst the early medieval levels tend to be above the water-table, cut features, such as deep pits and wells, are not, and thus there is considerable potential to recover quite detailed dating evidence for Carlisle's early history.

It is clear that, whilst Roman urban life in Carlisle decayed, people continued to live within the later bounds of the medieval city throughout the early medieval period. The nature of the settlement changed, though, as did the focus, seemingly from the Roman fort at the north-western end of the settlement to the area around the present cathedral. At the beginning of the period, it seems that the citizens thought of themselves as Romano-British, and continued to enjoy and be proud of their urban life for some considerable time, but then a change becomes visible in the record, so that by the eighth or ninth century it is the religious life of the settlement that is highlighted by the archaeological evidence. It is clear that there was a renewed focus on Carlisle after the Norman takeover, with royal support to rebuild the city into a vibrant economic centre, but how large a task this actually was, and what exactly this meant physically, are still questions to be addressed by future work.

* * * * *

Suggested Further Reading

R. N. Bailey and R. J. Cramp, *The British Academy Corpus of Anglo-Saxon Stone Sculpture in England. Volume II: Cumberland, Westmorland and Lancashire North-of-the-Sands* (Oxford, 1988)

B. Colgrave and R. A. B. Mynors (eds), *Bede's Ecclesiastical History of the English People* (Oxford, 1940)

J. Earle and C. Plummer (eds), *Two of the Saxon Chronicles* (Oxford, 1892)

N. Higham, *The North to AD 1000* (London, 1986)

W. E. Kapelle, *The Norman Conquest of the North: The Region and Its Transformation, 1000–1135* (London, 1979)

M. R. McCarthy, *A Roman, Anglian and Medieval Site at Blackfriars Street* (CWAAS, Research Series, 4, 1990)

M. R. McCarthy, *Roman Carlisle and the Lands of the Solway* (Stroud, 2002)

M. R. McCarthy, *The Roman Waterlogged Remains and Later Features at Castle Street, Carlisle: Excavations 1981–2* (CWAAS, Research Series, 5, 1991)

R. M. Newman, 'The early medieval period resource assessment', in M. Brennand (ed.), *The Archaeology of North West England: An Archaeological Research Framework for North West England. Volume 1: Resource Assessment* (Manchester, 2006), pp. 91–114

D. Rollason, *Northumbria, 500–1100: Creation and Destruction of a Kingdom* (Cambridge, 2003)

J. Zant, *The Carlisle Millennium Project: Excavations in Carlisle 1998–2001. Volume 1: The Stratigraphy* (Lancaster, 2009)

Chapter 6
The Defences of Medieval Carlisle

Henry Summerson

A stronghold before it became anything like a town, Carlisle remained a stronghold even after it had developed all the characteristic features of urban life. When King William Rufus occupied the site in 1092, his first action was to build a castle there. If its previous ruler, Dolfin, gave allegiance to anybody it was to the king of the Scots, and this annexation of territory provoked Scottish resentment. Carlisle was disputed territory until 1237, when the Treaty of York confirmed its status as part of England, and though nearly 60 years of peace followed, King Edward I's claims to Scottish overlordship led in 1296 to the outbreak of Anglo-Scottish hostilities, so that city and castle stood at the centre of a war-zone for over 250 years. The threat of attack hung almost continuously over medieval Carlisle, doing much to dictate its physical form and to shape the lives of those who lived there (Figure 6.1).

Modern scholarship has shown that many medieval castles were intended primarily to proclaim the status and power of their builders. But the castle Rufus built at Carlisle, which his successors greatly extended and elaborated, was intended first and foremost to serve purely military purposes, by controlling and protecting a strategically important position where several roads and rivers met (Figure 6.2), and by acting as a base for offensive and defensive operations. The town that developed literally at the castle gate was soon inextricably involved in the castle's military function. In the very early days of Anglo-Norman occupation the two were apparently kept separate, each behind its own walls; but around 1168 a new gate for the castle was built, opening into the town, while the town's walls were continued northwards, to join those of the castle's south curtain. Henceforward the town constituted a massive defensive outwork for the castle. The latter's position at the northern end of Carlisle, overlooking the flood plain of the River Eden, was such as to make it almost invulnerable to direct attack except from the south; and after 1168 the Scottish invader or English rebel who aimed to capture it had to break into the town first. Surrounded by a continuous sequence of fortifications, castle and town together formed a single powerful defensive unit, and as such constituted a vital part of the defences of northern England.

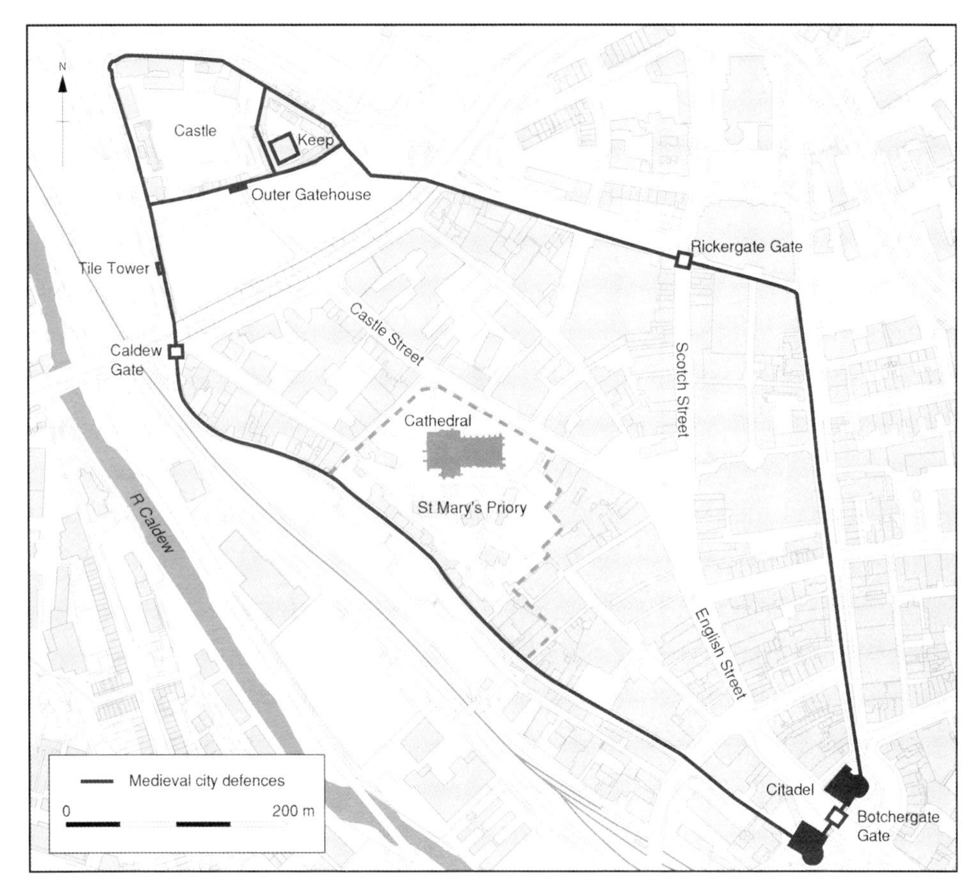

Figure 6.1. Map of the medieval defences in Carlisle

A Beleaguered Community

Carlisle needed all its defensive strength, for it was many times attacked, and even more often threatened. In 1135 it was taken by a trick, when King David I of Scots and his retinue were able to take possession after pretending that they only wanted lodging there. Once admitted, the Scots strengthened their hold on Carlisle by improving its defences. Returned to English rule in 1157 by David's grandson, Malcolm IV, Carlisle was attacked by Malcolm's brother, William the Lion, in 1173 and again in 1174, when it was nearly forced to surrender (Figure 6.3). Then, in 1216 – at a time of civil war in England – disaffected townsfolk surrendered the city to William's son, Alexander II, whose soldiers then mined and battered their way into the castle. Carlisle was again returned to English rule a year later, and for most of the thirteenth century peace reigned in the city, broken only briefly in 1264, when followers of Simon de Montfort occupied the castle and released the

Figure 6.2. An aerial view of Carlisle castle, 1987 (*by courtesy of Cumbria County Council*)

prisoners there. But things changed drastically for the worse in 1296, with a determined Scottish attack on Carlisle that took the city by surprise and nearly succeeded, and a further threat a year later, when William Wallace ravaged his way up to the walls. For nearly 20 years the wars mostly continued in Scotland, but in 1315 King Robert I (Robert Bruce) led an all-out attack on Carlisle, only to be thwarted by a resolute defence led by Sir Andrew Harclay and by the year's incessant rain, which turned the approaches to the walls into a quagmire.

There followed repeated Scottish attacks on and round Carlisle. In 1326 there was an attempt to capture the castle by night, while the mid-1340s saw a whole series of alarms and excursions, with rumours that war-weary Cumbrians were plotting to surrender Carlisle to

Figure 6.3. The seal of William I (the Lion), king of Scots, who besieged Carlisle in 1173 and 1174, from an engraving, *c.* 1890

the Scots, and a number of incursions that devastated the city's suburbs. The capture of King David II in 1346 brought an uneasy peace to the Borders, but by the late 1370s hostilities were beginning again. In 1383 – despite the truce that was still in force – Scottish archers shot fire into the city, destroying one of its streets, while two years later another invading army briefly threatened to lay siege to Carlisle. Further destruction around the city followed in 1388–9, while the first decade of the fifteenth century saw yet more raiding and fighting, with what was referred to as 'a great battle' being fought near Carlisle in 1406. The installation of guns, first in the castle and then on the city walls, may have helped keep attackers at arm's length, but it could not deter them completely. There was yet more devastation outside the walls in 1449; and in 1461, in the confusion generated by the Wars of the Roses, a determined attempt was made to break through them by an army of Scots and Lancastrians. Probably not since 1315 had Carlisle been in such danger. The attackers damaged the walls (perhaps they had brought cannon with them) and set fire to the gates, and eventually they seem to have forced their way into the city. But the defenders held out in the castle until a Yorkist army came to their relief and scattered the enemy (Figure 6.4). Despite still more raiding around Carlisle in the early 1480s, the decades after 1461 were relatively peaceful ones; but the danger from the north persisted, and the city was lucky to escape attack by a large Scottish army in 1522, a threat renewed a year later. Nor was it only Scots who might endanger Carlisle, for in 1536 the forces of the Pilgrimage of Grace tried to occupy the city, and in February 1537 made a direct attack on its walls, only to be defeated by a relieving force. It was primarily this last crisis that led to a radical reshaping of Carlisle's defences, with major works in the castle and the construction of a citadel at the southern end of the town (Figure 9.3).

Settling Responsibilities

The city and castle that thus developed together, and faced the same dangers together, soon possessed an impressive set of stone fortifications. By 1173 the castle's mighty donjon was already 'the great ancient keep' (Figure 6.5), while the town was surrounded by a wall that only steel picks could hope to demolish. So handsome were Carlisle's defences that a twelfth-century poet could describe Carlisle under siege as 'resplendent in its beauty'. At that time the crown shouldered the responsibility for the whole of this strategically important complex. King Henry I (1100–35) not only started work on the keep but also provided the town with walls. As late as 1190 the gates of Carlisle were built at the crown's expense. In the more peaceful conditions of the thirteenth century, the king remained responsible for the castle, at least in theory – in practice it was sadly neglected, and in a state of advanced decay by the mid-1250s. But when the townsfolk acquired rights of self-

Figure 6.4. A fifteenth-century illustration of a medieval town under siege showing a wooden siege-tower and cannon, from British Library, MS Royal 14 E.IV, f. 281v (© *The British Library Board*)

government in 1231, they seem also to have been saddled with the burden of maintaining their own walls. The king was prepared to provide assistance, in the form of grants of murage, which licensed the city authorities to take tolls from specified goods brought into Carlisle for sale, and to spend the proceeds on the walls. Starting in 1232, such grants were made at regular intervals throughout the thirteenth and well into the fourteenth century. But their administration was dogged by hardly less regular allegations of corruption, which may have been justified, but may also have resulted from incompetence on the part of those who collected and spent the money. It is also possible that the tolls simply did not raise enough money, something that those who paid them may not have appreciated when they saw that their involuntary contributions were making no obvious difference.

Figure 6.5. The keep of Carlisle castle (*photograph: Mark Brennand*)

It was always accepted that the king bore an underlying responsibility for all the defences of Carlisle. It was to him or his officers that charges of misuse of murage receipts were made, and when in the early 1290s a dispute arose between the cathedral canons and the Dominican friary, during which the canons obstructed the drain which carried the friary's sewage under the city walls with a pile of stone and timber, the verdict in the resulting lawsuit found that because the blockage made the wall easier to climb for anyone who attacked the city in wartime, it was 'to the king's loss and detriment'. Then the outbreak of Anglo-Scottish hostilities in 1296 made the defensibility of Carlisle a matter of urgent concern for the crown. In the castle this led to numerous works of repair and the occasional addition of new buildings, such as the tower erected at the south-east corner of the inner ward between 1307 and 1312. For the city it meant a steady encroachment on the townsmen's control of their own affairs, and an accompanying intrusion into urban life of military preoccupations and values. The Scottish attack of 1296, when the city was taken unawares and the besiegers were only just beaten off by the combined efforts of all the inhabitants, including the townswomen, probably made it clear to the king's government that a place of such strategic importance could not be left safely in the hands of amateur defenders. Nevertheless, the crown's resources were not unlimited, while the civic authorities remained attached to their rights of self-government, and it took some time for agreement to be reached as to how responsibility for the defences should be shared.

In 1296 Carlisle's long-standing administrative independence was in abeyance, having been rescinded in 1292, and it was probably under direction from the castle that the city's defences were enlarged for the first time for over a century, by the digging of substantial ditches outside the walls. They may have been principally intended to protect the gates, which seem to have acquired drawbridges over them. But the ditches, which became full of water, were clearly a considerable inconvenience to those on whose property they were made. They needed constant repair and renewal, apparently because they were often neglected, or even surreptitiously filled in. This was just one of the ways in which the townspeople's civilian interests could conflict with their military role (their persistence in trading with Scotland, despite numerous prohibitions, was another). But when the city was faced with direct attack, then its inhabitants had no choice but to act with the castle garrison in mutual self-defence. This can be clearly seen in the siege of 1315 (Figure 6.6). Although the Scottish attack fell on the city walls, resistance was organised and led from the castle. Sir Andrew Harclay had all the city gates blocked up with stone, burned houses outside the walls to prevent their providing cover for attackers, and demolished at least one house within the city in order to use its materials to strengthen the battlements. He probably set up his command post in or near what is now known as the Tile Tower (Figure 6.7), in the stretch of wall linking the castle's south face with the city's west wall: it was apparently this structure that was referred to in 1388 as 'the tower called Harkeleyes'. He commanded a garrison of several hundred soldiers, but the contribution of the townsmen, not least in keeping watch upon the walls, was clearly essential, and a year later King Edward II rewarded them by regranting to Carlisle its rights of self-government.

It is emblematic of the symbiotic relationship between city and castle at this time that, when in 1323 their walls were found to have been well-nigh shattered by incessant hard usage, a continuous wooden palisade going round the entire defensive complex was constructed to protect both city

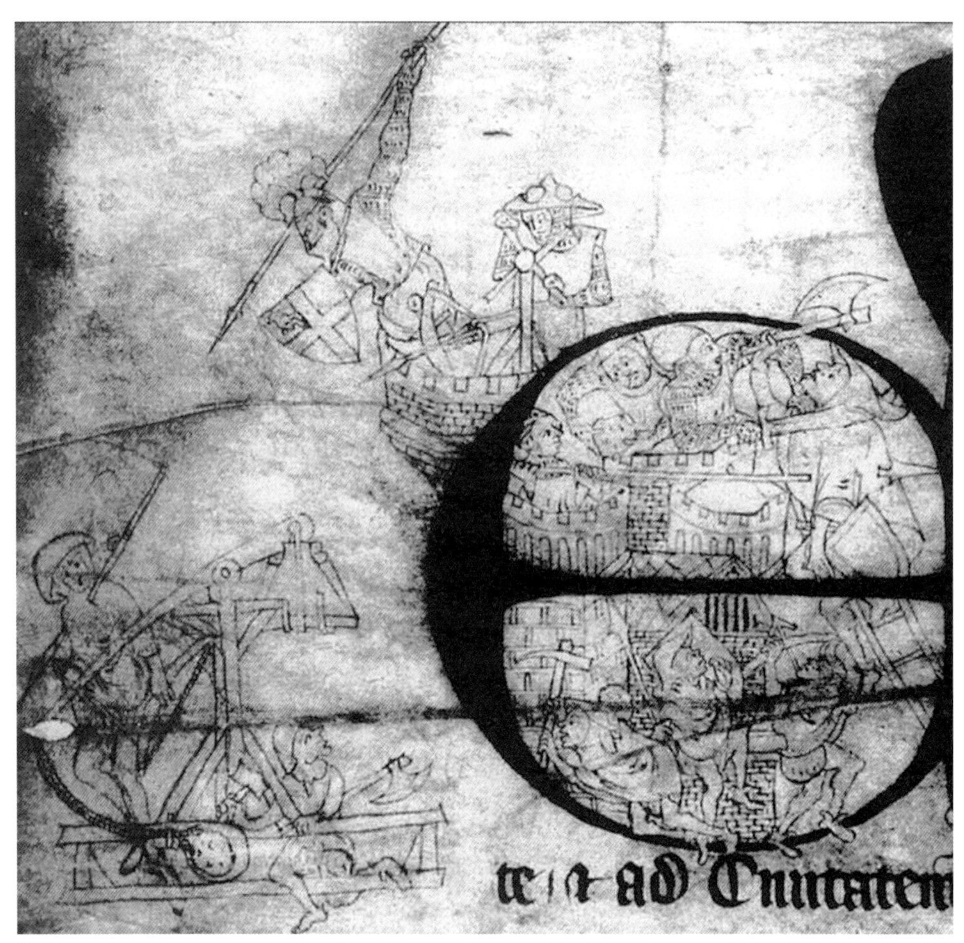

Figure 6.6. A depiction of the siege of Carlisle in 1315, with Sir Andrew Harclay (identifiable from the coat of arms on his shield) leading the defence (*by courtesy of Tullie House Museum and Art Gallery, Carlisle*)

Figure 6.7. A stretch of west-facing medieval wall, including the Tile Tower (*photograph: Mark Brennand*)

and castle while the stonework was repaired. But when the Scottish threat eased temporarily, the crown became less willing to finance the upkeep of the town defences, and returned to traditional methods for maintaining them. Another grant of murage was made in 1336, and when large-scale hostilities resumed in the Borders in the mid-1340s, there are clear signs that the central government expected the civic authorities to continue to maintain Carlisle's walls. But two inquests held in 1348 recorded that 'the king is bound to do the necessary repairs, which cannot be suitably effected for less than £500', while the townsfolk 'have had no means assigned to them wherewith to do the repairs, and are not bound to do them, being too much burdened with watches and other efforts for the safety of that city'. The unending conflict that made repairs essential had also so impoverished the people of Carlisle that they were incapable of carrying them out.

Patterns of Cooperation

The result was a shift in the balance of responsibility. From the mid-fourteenth century it was finally accepted that the king should maintain all the defences of Carlisle, including the city walls. He might make grants of money for their upkeep, or provide timber from Inglewood Forest; in 1354 he gave both, instructing that 12 oaks and 100 marks (£66. 66p.) be supplied for repairs to walls and gates. But he could also direct that money from Carlisle itself be used for this purpose, ordering that the city's fee-farm – the annual sum due to the crown in return for the city's right to self-government, set at £80 in 1316 – should be spent on the defences instead of being paid to the exchequer. Occasionally this was done after the event; in 1382, for instance, the fee-farm was pardoned to reimburse the citizens for putting their defences in order. But more often the crown responded to petitions for help by directing that the fee-farm be spent in this way, sometimes wholly on the city walls, sometimes on city and castle together. To ensure that the money was disbursed as ordered, commissioners were appointed by the crown to keep watch over expenditure and works. Very often the task was entrusted to the warden of the West March, in the later Middle Ages the king's most important representative in the North-West, with a residence in Carlisle castle from which he oversaw the defence of the region. Thus in 1382 the fee-farm was pardoned after Lord Scrope, who was then March warden, had certified that £80 had indeed been spent on recent works. And when in 1386 the mayor and one of his fellow-citizens were directed to spend £40 on the city defences and £40 on the castle walls, they were to act 'under the supervision and direction' of John, Lord Neville, his son Ralph, and Sir Thomas Clifford; all three were members of leading northern families, while Ralph Neville and Thomas Clifford were joint wardens of the West March and keepers of Carlisle castle. It is hard to imagine more authoritative oversight.

Although works on city and castle were often in progress simultaneously, the former's defences always received much less royal money than the latter's. Between 1378 and 1385 the castle's gatehouse was replaced at a cost of at least £500 (Figure 6.8), considerably more than is known to have been spent on the town walls in the entire second half of the fourteenth century. The first guns recorded at Carlisle were placed in the castle – two in 1380, and three more in 1384, nearly 50 years before the city had any. But when the city did acquire guns, it was at the crown's expense. In the late 1420s the defences were found to be in a deplorable state after years of neglect. The steps taken to restore them illustrate how king and townsfolk now cooperated in carrying out necessary works. The money for repairs came from the citizens

Figure 6.8. The gatehouse of Carlisle castle, rebuilt at considerable expense between 1378 and 1385 (*photograph: Mark Brennand*)

themselves. Thus in 1429 it was ordered that for three years the fee-farm should be spent on putting the walls and gates in order, and when in 1431 it became clear that this was not going to be sufficient, the order was repeated, making available a total of £480. But this large sum was not entrusted to the mayor, or even to the warden of the March. The crown now employed a clerk of the works, John Skipton, to oversee the maintenance of strongholds in the Borders, and a series of indentures records his receiving the money each year from the mayor of Carlisle. There was not enough to pay for military stores as well, and these were funded directly from the exchequer. Again the money was supplied to Skipton, who bought what was needed and handed it over to the city authorities. Cannon had apparently been provided in 1430. Two years later the mayor acknowledged receiving stores including longbows, crossbows, saltpetre and sulphur to make gunpowder, and a total of 543 'gunstones'. Such measures were not only a safeguard against peculation; they also ensured that essential works were carried out with appropriate expertise. But tasks that did not require specialised skills were still left to the townsfolk. In the fifteenth century it was the city authorities which organised the keeping of watch on the walls at night, took precautions against buildings being erected too close to the walls, and ensured that the city ditches were kept in repair.

The same pattern of responsibility was still being maintained in the 1490s, when King Henry VII appointed Sir Henry Wyatt as captain of Carlisle. Wyatt's post gave him control of all the defences, and he used it to carry out repairs from which the city authorities were totally excluded. But when they were completed, Wyatt returned the walls and the inner gates to the mayor (the outer gates were controlled from the castle, where their keys were kept), having had the walls cleared of ivy and the roofs of the gates and towers restored, and also provided the mayor with guns, gunpowder, bows and arrows. Although the townsfolk were clearly expected to keep their defences in the state in which they had just received them, this arrangement broke down because in 1500 Henry VII, anxious to save money, entrusted castle and city to Thomas, Lord Dacre, who as warden of the March undertook to maintain the defences of both, but in practice paid no attention to either. Years of decay followed, with the result that by 1540 the city was regarded as effectively indefensible. With war against Scotland imminent, the problems of Carlisle's defences had become such as to call for radical solutions.

The View from Outside

For the Scots, or indeed for anyone coming to Carlisle from the north, the approaches to the city were dominated by the castle, set up on a prominent bluff overlooking the River Eden (Figure 6.9). The whole complex of walls and towers remained an impressive one. Ghillebert de Lannoy, a Burgundian

Figure 6.9. Carlisle from the north-west, with the castle dominating the approaches to the city, from an engraving by Nathanial Buck, 1739

soldier and diplomat who passed through Cumberland in 1431, described Carlisle as 'a very pretty little town, enclosed with walls and possessing a very fine cathedral and castle' – although since there were works in progress on those walls at precisely this time, he may not have looked very closely. The castle could be entered only through the city, whose walls were pierced by three defended double gates and reinforced by a number of towers, said to be six in 1491. A mid-sixteenth-century plan shows that most of the towers were placed on the east side, the sector nearest to the Eden bridge and presumably for that reason the one thought most likely to be attacked, with only one tower on the west (Figure 9.2). Two of them have recorded names: the 'Beaumond' Tower and the 'Spring' or 'Springold' Tower. The latter, which was described in 1565 as 'the chief and principal defence of the town walls', was doubtless so-called because it contained a springall, a powerful missile-firing engine; it may have been the tower represented on the west side of the walls, placed close to the southernmost of the city's three gates, the Botchergate Gate, which was perhaps regarded as in particular danger because it was the only one which could be reached without crossing a river first.

Although the plan may have been made to accompany a report on Carlisle's defences for consideration by royal officials, the state of the town walls did not only concern the crown, or even those who lived within them. In wartime Carlisle became the principal place of refuge for the country around. In 1378 it was the commons of Cumberland, not the citizens of Carlisle, who petitioned for repairs to castle and city precisely because it was 'the chief resort and point of governance' for the entire county. Several Cumbrian landowners, lay and ecclesiastical, when disposing of properties in the town, made provision for the possibility that they might still need to occupy them if the Scots invaded the region. Moreover, as the city's population grew in the twelfth and thirteenth centuries, so suburbs developed outside the walls, and their inhabitants might need to take refuge inside the walls if the danger outside them became too great. In the Scottish attack of 1296 a number of the fishermen who had nets in the River Eden had been killed; for their successors, and others like them, the city's defences could be literally life-saving. However, although the city's function as a place of refuge would have increased the pressure on its food supplies, it must have also augmented the manpower available to defend it. In April 1314 the Scots who had ravaged north Cumberland were said to have decided against an attack on Carlisle, 'because of the knights and country people who were assembled there'.

Soldiers and Citizens

For those who lived inside the walls, the responsibility for defending them was probably allocated according to circumstances. In wartime, and especially when it looked as if Carlisle might be attacked, it is likely that the burden was principally shouldered by professional soldiers commanded from the castle. At moments of crisis their number could be considerable, at least in proportion to the total population of a small town. Around the end of 1314, for instance, there may have been nearly 540 soldiers in Carlisle. Admittedly that was a time of exceptional danger; but early in 1384, with renewed Anglo-Scottish hostilities imminent, the castle was said to have a garrison of 150 men, and the city one of 120, certainly enough to take the lead in manning the walls. Such numbers also created problems of accommodation. The peacetime garrisons of medieval castles were usually small, enabling them to live in the buildings they were employed to protect. But a total of 270 men was far more than Carlisle castle could accommodate, making it necessary for many of them to be billeted on the townsfolk. Not everybody welcomed this, and in 1385 Sir Thomas Ros of Kendal, a powerful figure in the North-West, secured exemption from having his town house commandeered in this way. It was a process capable of abuse – a year later the citizens complained that soldiers had 'entered and taken up their abode in their houses without paying any rent or making any agreement with the owners'. But when fairly administered, it offered townspeople the chance to make some money, and may also have made them feel more secure.

It is clear that there was easy access to the castle from the city, as indeed there had to be, since the castle had important civilian functions. The sheriff of Cumberland maintained an office in it, with an 'exchequer' in the outer gatehouse, and it was also the site of the county gaol. Court sessions, too, were held there – in 1370 the costs of works on the castle included a small sum spent on 'the repair of the motehalle against the arrival of the justices'. The king's justices may have sat in the gatehouse, or perhaps they conducted proceedings in one of the buildings in the outer bailey. The castle must also have provided both business and employment for the townspeople, whether as tradesmen supplying food and clothing, or as artisans working on repairs to walls and buildings, or as wage-earners employed as servants, cleaners and cooks. In such circumstances, it is hardly surprising that in 1470 the townspeople, acting on King Edward IV's behalf under the leadership of the bishop, were able to capture the castle from Warwick the Kingmaker, the warden of the March – no doubt they took it by surprise, in a sudden attack on its most vulnerable side.

Constant interaction between castle and city could also make for friction, of course. A serious outbreak of violence in 1345, when members of the garrison ran riot in the streets and killed at least three people, including one of the city's bailiffs, caused serious concern at Westminster. It was a year of open war in the Borders, and the government appreciated that if the 'dissensions and discords' were not checked, Carlisle would be at serious risk from a Scottish attack that was known to be imminent. The violence originated in the exceptional difficulties of the 1340s, and above all in the crown's repeated failure to pay the castle garrison, which as a result was only able to maintain itself by taking goods from the townspeople without paying for them. At other times relations were better, if not necessarily more peaceable in their results. A dispute over the election of a prior of Carlisle Cathedral Priory in the 1380s led to considerable disorder, during which a group of canons were said to have recruited 'soldiers of the town and castle' to intimidate their opponents. Perhaps some of them had been billeted on the citizens, making it easier to enlist their services.

The military character of Carlisle, which can only have been enhanced by the intermittent presence of large numbers of troops, must have been further intensified by the need for the townsmen to contribute actively towards their own defence, above all by keeping watch on the walls at night (Figure 6.7). Unquestionably a burdensome duty (and also a dangerous one – in 1543 a watchman fell to his death from the walls one night), it was one of the responsibilities whereby the townsfolk claimed in 1318 to be 'much vexed and charged'. Again, in 1341 'continual watches on walls and gates' were said to be a contributory factor in the citizens' impoverishment; while in 1386 the king had to order the March wardens to compel them to keep watch upon their walls. Perhaps it was as a result that a new officer appeared, the 'serjeant of the watches of the town and castle of Carlisle'. His residence was in the 'Beaumond' Tower, which suggests that he was principally concerned with the city's defence. But before long his responsibilities seem to have been transferred to the mayor, and it was under the mayor's leadership that the townsmen became involved in a lengthy quarrel, between 1430 and 1449, with the cathedral canons over the contribution the priory should make to keeping watch on the walls at night. The canons pleaded that all that was required of them was 'to pray for the good estate of the king and the realm day and night', and perhaps unsurprisingly the pious Henry VI agreed, and granted them – and presumably their numerous tenants – exemption. This must have created a shortfall in manpower that others had to make up, but it may also have created opportunities. It had become acceptable practice for richer townsmen who did not want to keep watch themselves to hire substitutes to act for them. In 1439, and again in 1440, one John Rome was sued in the mayor's court for money he owed his deputies 'for watching for him by night on the walls of Carlisle'. Probably there were many poor men glad to supplement their incomes by replacing their social superiors in this way, and after 1449 they could hope to do so more often.

Living on the Defensive

The defences not only made constant demands on the pockets, time and strength of the townsfolk; they also constituted a perpetual reminder of their vulnerability, as indeed did the fact that those defences were often less formidable than they appeared. In the fifteenth-century ballad of Adam Bell, two of the comrades of the imprisoned outlaw William of Cloudesly, intent on rescuing him, are at first unable to enter Carlisle because all its gates are closed (eventually they trick the porter of one of them and break his neck), suggesting a city effectively secured against attackers. Yet the fact that the rescuers are only alerted to William's plight by a boy who escapes from the town through a gap in its walls indicates that in fiction, as in reality, the image of the city's defensibility could be misleading. It is hardly surprising, therefore, that besides looking to the king for protection, Carlisle should have invoked a supernatural guardian as well. By the fourteenth century the cathedral was the centre of a celebrated cult of the Virgin Mary, for reasons vividly explained by the chronicler Henry Knighton, who tells how in 1385, when the Scots were attacking the city:

> a woman appeared and declared that the king of England was coming with his army, and when they looked, they seemed to see the king's standard advancing, and thus dismayed they abandoned their ladders on the wall, and their machines, and fled. And the woman was believed to have been the glorious Virgin Mary, Carlisle's patron, who ever watches over her townsmen.

During the fifteenth century there came to be a notable statue of the Virgin in the cathedral, and it is significant that while the medieval seals of several other towns and cities were engraved with images of walls and towers, that of Carlisle bore the city's arms on one side and the Virgin and Child on the other (Figure 6.10). It was the Virgin Mary, at least as much as the 'right fayre and strong wal' described by John Leland in 1539, who constituted the townspeople's ultimate recourse in times of danger.

Figure 6.10. Carlisle's celestial defender: the Virgin and Child as shown on the city's seal, from an engraving, *c.* 1883

Prominent among the strains arising from Carlisle's military role was the constant disruption that war inflicted on the city's other functions, and especially on its position as a commercial centre of considerable regional importance. The defensive duties forced on the townsmen, along with the constant threat, and frequent reality, of interruptions of trade through Scottish raids and devastation, were among the pressures that they intermittently claimed were making life intolerable for them, leading to repeated declarations that they were preparing to leave and settle elsewhere. The threat to abandon the town was not an idle one – during 'le Sege tyme' of 1461, when Carlisle was nearly captured by the Scots and Lancastrians, a number of inhabitants went over to the enemy, and were subsequently put out of the city for their disloyalty – but such a threat was also a useful one for the citizens to be able to make. The king needed the involvement of the townsmen in the defence of a place vital to the defence of the Borders, and could be induced to make financial concessions in order to secure it. But in return he required the townsmen to participate effectively in the defence of the city, and he eventually appears to have succeeded. When the citadel was planned in the late 1530s, it was intended that it and the castle should together provide for the defence of the whole site of Carlisle, the city's walls being too dilapidated to be worth repairing. But now the inhabitants, far from threatening to leave, declared that they were ready to 'spend their goods and lives' in the defence of their city. In 1545 it was 'good constitutions and statutes' that were required to ensure that Carlisle was properly defended, not fighting spirit, and in 1561 the city's Dormont Book, its first comprehensive collection of statutes, contained several regulations for civic security, including a clause in the mayor's oath to 'see or cause to be sene nyghtly the watchmen of the walles of this citie trewly set serchet [inspected] and kept'. The effort involved in securing the walls may still have been grudged, but the necessary commitment was at last being made.

Having to live within walls (or, for the inhabitants of the suburbs, below them), along with the proximity of the castle, affected the lives of the people of Carlisle at every level. An awareness of the city's defences is constantly apparent in Carlisle property deeds, where the tenements they dispose of are repeatedly defined by reference to such features as 'the lane that runs below the wall of Carlisle', or 'the gutter that leads to the king's wall', or 'one tenement inside the Caldew Gate inside the walls of Carlisle', or 'the road that runs below the walls of Carlisle towards the castle', or 'the path that leads towards the "upcome" of the city wall' – the 'upcome' must be one of the flights of steps giving access to the battlements, shown on the map of the city and castle of *c.* 1560 (Figure 9.2). Carlisle's defensive role, embodied in those walls, had contradictory effects. It led to frequent royal interference with the city's rights of self-government, and often played havoc with its trade, but it also justified many claims on the support of the crown, and fostered an important, and doubtless profitable, cult of the Virgin. The very fact that the defences of Carlisle could be seen in different perspectives brings out the extent to which they moulded the way its inhabitants saw the city that was their home, and also the way they saw the wider world. Protecting their bodies, homes and livelihoods, those defences had a profound effect on their feelings and perceptions as well.

The Sixteenth-Century Aftermath

When in the 1540s the citadel was built, and the city walls were at first written off as too decrepit to be restored, but subsequently reprieved and rebuilt (over £800 were spent on them in the mid-1550s), England was still usually at odds, and often actively at war, with Scotland. But Scotland's Protestant Reformation, which in 1560 strained her traditional alliance with France to near-breaking point, made for much better relations with England, also committed to Protestantism following the accession of Elizabeth I. Peace was also furthered by dynastic considerations, as James VI of Scots looked increasingly likely to become Elizabeth's successor. Against this background, the age-old defences of northern England began to look obsolete. The disorder generated by centuries of Border warfare was not speedily repressed. Indeed, it became all the greater as national governments, no longer concerned about the security of their outlying provinces, largely lost interest in trying to control the reivers and riding clans who occupied themselves in robbing one another there. To an increasing extent Elizabethan Carlisle became little more than a centre for ineffective police operations, and is now principally remembered (thanks to an exciting but historically unreliable ballad) for the escape of 'Kinmont Willie' – William Armstrong of Kinmont – from the castle on the night of 13 April 1596, an episode involving the 'springing' of a ruffian by a band of his associates, helped by inside information. When James VI did indeed become James I of England in 1603, thereby calling into question the whole concept of an Anglo-Scottish Border, this seemed to mark the end of Carlisle as a military establishment. That was certainly the view from Westminster. 'I think', minuted Lord Treasurer Buckhurst, as he docked the sheriff of Cumberland's claim for expenses, 'in future noo allowance at all to be made in like cases in respecte of the quietnes of that cuntrye which is nowe likelye to ensue'.

★ ★ ★ ★ ★

Suggested Further Reading

R. A. Brown, H. M. Colvin and A. J. Taylor, *The History of the King's Works. Volume I: The Middle Ages* (London, 1963)

J. A. A. Goodall, 'The great tower of Carlisle castle', in M. R. McCarthy and D. Weston (eds), *Carlisle and Cumbria: Roman and Medieval Architecture, Art and Archaeology* (British Archaeological Association, Conference Transactions, 27, 2004), pp. 39–62

M. R. McCarthy, 'Excavations on the city defences, Carlisle', *CW2*, 80 (1980), pp. 69–78

M. R. McCarthy, H. Summerson and R. G. Annis, *Carlisle Castle: A Survey and Documentary History* (English Heritage Archaeological Report, 18, 1990)

N. Pounds, *The Medieval Castle in England and Wales: A Social and Political History* (Cambridge, 1990)

H. Summerson, *Medieval Carlisle: The City and the Borders from the Late Eleventh to the Mid-Sixteenth Century* (CWAAS, Extra Series, 25, 1993)

H. Summerson, 'Responses to war: Carlisle and the West March in the later fourteenth century', in A. Tuck and A. Goodman (eds), *War and Border Societies in the Middle Ages* (London and New York, 1992), pp. 155–77

H. L. Turner, *Town Defences in England and Wales: An Architectural and Documentary Study, AD 900–1500* (London, 1971)

Chapter 7
The Medieval Church in Carlisle

David Weston

The period covered by this chapter (1092–1540) begins with the final stages of the Norman conquest of England, and it ends with the Reformation, when King Henry VIII severed ties with Rome and undertook the Dissolution of the monasteries. This was an era of profound significance for the development of English church life, and the evidence concerning Carlisle usefully illuminates the processes of continuity and change at a local level (Figure 7.1).

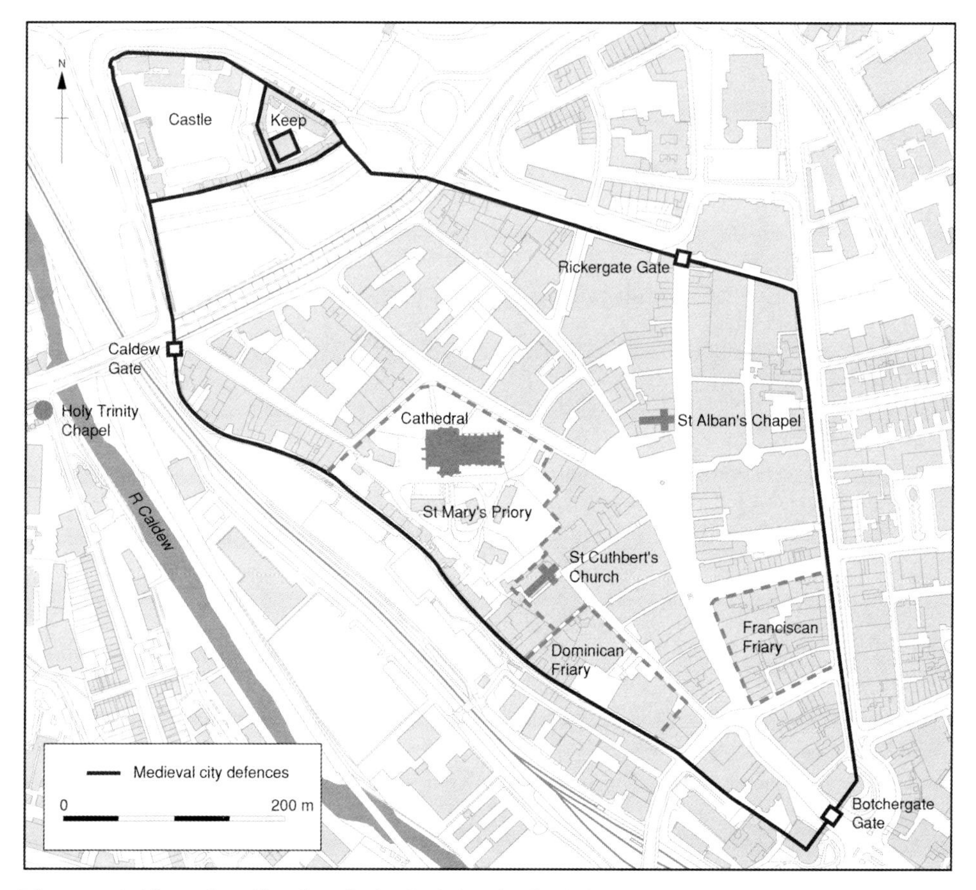

Figure 7.1. Map of medieval ecclesiastical sites in Carlisle

The Church in Carlisle in 1092

The year 1092 saw the establishment of Norman power in Carlisle in both secular and ecclesiastical terms. On the one hand, Dolfin was replaced as the local ruler, and the castle was built as a potent symbol and tool of Norman royal dominance. On the other, the Scottish episcopal authority exercised in the region by the bishop of Glasgow was curtailed, and the archbishop of York began to bring Carlisle more firmly under his control.

Further details are sparse, and so the actual state of church life in Carlisle in 1092 is not easy to reconstruct. But, certainly, the statement by the chronicler John of Worcester, that Carlisle had been left virtually abandoned after the Viking raid of 876, must be set aside. Accumulating evidence from archaeological excavations, especially from burials, shows that Carlisle was occupied and relatively flourishing. Indeed, there are strong indications that the two parishes of St Mary and St Cuthbert in Carlisle were pre-Norman in origin, and this may also be true of the chapelry of St Alban.

The likely location of pre-Norman St Mary's is suggested by the position of the ninth- and tenth-century cemetery found in the course of the excavation in 1988 to create the underground Cathedral Treasury, on the site of the cathedral's demolished north nave aisle. The location of pre-Norman St Cuthbert's was almost certainly on the site of its present eighteenth-century successor (see below, p. 110).

The Augustinian Priory of St Mary

The first major development of the Church in Norman Carlisle occurred with the arrival of King Henry I in person in 1122, when he came to consolidate his authority in the region and to strengthen the frontier with Scotland. Part of Henry's plan involved the foundation of an Augustinian priory in Carlisle, with his chaplain Athelwold, prior of the Augustinian house of Nostell in Yorkshire, as its first prior. In order to support this new foundation, which was dedicated to St Mary, the king endowed it with property formerly belonging to Walter the priest, a wealthy Norman, whose lands had recently passed into the crown's hands. This property included the parish churches of St Cuthbert, Carlisle, and St Michael, Stanwix, and land in Linstock, Rickerby, High Crosby, Low Crosby, Walby, Brunstock, and the two Carltons. The church of St Mary was demolished and relocated within the five bays at the west end of the nave of the new priory church, while St Mary's parish became part of the priory's endowment.

The Cathedral Priory

When Henry I founded St Mary's Priory in 1122, it is likely that he already planned to make its church the cathedral of a new diocese of Carlisle.

Begun in 1133, this diocese was the last to be created in England until after the Reformation. The new cathedral was also unique in being served by Augustinian canons, because the other seven monastic cathedrals in England were all served by Benedictine monks. The Augustinians, who belonged to an order that had recently arrived from the Continent, were not technically monks, and their rule allowed them to exercise a wider range of ministries in parishes and hospitals.

Athelwold, the first prior of St Mary's Priory, became bishop of the new diocese while initially retaining the office of prior. The creation of the new see was undoubtedly intended to resolve the complex issue of ecclesiastical jurisdiction in Cumberland, and to help to create stability in an unsettled frontier zone. It also seems significant that the new priory-cum-cathedral was constructed across the line of the old Roman road now known as Blackfriars Street. This suggests that the Normans were imposing a new physical layout on Carlisle, in step with their determination to assert their hegemony within the region.

Building work on the cathedral priory would have been helped by the availability of suitable stone in and near Carlisle. Stone from the remains of Roman buildings and walls was re-used for the priory church's exterior walls, while for interior wall-surfaces stone was probably freshly quarried locally. The parish church of St Mary would have continued in use until the new building was sufficiently advanced for it to be demolished and established in the nave of the cathedral.

In the medieval period, the cathedral priory church went through four main building phases. The first phase was in the Norman, or Romanesque, style of the twelfth century. Thus the original church was cruciform or cross-shaped, consisting of a nave of seven bays with an aisle on either side, a tower at the crossing between the north and south transepts, which had apsidal or semi-circular chapels on the east side, and an aisled sanctuary probably with an apsidal end (Figure 7.2). No part of this building east of the crossing now exists above ground, but three blocked arches and traces of a roof-line on interior walls provide indications of its overall scale.

It is noticeable that the four pillars supporting the tower have sunk by up to 30 centimetres, with consequent distortion of the adjacent arches. The causes of this subsidence were the presence of underground water and the variable nature of the subsoil. Two wells within the church near the tower provide evidence of the water, and excavation in 1988 revealed occupation levels to a depth of over three metres.

There was probably a screen between the first two bays of the nave, where the choir stalls of the canons were located, and the remaining five bays, which served as the parish church. This suggestion is strengthened by the presence of a doorway (now blocked) in the south nave aisle, which would have been used by the canons for access to and from the adjacent cloister. There was

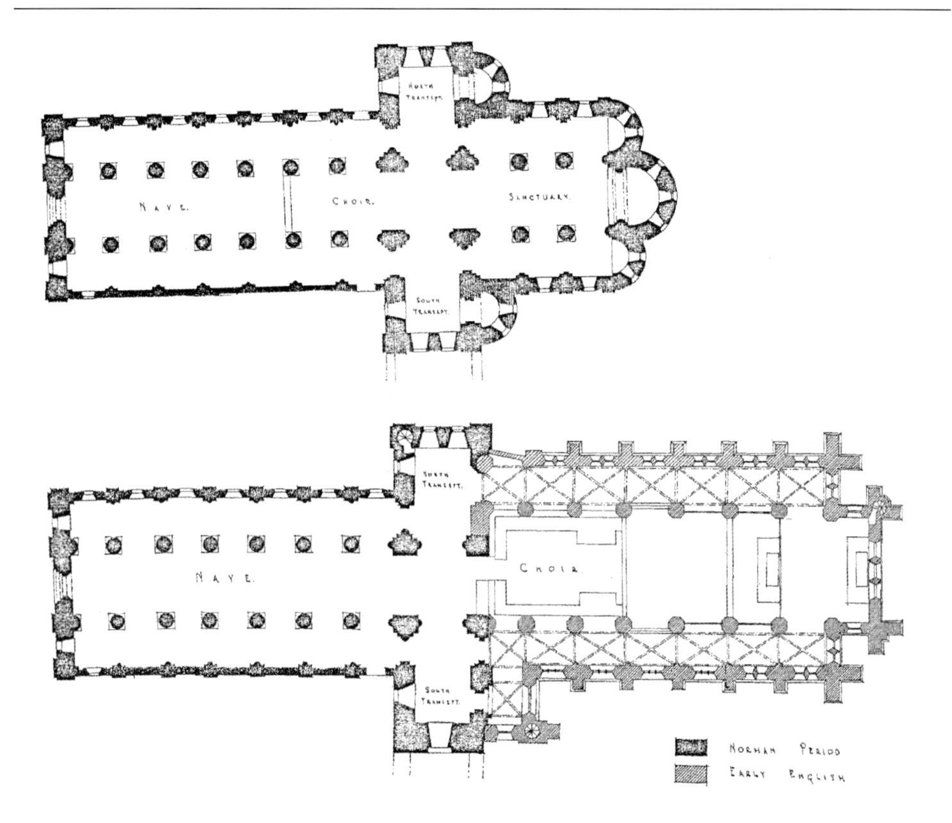

Figure 7.2. Plans by C. G. Bulman of the twelfth-century Norman cathedral and the thirteenth-century extension in Early English style

no doorway at ground level in the south transept until the mid-nineteenth century, but a night stair provided access to the canons' dormitory in the east range of the cloister. The demolition of five bays of the nave and the west end of the cathedral in the 1650s gives the building its foreshortened appearance.

Noteworthy exterior features of the surviving architecture are the zigzag decoration of the clerestory, or top level, windows and the grotesque heads forming the corbel-table, which supports the parapet around the base of the roof. The interior stonework consists of red sandstone, with distinctive zigzag patterns around some of the arches, and scallop and cushion style capitals at the top of the pillars of the nave. All interior surfaces of the walls would have been painted. In the Norman period, this tended to take the form of white paint on plastered walls, with red lines drawn in rectangular shapes to suggest the outline of the stones. There is also some evidence that details of the capitals at clerestory level were picked out in colour.

The second of the four chief phases of building-works arose from dissatisfaction with the constraints of the small Norman sanctuary or choir. It was demolished, probably on the initiative of Hugh of Beaulieu, bishop of Carlisle (1219–23), and during the thirteenth century it was replaced by a much longer, taller and wider choir in the new Early English Gothic style (Figure 7.2). The greater width was achieved by adding an extra four metres to the north side of the choir. This gives to the cathedral its irregular shape when viewed inside from the east end looking west. The extension made the cathedral's appearance much more impressive, and enabled it to accommodate a growing influx of pilgrims. The character of the new work, with its lancet windows and dog-tooth and nail-head decoration, is now clearly seen only in the walls of the north and south choir aisles, because the newly constructed choir was badly damaged in a fire of 1292. Since, however, the choir aisles had stone vaulting as distinct from the wooden roof of the choir, they were relatively unaffected by the fire, whereas the choir roof was destroyed.

This disaster led to the third main phase of the building of the cathedral. Throughout the fourteenth century, the choir was under reconstruction in the new Decorated Gothic style, which was more ornate and allowed for larger windows as engineering skills advanced. This rebuilding largely retained the dimensions of the earlier work, but gave to the cathedral several of its most important surviving features (Figure 7.3). The great east window is notable for its stone tracery, and it retains in the upper section much of its original fourteenth-century glass. It is what is known as a 'doom window', showing Christ seated in judgement at the top, with figures rising from their graves and small scenes of heaven and hell. The ceiling, although heavily restored, retains its original form and main timbers. Twelve of the fourteen capitals at the top of the pillars of the choir incorporate scenes known as 'the labours of the months', a characteristic contemporary form of decoration.

The last of the four phases of medieval building came as a result of the fall of the tower onto the north transept in 1380. Although this catastrophe was blamed on a storm, the insecure foundations of the tower and consequent subsidence are likely to have been contributing causes. The rebuilding of both the tower and the north transept took place soon after 1400, by which time the Perpendicular Gothic style had come into fashion. This new style marked a move away from the curving and flamboyant lines of the Decorated style to straighter lines and more rectangular shapes. It is seen in the windows of the tower, in the unglazed interior window high up in the crossing facing the north transept, and in a window at the west end of the north choir aisle. The cathedral's oldest bell and choir stalls, with their 46 misericord seats, are of about the same date.

Around 1465 Thomas Gondibour was appointed prior. His practice of having his initials carved on work that he initiated identifies his extensive campaign to improve and beautify the cathedral and its other buildings. This work includes the paintings on the backs of the choir stalls, which depict the twelve apostles and the lives of St Antony of Egypt, St Augustine of Hippo, and St Cuthbert.

Figure 7.3. The cathedral's fourteenth-century choir and east window (*by courtesy of the Dean and Chapter of Carlisle Cathedral, © James Armstrong*)

When King Henry VIII dissolved St Mary's Priory on 9 January 1540 it would have been at the peak of its material condition. But, in a rapidly changing world, monastic communities proved easy prey for a cash-strapped king and a land-hungry nobility and gentry. Only the fact that Carlisle's priory church was also a cathedral saved it from destruction. The destruction it did suffer occurred in the mid-seventeenth century; yet even today Carlisle cathedral bears impressive testimony to the authority, power and splendour of the medieval Church.

The Monastic Quarters

While Carlisle's cathedral priory church went through its progressive changes in successive centuries, the priory's monastic buildings were also being developed (Figure 7.4). The remains of the cloister on the south side of the cathedral provide architectural evidence that the east range of buildings, containing the canons' dormitory, was in thirteenth-century Early English style, whereas the refectory, called the fratry, on the south side was built later. The fratry is complete, but it was rebuilt in the fifteenth century, altered in the eighteenth century, and restored in the late nineteenth century. Adjacent to the cloister's east range was the octagonal chapter house: only the entrance doorway remains above ground, but its tiled floor survives one metre below

Figure 7.4. Suggested reconstruction by Sir Charles Nicholson of the cathedral, the cloister with the fratry (foreground), the dormitory range, and the octagonal chapter house on the eve of the Reformation

ground. The cloister's west range, which would have included the cellarer's offices, has completely disappeared – as has the great part of the nave of the cathedral, which constituted the north side of the cloister.

The cathedral and its associated structures are the only medieval ecclesiastical buildings that can still be seen in Carlisle. For other aspects of Carlisle's medieval religious history, the evidence is archaeological and documentary.

St Cuthbert's Church

The parish of St Cuthbert was one of the two ancient parishes of Carlisle. The present St Cuthbert's church was built in 1778, but it stands on the foundations of a much earlier church. Clues to its antiquity are its unusual orientation, which is north-east to south-west instead of the usual east to west, and some fragments of medieval glass set into one window. The likely reason for its orientation is that it was built on the foundations of a Roman building that had stood end-on to the Roman road that is now Blackfriars Street. The date of the first church on this site is uncertain, but it is likely to go back to the seventh century and to have been associated in some way with St Cuthbert's visits to Carlisle in 685–6.

The St Cuthbert's church of 1092 was probably the second church on the site, having been rebuilt after the destructive Viking raid of 876. The first certain fact known about it is that it had belonged to the Norman, Walter the priest. As already mentioned, it passed from Walter to King Henry I, who in turn gave it to St Mary's Priory as part of its foundation endowment. Possibly the church was rebuilt at this time, as seems also to have been the case with Stanwix church, another of Walter's properties given to the priory by the king. What is clear is that St Cuthbert's church was destroyed in May 1391 by a fire that devastated much of Carlisle.

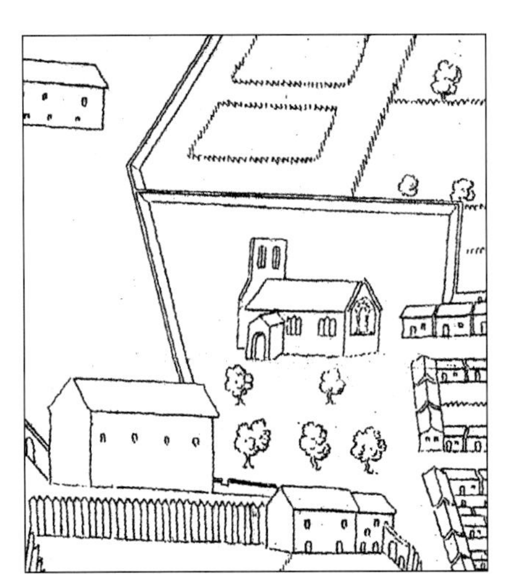

Figure 7.5. A depiction of St Cuthbert's church based on the map of Carlisle of *c.* 1560

The church must therefore have been rebuilt in about 1400, no doubt in the Perpendicular Gothic style of the period. This is the St Cuthbert's church illustrated on the map of Carlisle of around 1560 (Figure 7.5). It is shown as having a tower without battlements at its west end, a porch on its south side, and a large east window.

Although St Cuthbert's church was dependent on the prior and canons of the cathedral priory, who appointed its clergy, it nevertheless had the important status of being one of only two parish churches in the city. It also had an exceptionally large parish, which incorporated the parish of St Cuthbert Without: the word 'Without' was used here to mean 'outside' or 'outlying', and it is thought that this detached area had been a royal gift to St Cuthbert in the seventh century. It was only after the Reformation, however, that St Cuthbert's church acquired its status as the civic church of Carlisle.

St Alban's Chapel

St Alban's chapel in Carlisle is known to have existed throughout the medieval period from at least 1201, when reference to it occurs in a pipe roll of the Exchequer. Henry Summerson, however, has argued for a possible pre-Norman origin on the basis that the Augustinian canons of St Mary's Priory would have resisted its foundation independent of them after the priory was founded in 1122. References to the chapel refer mainly to its associated cemetery, the boundaries of which can to some extent be traced (Figure 7.6).

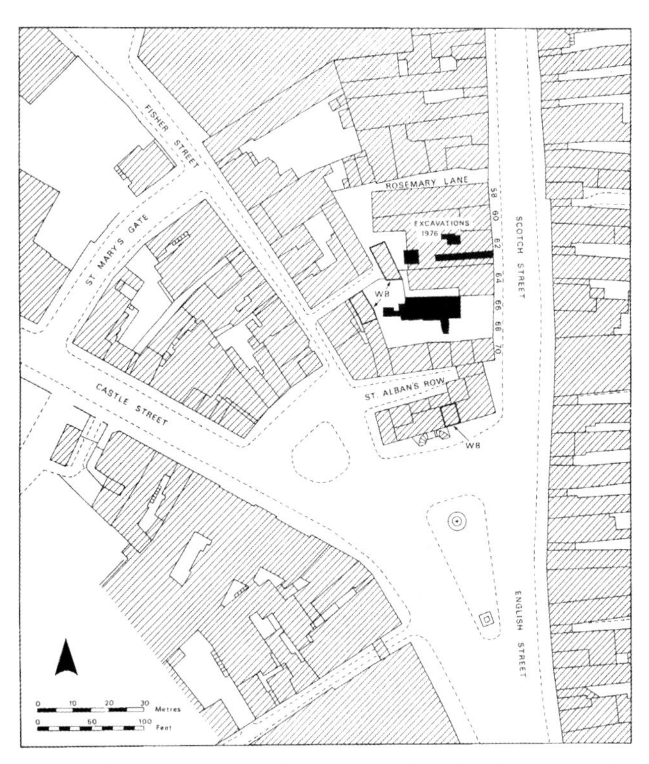

Figure 7.6. Map of the location of St Alban's chapel (*by courtesy of Tullie House Museum and Art Gallery, Carlisle*)

Documentary evidence was substantially supplemented by the results of an excavation in 1988, in the course of rescue archaeology on the site of 66–68 Scotch Street, now Waterstone's bookshop (Figure 7.7). This work uncovered part of the foundations of the chapel and associated burials both inside and outside the building. The excavation also showed that the chapel had been extended several times, with the foundations of new walls cutting into existing graves. One extension may be explained by the creation at St Alban's of a chantry chapel for Robert of Tebay in 1385. The archaeology suggests that

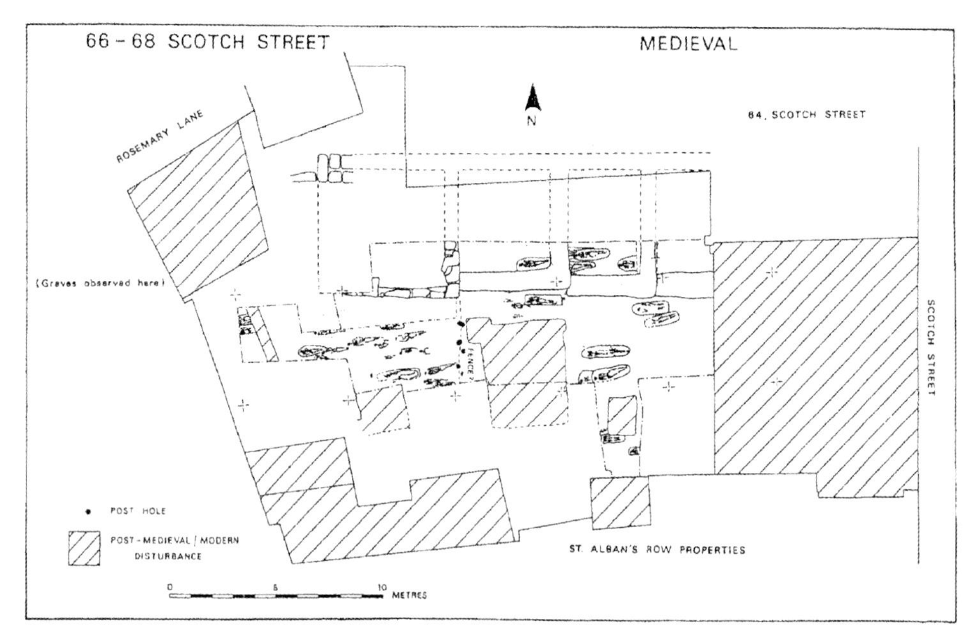

Figure 7.7. Plan of the 1988 excavation of the site of St Alban's chapel (*by courtesy of Tullie House Museum and Art Gallery, Carlisle*)

the cemetery probably did not extend beyond Rosemary Lane to the north, and that Scotch Street marked its eastern boundary. A document of 1348 also indicates that the town hall, the flesh shambles (butchers' stalls), and a house in St Alban's Row, defined its southern and western boundaries.

St Albans's chapel, as distinct from its cemetery, features only rarely in surviving medieval records. But one important issue did arise on 20 October 1356, when Bishop Gilbert de Welton raised the question of whether the chapel had ever been consecrated, and appointed a commission to look into the matter. The commissioners reported on 12 November that although services had been celebrated in the chapel, and bodies had been buried in the graveyard, they had found no evidence of its consecration. In consequence, all services were temporarily forbidden by the bishop. Thereafter archaeological evidence suggests that burials did continue, and so did services and gifts to the chapel's chaplains and its fabric. Since the chapel had acquired the status of a chantry, it briefly survived the dissolution of Carlisle's priory and friaries. A survey made in 1546 recorded that the chantry possessed lands worth £2.17s.8d. and plate and ornaments worth £1.15s. But it was dissolved with all other chantries in 1549 under legislation of King Edward VI, and its lands were sold to Thomas Dalston of Carlisle and William Denton of London. The chantry building and cemetery do not appear on the map of Carlisle of *c.* 1560, which shows that the site was soon built upon (Figure 9.2). St Alban's Row and a Civic Trust plaque on the site roughly mark their location.

Holy Trinity Chapel

Documentary sources of the early fourteenth century provide evidence for the existence of a medieval chapel dedicated to the Holy Trinity in Caldewgate, outside the city walls. Its location is perhaps confirmed by the discovery of a number of burials beneath Bridge Street in 1959, in the course of digging a sewer-trench. The chapel cannot have survived for long, given the very slight evidence concerning it. The reason for its disappearance is likely to have been its undefended position on the northern outskirts of the city and its consequent vulnerability to Scottish raids.

The Friaries

The founding of orders of friars in the thirteenth century had a transforming effect upon Western Christendom. The Franciscans or Grey Friars, founded by St Francis in 1209, and the Dominicans or Black Friars, founded by St Dominic in 1220, reflected the realisation that the traditional pattern of parochial clergy in parish churches and monks and canons in monasteries was not meeting the changing needs of the Church and the world. The Dominicans arrived in England in 1221 and the Franciscans in 1224. The fact that both orders quite independently set up friaries in Carlisle in 1233 shows that they not only saw opportunities to work there, but considered the city wealthy enough to support them, given their dependence upon alms. The simplicity and poverty of the friars' lives contributed to their popularity, and most friars had received a better education than other clergy – indeed, it is known that the Franciscans ran a school in Carlisle. Both orders also enjoyed some significant royal patronage in Carlisle, notably from King Henry III (1216–72). The friars, unlike the canons at the cathedral, tended not to be local men, to judge from their surnames, and they travelled widely. Fourteenth-century records indicate that their numbers in the two friaries were about 16 Dominicans and about 20 Franciscans, but by 1534 their numbers had fallen substantially to four Dominicans and nine Franciscans. And a few years later almost every trace of the friaries above ground would disappear.

The Franciscan Friary – Grey Friars

According to the so-called Lanercost chronicle, the Franciscans arrived in Carlisle on about 15 August 1233. They were given a house inside the city walls on a site that is known but is now marked only by a lane called Friar's Court. The friary is shown as a rough outline sketch on Stefan von Haschenperg's map of Carlisle of around 1542. It was located on land between the modern Devonshire Street and Bank Street, close to the east wall of the city, on a site of about one and a half acres. The 1560s map roughly identifies the site where the Franciscan friary had stood, but by this date it had already been closed, demolished and left as an open space (Figure 7.8).

The friars' first building was destroyed in a fire of 1251, which seems to have particularly affected the east side of the city. King Henry III's response was to provide the citizens with timber from Inglewood Forest, while the friars were specifically granted 40 oaks and £20 for their church. The benefits of their rebuilding were short-lived for the Franciscan friary was again destroyed in the fire of 1292.

It is recorded that after the closure of the Franciscan friary in 1539, building materials from it were used by Sir Thomas Wharton for the repair of the castle, the citadel and the city walls. In 1998 four pieces of sculptured stone were found in a cellar in a Devonshire Street property, and these are likely to be fragments from the friary.

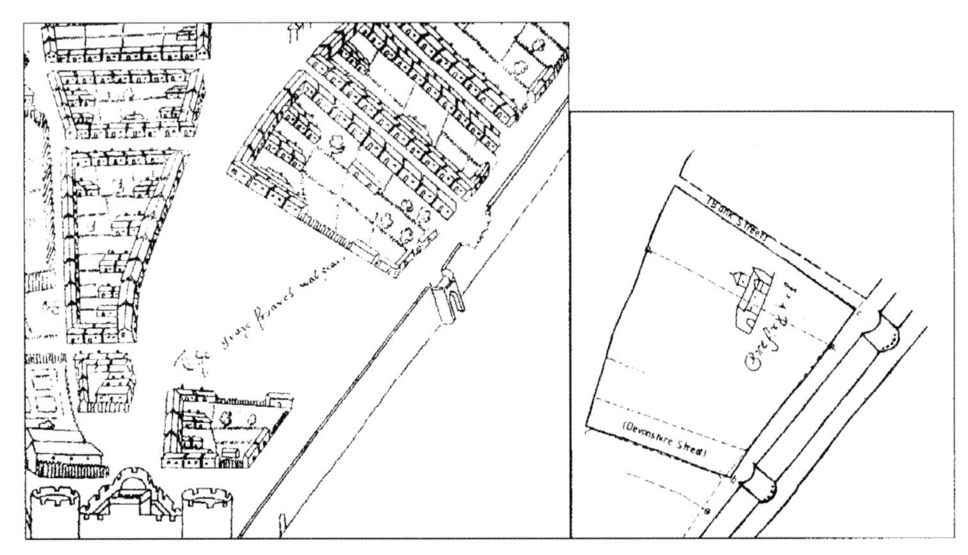

Figure 7.8. The location of the demolished Franciscan friary from the map of Carlisle of *c.* 1560, with Stefan von Haschenperg's sketch of the friary, *c.* 1542 (both redrawn)

The Dominican Friary – Black Friars

The Dominican friars arrived in Carlisle on about 29 September 1233 and settled initially just outside the city walls to the south. On 12 September 1236 King Henry III allowed them 20 oaks from Inglewood Forest for their buildings. However, this first house of the Dominicans obstructed the highway and they had to move to a new site. They had established themselves within the city by May 1238, and they received permission in 1240 to create a drain under the city wall from their living quarters (Figure 8.3). The general location of the Dominican friary is identified today by Blackfriars Street, and the precise location is revealed by the 1560s map and by the report of the archaeological excavation on that site in 1977–8 (Figure 7.9). This excavation uncovered part of the Dominican church, a section of its cemetery, and fragmentary remains of other friary buildings.

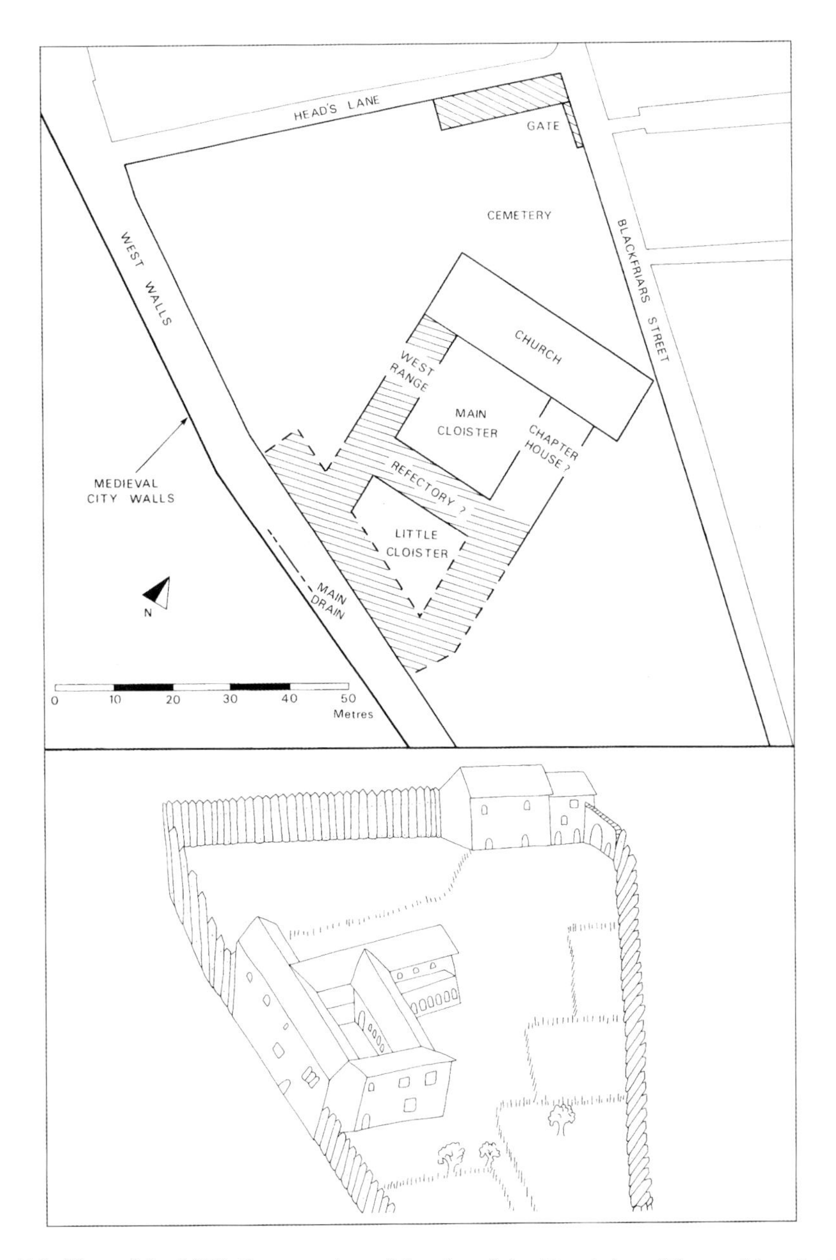

Figure 7.9. Plan of the 1977–8 excavation of the site of the Dominican friary, with a depiction of the surviving buildings based on the map of Carlisle of *c.* 1560 (*by courtesy of Tullie House Museum and Art Gallery, Carlisle*)

The chronicler Walter of Guisborough records that the Dominican friary was saved with the greatest difficulty from destruction by the fire of 1292. In 1334 New Bank Lane was built as an entrance road from the market place to the main gate of the friary. The appointment by the Dominicans of John Aglionby, a prominent citizen, to oversee the safeguarding of their lands and possessions in 1464, has been interpreted as suggesting that they were in financial difficulties at that time. The site of the friary included a stone church with a lead roof and two bells, conventual buildings, two stables, store rooms, a kiln house, gardens, an orchard and a burial ground. It consisted of about two acres of land in 1539, by which date much of it was already lying waste following the dissolution of the friary. The 1560s map shows some surviving stone buildings on the site, but not the church. One of these buildings was described as 'well and strongly built', and it was set aside for use by the king's council and by the March warden. This building later fell into ruin, but the excavation of the site in 1977–8 shed important new light upon it.

The Hospitals

Hospitals were an important feature of life in medieval England. They were in effect religious communities as well as establishments to care for the sick and elderly, and sometimes specifically for lepers. For health reasons, they were located outside the towns and cities with which they were associated. Two are named in the records of Carlisle: the hospital of St Nicholas, a favourite dedication for hospitals, and the hospital of the Holy Sepulchre. As for the latter, its history and role, as well as its location, are obscure. It functioned for a while in the thirteenth and early fourteenth centuries; but it seems that thereafter Carlisle could not sustain two hospitals because of the difficulties posed by Border warfare and the Black Death. The hospital of St Nicholas, by contrast, is much better recorded.

The Hospital of St Nicholas

St Nicholas's Hospital was probably a royal foundation dating from the mid-twelfth century. A petition, submitted by the hospital to King Edward I in about 1300, claimed that Henry II had granted the wardenship of the hospital to Bishop Athelwold, which must have occurred not later than 1156. This is not inconsistent with the claim by the canons of St Mary's Priory that the hospital had been 'theirs from the foundation of their church by the gift of the kings, their founders', given the fact that Bishop Athelwold had been the first prior.

The hospital was located on a known site half a mile (0.8km) south of Carlisle's city walls (Figure 7.10). It was intended for the care of lepers,

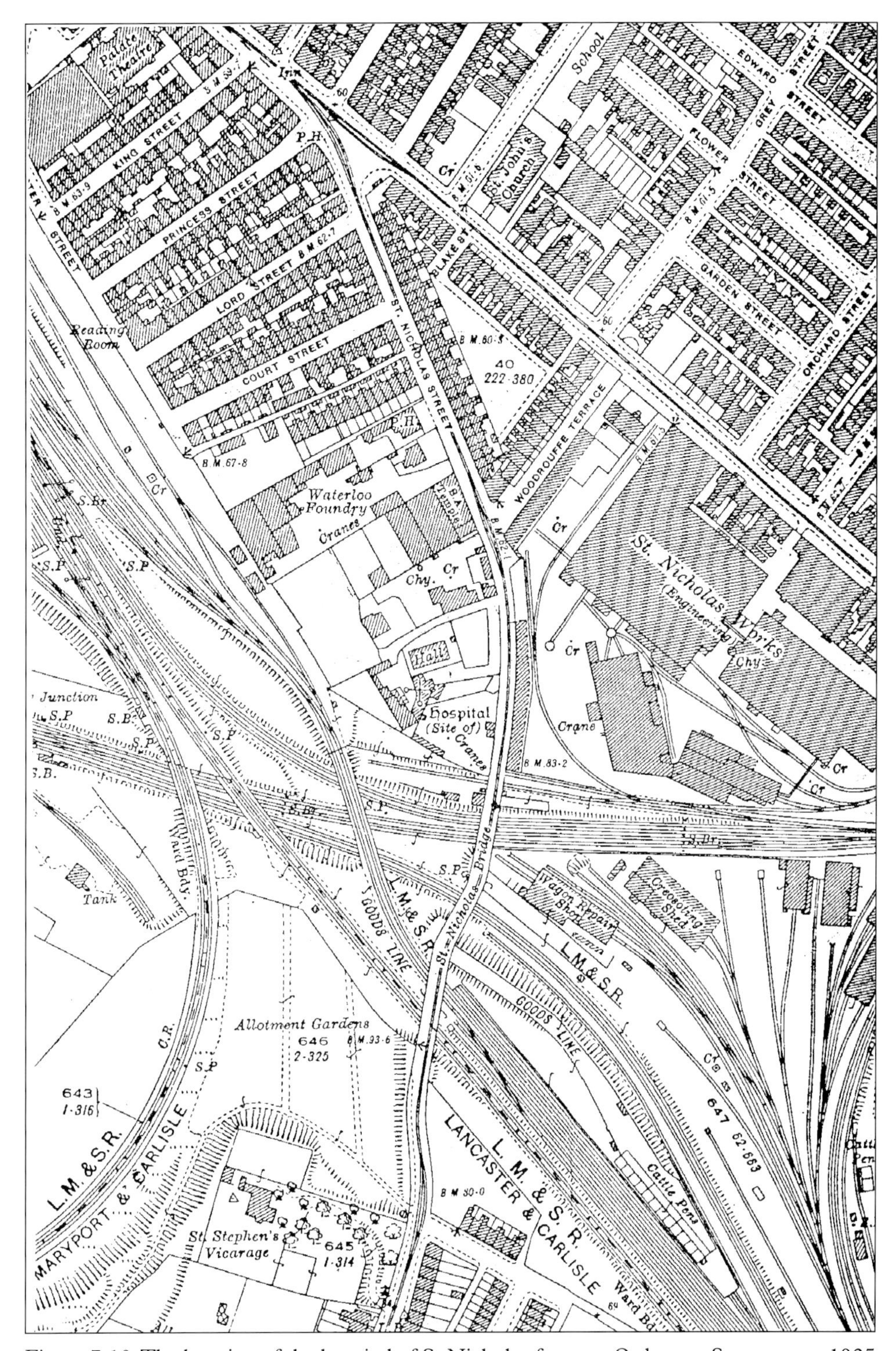

Figure 7.10. The location of the hospital of St Nicholas from an Ordnance Survey map, 1925

although no certain evidence of this role has survived from before King John's letter of protection of 1201. Instructions sent to the sheriff of Cumberland in 1246 refer to three acres of land held by 'the lepers of Carlisle'. In 1341 an inquest recorded that the citizens of Carlisle had long before granted to the hospital a bottle of ale from each brew-house every Sunday and a loaf of bread from each baker every Saturday, on the condition that it received the lepers of the city on the presentation of the mayor and citizens. It seems likely, however, that by 1292 the role of the hospital had changed to that of the long-term care of 12 infirm men under the direction of a master and chaplain.

Oversight of the hospital passed from the Augustinian canons at the cathedral priory to the bishop of Carlisle at some date between 1218 and 1223. Then, in 1292, it passed from the bishop to the king, with each in turn being keen to acquire the right to appoint the master. A disadvantage of the hospital's location outside the city walls was its vulnerability to attack. In 1296 a Scottish raid led by the earl of Buchan burned the hospital. This may have caused a drop in morale, because an inquiry in 1335 into the affairs of the hospital found that the rules 'were not observed as they used to be, for 36 years past or more'. The inquiry, however, did reveal that the hospital was 'much improved' by its present master. But any improvement was short-lived, for in 1337 the Scots again burned the hospital and also Rose Castle near Dalston, the bishop's residence. In 1340 a further commission, which included the bishop, came up with a more damning report of the hospital's mismanagement and financial corruption. It had become so poor that its goods were not sufficient to support the inmates and the master. The arrival of the Black Death in 1349 added a further blight on the whole region. The fact that difficulties continued at St Nicholas's is confirmed by an order of 1396 for a commission to inspect the hospital, 'where, by the carelessness of the masters and ministers, notorious defects exist'. Moreover, a parliamentary statute of 1414 shows that the decline of hospitals was, at that time, a nation-wide phenomenon.

In 1477 the cathedral priory petitioned King Edward IV to be given the hospital as an asset to boost its own finances. The king granted their request, to take effect on the death or resignation of the current master. This was on condition that the priory supplied one of its members, who would be known as the king's chaplain, to celebrate masses in perpetuity for the king and queen and their children. This condition was duly fulfilled, and thereafter the master of the hospital was one of the canons of the cathedral. In 1535 the chaplain of the hospital received 46 shillings per annum, and its three poor beadles, or bedesmen, nine pence per week. After the dissolution of the cathedral priory of St Mary in 1540, and on its re-foundation as the cathedral of the Holy and Undivided Trinity in 1541, the hospital of St Nicholas passed to the ownership of the dean and chapter. The hospital survived until 1645, when it was destroyed in the siege of the city by the Scottish army.

No part of the hospital remains above ground, but *The Carlisle Patriot* reported on 18 October 1834 that 'in cutting the ground for the Newcastle and Carlisle Railway, at St Nicholas, near this city, a very ancient burying ground has been turned up'. It was further recorded in 1838 that, in the course of the railway's construction, 'a considerable quantity of human bones and some urns were found'. It was also stated that a few years before 'a stone coffin containing a chalice of pewter' had been dug up on the site (Figure 7.11). This would have been the burial of a priest, probably a master or chaplain, with a base metal chalice of the type specifically used for burials.

The railway development and rebuilding on the hospital's site have substantially reduced the opportunities for excavation; but some investigation of the area was undertaken in 1996–7. Perhaps unsurprisingly, the results were complex, disappointing and inconclusive as far as the hospital was concerned. Roman activity on the site was more evident, and specifically Roman burials were found. The medieval pottery was likely to relate to the hospital, but no buildings were clearly identified and no new information about the hospital emerged.

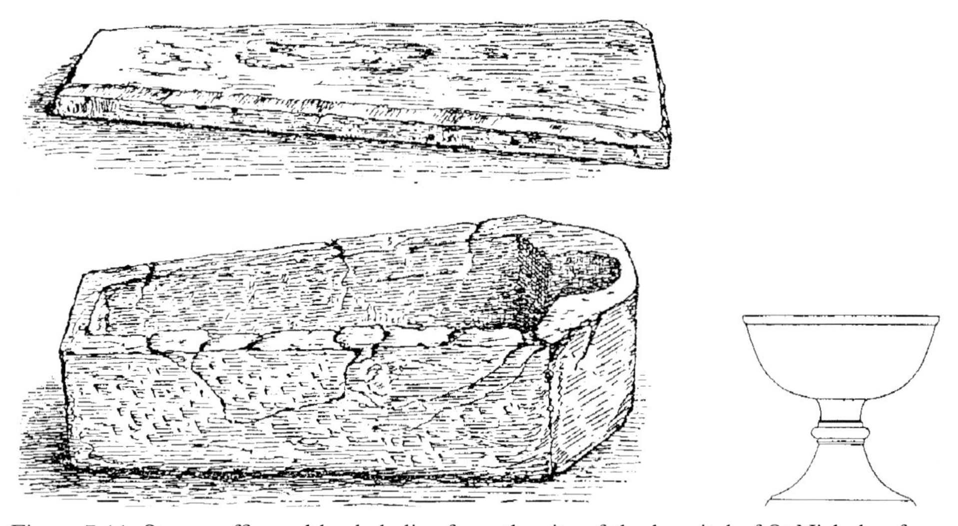

Figure 7.11. Stone coffin and lead chalice from the site of the hospital of St Nicholas, from sketches by Linnaeus Hope, *c.* 1906

Conclusion

Although Carlisle has lost many of its medieval ecclesiastical buildings, including a parish church, two chapels, two friaries and two hospitals, it is nevertheless possible to draw up a reasonably full picture of the medieval Church in Carlisle. Other cathedral cities, such as Durham and York, achieved greater wealth and power; but Carlisle was without doubt a major religious centre in the outer zone of the medieval kingdom of England. Then, with the Reformation, came the dissolution of Carlisle's priory and friaries, a consequent reduction in the number of clergy, and radical changes in public worship and personal piety. So it was that the time-honoured religious traditions of medieval Christianity were brought to a juddering halt, and a new age had begun.

★ ★ ★ ★ ★

Suggested Further Reading

H. Barnes, 'On a stone coffin and chalice found at St Nicholas, Carlisle', *CW2*, 6 (1906), pp. 292–300

P. Cracknell, 'Four pieces of sculpture from Devonshire Street, Carlisle', *CW2*, 98 (1998), pp. 306–9

C. Howard-Davis and M. Leah, 'Excavations at St Nicholas Yard, Carlisle, 1996–7', *CW2*, 99 (1999), pp. 89–115

B. C. Jones, 'St Alban's church and graveyard, Carlisle', *CW2*, 90 (1990), pp. 163–81

B. C. Jones, 'The topography of medieval Carlisle', *CW2*, 76 (1976), pp. 177–96

M. R. McCarthy, *A Roman, Anglian and Medieval Site at Blackfriars Street* (CWAAS, Research Series, 4, 1990)

D. Perriam, 'An unrecorded Carlisle church: the church of the Holy Trinity, Caldewgate', *CW2*, 79 (1979), pp. 51–5

R. L. Storey, 'The chantries of Cumberland and Westmorland', *CW2*, 60 (1960), pp. 70–1

H. Summerson, *Medieval Carlisle: The City and the Borders from the Late Eleventh to the Mid-Sixteenth Century* (CWAAS, Extra Series, 25, 1993)

D. Weston, *Carlisle Cathedral History* (Carlisle, 2000)

W. G. Wiseman, 'The hospital of St Nicholas, Carlisle, and its masters: Part 1', *CW2*, 95 (1995), pp. 93–109; 'Part 2', *CW2*, 96 (1996), pp. 51–69

W. G. Wiseman, 'The medieval hospitals of Cumbria', *CW2*, 87 (1987), pp. 83–100

Chapter 8
Life in Medieval Carlisle

Frank Giecco

The beginnings of medieval Carlisle are notoriously difficult to pinpoint. With our current knowledge it is impossible to speculate on the size and layout of the pre-Norman settlement. A date of 1092 has generally been accepted as the conventional beginning of what we now recognise as Carlisle, when the site was chosen by King William Rufus as a strategic stronghold to stabilise the north-western border with Scotland.

The Layout of the City

Medieval Carlisle was clearly defined by its city walls, which enclosed an area measuring approximately 23 hectares or 57 acres (Figure 8.1). The city walls extended from the castle and along West Walls to the Botchergate Gate, which marked the southern limit of the city. The eastern section ran along today's Lowther Street, turning north along East Tower Street and back to the castle. The volatile history of medieval Carlisle is well documented, with the city existing as a vulnerable garrison town for much of the fourteenth and fifteenth centuries. The reason for stationing a permanent garrison at Carlisle was its strategic position as a bulwark against Scottish raids into the North-West, and that garrison clearly demonstrated the English crown's desire to hold onto Cumberland and to defend England's northern boundary. The skyline of the city would have been dominated by the cathedral and castle. By the early thirteenth century religious institutions such as the cathedral, the priory, St Cuthbert's church and the two friaries occupied around one-third of the total walled area. The street-plan had also been largely established by this period with burgage plots set out along all the major streets. Burgage plots were narrow property divisions set out at right angles to the street, thus allowing each plot a presence on the street frontage and a long yard behind. The plots often measured approximately five metres in width and 60 metres in length, and the tenants to whom they were rented out would have formed the urban elite. The burgage plots of Carlisle were owned by the crown, although by the fifteenth century many plots had been acquired by the city's religious houses.

The religious houses, occupying a central position within the city, may have created more economic stimulus than the castle's garrison, being significant

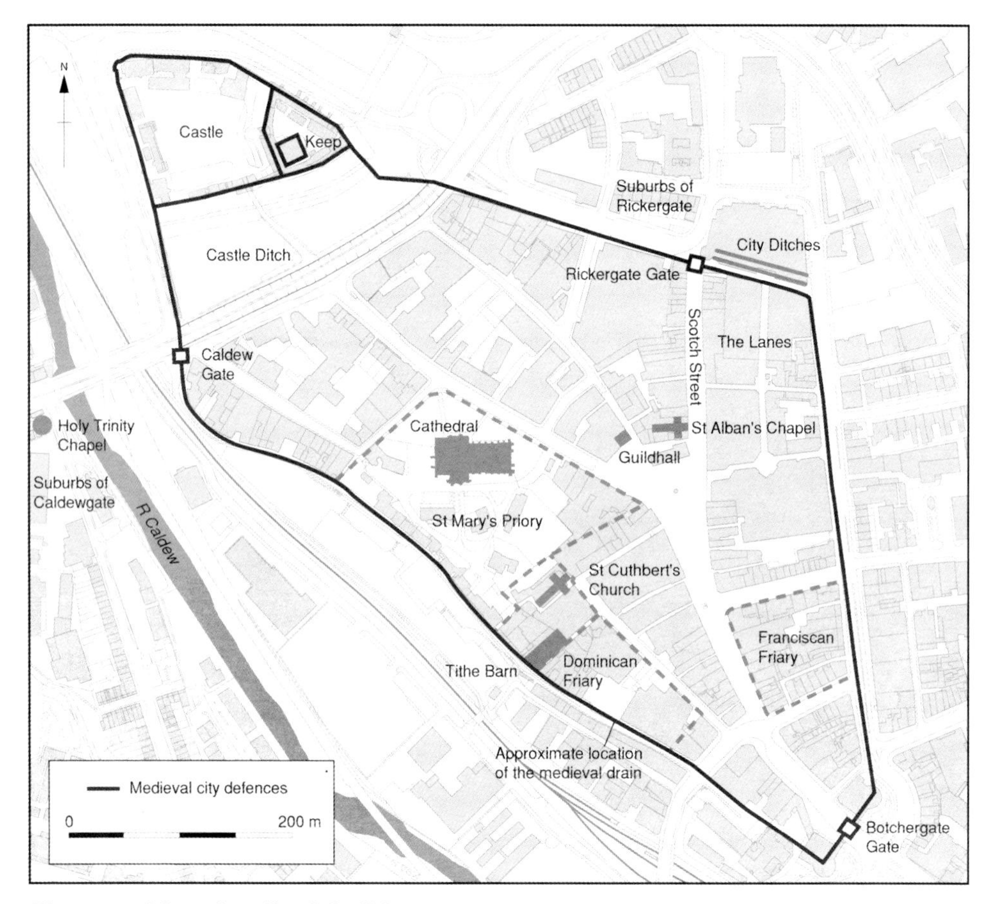

Figure 8.1. Map of medieval Carlisle

patrons of local tradesmen and merchants, as well as providing centres of education. From the Middle Ages until the late eighteenth century, Carlisle was more or less confined to the land within the city walls, apart from three ribbon-like suburbs outside the three city gates: Botchergate, Rickergate and Caldewgate. Defensive ditches were later added outside the city walls, and may have been maintained only in periods of open warfare. It is likely that the Carlisle of the thirteenth century was much less impressive in terms of size and population than its Roman predecessor, which appears to have been more intensively built up and had larger suburbs. There is documentary evidence of substantial Roman structures still standing in the twelfth century, and the continuity between the Roman town and the medieval city is further highlighted by the street-layout, with both Botchergate and Rickergate following the alignments of Roman roads. The unusual alignment of St Cuthbert's church, which is aligned north-east to south-west, was probably due to its respecting a street frontage along a Roman road.

The Population

The population of Carlisle would have been fairly small and relatively stable throughout the medieval period. In the early twelfth century, it was supplemented by communities imported from the southern estates of the Norman lords who were given lordships around Carlisle. This modest plantation was undoubtedly reinforced by an influx of population from the locality to create the beginnings of what we would consider an urban centre. It is impossible to put an accurate figure on the population of Carlisle in the twelfth century, but by the fourteenth and fifteenth centuries a population in the order of 1,500 has been suggested through the analysis of poll tax returns and rents paid. This is a relatively small number for a regional centre even by medieval standards, and compares poorly with an estimated population of 4,800 in Newcastle and 11,000 in York. The population would, however, have been supplemented by a garrison that in times of war could be counted in the hundreds.

The Economy of the City

During the thirteenth century, Carlisle saw an extended period of peace and prosperity after the Scottish siege of 1216, due in no small part to an increase in trade with Scotland. Nevertheless, this period of peace was to descend into violence and disorder throughout much of the fourteenth and fifteenth centuries, with Carlisle's vulnerable military position severely affecting trade and growth. This must undoubtedly have had a detrimental effect on the overall wealth of the city's markets and urban population in general, so that medieval Carlisle was looked upon as poor and isolated compared with other English cities. The mainstay of Carlisle's economy was in wool and hides, as was dictated by the region's pastoral economic base. Wool is known to have been processed into cloth, both dyed and undyed, with hides being used to manufacture leather goods, and a fulling-mill of 1292 is the first known industrial structure to be recorded in the surviving documentary record.

Although warfare undoubtedly did disrupt trade and commerce, some level of compensation must have been provided by the fact that a garrison was permanently stationed in the city. Carlisle was also the seat of regional governance, and on both counts it attracted significant funding from the crown. Tradesmen and industry would have been required on a large scale in times of war, and even in times of relative peace the garrison and the administrative staff would have required significant support from the locality. For example, during the stay of King Edward I in Carlisle for much of 1307, the entire royal court and Parliament followed, thus making Carlisle the centre of English government and *de facto* 'capital city'. This sudden elevation of Carlisle's status must have produced a huge, if short-lived, boom to the local economy and population.

The trades that could be supported by the garrison were wide, ranging from tanners, millers and coopers to blacksmiths and whitesmiths. In the surviving documentary records, there are details of the large orders placed with local merchants for everything from iron bars to loaves of bread. It has proved extremely difficult to assign individual trades to specific areas of Carlisle, although some trades that required a constant water-supply, such as the tanneries and corn mills, were situated outside the city walls, where they utilised the water-supply from the rivers Caldew and Eden. White metal-working is known to have taken place on Caldewgate in the fourteenth and fifteenth centuries, and recent excavations have revealed bronze-working in this area. The raw materials to support this industry, including lead and copper, may have been sourced from mines in the Calbeck Fells, which are known to have been mined from at least 1319, with iron ore coming in from west Cumbria.

The fact that Caldewgate is on the western side of Carlisle, closest to the probable sources of raw materials, makes it tempting to view the Caldewgate area as an industrial suburb specialising in the production of metal products. Other industries may have concentrated in specific parts of Carlisle, but due to the limited amount of available archaeological evidence from within the walls and suburbs it is not possible to know their extent and distribution. Traces of a possible tannery recorded during excavations in the Lanes (now the Lanes shopping centre) indicate that one of the most foul-smelling of trades could take place within the walled town, and offer a note of caution to anyone trying to establish the location and distribution of trades to specific areas of the medieval city.

Each of the significant industries would have been supported by a guild, and the eight guilds of Carlisle known to have been established by the fifteenth century were made up of butchers, merchants, shoemakers, skinners, smiths, tailors, tanners and weavers. The guilds were latterly housed in the Guildhall on the corner of Fisher Street, and it is perhaps significant that the Guildhall, a townhouse of early fifteenth-century construction, is the only surviving medieval house in Carlisle (Figure 8.2). The building is of timber-framed construction with the exterior frame infilled with fired clay tiles, and it gives some idea of how the architecture in the centre of Carlisle may have appeared during the fifteenth century. Other than the substantial religious and military structures of Carlisle, most buildings would have been modest affairs constructed primarily of timber and roofed with thatch, with this still being the case even up to the early eighteenth century.

The use of wood as the building material of choice was no doubt due to its ready availability from the plentiful forests of northern Cumbria and in particular Inglewood Forest. The disadvantage of this reliance on timber and thatch was that the town was extremely vulnerable to fire, especially in times of conflict. Substantial parts of the city were destroyed on at least four

Figure 8.2. The Guildhall, built in 1407, from a lithograph by Matthew Nutter, 1833 *(by courtesy of Tullie House Museum and Art Gallery, Carlisle)*

separate occasions, with the fires of 1251 and 1292 devastating much of city. The use of timber and the impact of numerous fires have resulted in scarce evidence for the homes and shops of medieval Carlisle's households and merchants, which is now confined to the archaeological and documentary record.

Other than the city walls and bridges, for whose maintenance the citizens of Carlisle were responsible, there does not appear to be any evidence of any other large civic projects, which again reflects the relatively impoverished state of the city and its inhabitants throughout much of this period. The most significant recorded evidence for any substantial medieval infrastructure relates to the substantial drains of the friaries, which were exclusively for the use of those houses. These drains are well recorded in the documentary record and a section of well-made stone culvert was recorded on the site of the Dominican friary in 1998 (Figure 8.3).

There is no evidence of a civic water-supply or of a significant municipal drainage system, and it is likely that each household would have been responsible for its own sanitation. Domestic water would have been provided by private wells, with most excavated examples of burgage plots containing

Figure 8.3. The medieval drain from the Dominican friary (*photograph: Matthew Town*)

at least one well, which is often the best preserved feature recorded during excavation. Initially most of the recorded wells in Carlisle were constructed out of timber, and often appear as large pits in unwaterlogged conditions, such as an example recorded on Scotch Street. In the later medieval period, domestic wells were more often constructed out of stone, and a particularly good example, with fine dressed sandstone as well as an elaborate timber pump, was recorded *in situ* at Scotch Street during excavations in 2003 (Figure 8.4). Once a well had gone out of use, the vast majority of excavated examples were reused as rubbish pits, often containing a treasure-trove of domestic objects and environmental remains.

Sewage would have been discarded into cess-pits and open sewers running along the street frontages. Archaeological excavation has revealed that livestock, including pigs, goats and hens, were frequently kept and sometimes butchered in the rear of the burgage plots. During periods of Scottish hostility and raiding, the population of Carlisle would have surged with an influx of people and their livestock seeking protection. Additionally, during market days and fairs the streets of the city would have thronged with livestock, and given the fact that the city was not provided with an effective level of sanitation, conditions must have been appalling by modern-day standards.

The first surviving map of Carlisle was produced around 1560 and shows a city that was well developed within the city walls, with the open space of the former Franciscan friary south-east of the city being shown as unoccupied (Figure 9.2). The three gates, of which unfortunately nothing survives, would have controlled access in and out of the city and collected tolls for goods leaving and entering it (Figure 8.5). The market place is clearly defined by the open space at which all the major roads converged and would have been crucial in the economic life of Carlisle, with the annual August fair undoubtedly being an important event not just for the city but for the whole region.

Figure 8.4. The late medieval well on Scotch Street (*by courtesy of North Pennines Archaeology Ltd*)

City Living: The Archaeology

The street-plans within modern Carlisle have changed little since the medieval period, and this has resulted in the current (largely nineteenth- and twentieth-century) buildings fronting the modern streets overlying their medieval predecessors, and in many cases removing the evidence of those buildings. Archaeological excavation itself has confirmed that substantial remains of Carlisle's medieval buildings are exceedingly hard to find. This is due partly to the fact that much of the present-day street-frontage is cellared, which in many cases has removed all traces of earlier structures. Much of the modern day city is constructed on a build-up of occupation material accumulated

Figure 8.5. The Caldew Gate from a lithograph by Matthew Nutter, 1833 (*by courtesy of Tullie House Museum and Art Gallery, Carlisle*)

over the last 2,000 years, which measures up to three metres in places. The deposition of these layers of soil often results in the oldest layers (prehistoric and Roman) having a far better chance of survival than more recent medieval and early modern layers. Nevertheless, archaeological excavation over the last 20 years has revealed pockets of well-preserved medieval archaeology within the city.

The largest excavations within the city walls were carried out on the Lanes between 1979 and 1983, and they revealed an extensive ground-plan of this area of medieval Carlisle. The distribution of buildings suggested a pattern of burgage plots fronting Scotch Street that was set out in the mid-thirteenth century, the result of a rare period of peace and economic growth in the medieval history of the city. All the buildings were fairly insubstantial timber structures with hard earth floors. A good example of a typical thirteenth-century building, recorded on Lewthwaite Lane, contained two rooms defined by a series of stone pads (for supporting timber uprights), beam-slots and post-holes. The plan of this building illustrates how ephemeral the archaeological remains can be, although longevity of occupation was suggested, and there is evidence that some of these medieval buildings were in continuous use into the seventeenth century. The remains left behind

Figure 8.6. The city ditches excavated in Rickergate beneath the modern Debenhams store (*by courtesy of Tullie House Museum and Art Gallery, Carlisle*)

for the archaeologist to discover can often be nothing more than a few pad stones, possibly a shallow gully, maybe a few post-holes, and perhaps a floor surface made up simply of compacted clay.

Other recent excavations of note in Carlisle include the series of Rickergate excavations (beneath Debenhams store), which centred on two substantial defensive ditches (Figure 8.6). A large assemblage of organic artefacts was recovered: for example, leather shoes, timber barrels, and a vast amount of animal bone, including a whole horse skeleton that had been thrown into the bottom of one of the ditches. Perhaps most remarkable of all was a water-carrier, comprising two leather bags that would have been carried by a horse (Figure 8.7). The use of the ditches as convenient rubbish dumps, filled with rotting carcasses, all manner of waste and fetid water, further indicates that the lack of sanitation continued into the later medieval period. The Millennium excavations on Castle Green, although primarily concerned with the Roman fort, revealed a section of the ditch that separated the medieval castle from the city, along with evidence of timber fences marking medieval property boundaries that extended up to the very edge of the city ditch. During both these excavations a remarkable amount of organic finds and environmental material was recovered due to the superb levels of preservation in the water-logged conditions. This is in marked contrast to most medieval levels in Carlisle, which are not waterlogged and therefore contain a fraction of the

Figure 8.7. A horse-borne water-carrier similar to that found in the city ditch, from the fourteenth-century Luttrell Psalter, British Library, MS Additional 42130, f. 201 (© *The British Library Board*)

evidence for the everyday items used and worn by the medieval inhabitants of Carlisle.

The redevelopment of 42–48 Scotch Street in 2003 provided the opportunity to investigate a site in the heart of the medieval walled town. The site contained a complex sequence of deep archaeological deposits measuring over three metres in depth, with the Roman layers being covered by a build-up of the ubiquitous 'dark earth' as seen throughout the city centre. A small narrow building, which was constructed onto this dark-earth layer in the earlier twelfth century, was divided into at least two rooms by an internal partition. The building was defined by crude cobble-wall foundations set in a shallow construction trench, which represented the only evidence for its existence, as no recognisable floor surfaces or occupation layers survived.

The lifespan of this building must have been relatively short, for it was cut through by cess-pits later in the twelfth century, with over 30 pits – dating from between the late twelfth and the fourteenth centuries – being excavated throughout the site (Figure 8.8). A dendrochronological (tree-ring) date of 1150 was obtained from preserved timbers within one of these pits. It is clear from the intensity and distribution of the pits that they related to a property or properties that fronted onto Scotch Street, though since no evidence of any property boundaries was found the area of excavation was perhaps entirely within one property boundary. The contents of these rubbish pits

Figure 8.8. A large thirteenth-century cess-pit on Scotch Street (*by courtesy of North Pennines Archaeology Ltd*)

produced a finds assemblage typical of domestic activity in the medieval period, including large quantities of pottery, butchered animal bone, stable sweepings and night soil.

The period of pit-digging was followed by a succession of at least three pottery kilns – the only recorded medieval pottery kilns discovered within Carlisle so far. The best preserved kiln (Figure 8.9) had an overall diameter of approximately 2.5 metres, and is highly likely to have been a simple open-topped, single-flued updraught kiln, which would have been wood-fired. Although nothing survived above ground level, the kiln superstructure was formed out of clay with a stone-flagged base.

Pottery wasters from this or the later kilns (dating to the fourteenth century) were recovered from a large pit situated adjacent to the firing pit, and fragments of the clay superstructure of the second kiln produced an archaeomagnetic date of 1370–1400 for the final firing. It is likely that the rear of this burgage plot acted as a small pottery, with the products being sold in a shop fronting Scotch Street, although any buildings associated with the workshop have been totally truncated by later activity.

This vividly illustrates how spatial boundaries between domestic and industrial life must have been very slight in medieval Carlisle. Industries that one would normally expect to find in the suburbs, such as potteries and tanneries, may have moved into the relative safety of the city in times of

Figure 8.9.The remains of a fourteenth-century pottery kiln on Scotch Street (*by courtesy of North Pennines Archaeology Ltd*)

hostility between England and Scotland. In any case, it is highly probable that many domestic and commercial properties within the city walls had small-scale industrial activities in the back plots, with industry being as much a factor of everyday life in the city as it was in the suburbs, regardless of the ever-present threat such industrial activity brought to a city largely constructed of timber and thatch.

Although the Scotch Street excavation produced an interesting sequence of structures in the back plot, it was the material discarded in the numerous inter-cutting cess-pits that yielded the most revealing information on the life of Carlisle's medieval inhabitants. Analysis of the soil samples taken from the pits disclosed a wealth of data on both the environment and activities that would have been unavailable from analysis of the structural remains alone. Plant remains included pollen and seeds, with fruit species of plum, apple, sloe and cherry – all indigenous species that could have been grown in orchards within the city walls. Flax seeds, possibly associated with the relief of diarrhoea and other stomach upsets, were also found in several of the cess-pits, and there were large quantities of moss, a medieval version of today's toilet paper.

Species represented from animal bones included cow, sheep, goat, horse, chicken and small quantities of fish, which indicates quite a varied diet and the possibility of some butchery taking place in the rear yards. Sheep wool, pig hair and chicken feathers were also recovered from several deposits. The presence of these hairs and feathers, combined with the fact that acorns and fat-hen (common feeds for pigs and chickens respectively) were recovered from several deposits, strongly suggests that pigs and chickens were kept in the back plots.

Parasite remains were recovered in some pits, their size suggesting that they were human in origin, indicating human faecal remains within cess-pits. Insect remains of species that consume faecal material and other rotting or stored organic matter were also recovered. Additionally various parts of adult grain weevils were found and they could have represented a serious threat to a relatively poor household by consuming its store of grain or other foodstuffs.

The Suburbs of Caldewgate

It is beyond doubt that life would have been hard for the average citizens living in the undefended suburbs of Carlisle over much of the medieval period, even by the standards of the day. Even during times of relative peace the suburbs could be decimated by flood, fire and plague. Much of what is now Caldewgate was given by King David I of Scotland (1124–53) to Hexham Priory, and it was still owned by the priory at the time of the Dissolution of the monasteries in the mid-sixteenth century. The area came under the jurisdiction of the bishop of Carlisle's manor of Caldcotes, and it is recorded that leases were held throughout the fourteenth and fifteenth centuries by members of the Goldsmith family, who manufactured silver and gold objects.

In contrast to the archaeology of the city centre, the medieval remains belonging to the suburbs are often just beneath the modern ground surface. In fact, recent excavations at sites along Botchergate and Caldewgate have unearthed medieval deposits at fewer than 20 centimetres beneath the modern overburden. What has also been confirmed during all recent excavations in the suburbs is the very poor level of preservation of metallic objects and bone, along with the expected absence of other organic remains due to the lack of waterlogged conditions. This results in the finds assemblages often being strongly biased towards inorganic artefacts such as pottery, which is far more resilient to the local soil conditions.

There is evidence that the chapel of the Holy Trinity was situated in an area called the Giant's Grave at the head of Caldewgate. The so-called chronicle of Lanercost gives a detailed description of the Scottish siege of Carlisle in 1315. The chronicle states that '[the Scots] erected an engine for casting stones near the church of the Holy Trinity, where their king [Robert Bruce] had placed himself, and continually threw great stones towards the Caldew Gate, and at the wall, but did no injury, or but little to those within, except that they killed one man'. Caldewgate is recorded as having been decimated by a cataclysmic flood in 1484, and it is unclear how much of the Caldewgate area was reoccupied in the aftermath of the flood during the late fifteenth and the sixteenth centuries. If the devastation was as long lasting as has been suggested, it perhaps helps to explain the abandonment of Holy Trinity chapel, because the suburb it served may have largely ceased to exist.

Recent excavations in the vicinity of this chapel, at the site of the Maltster's Arms, revealed a period of intense industrial activity extending from the early fourteenth century through to the fifteenth century. The site was occupied by a succession of three timber workshop buildings and six associated furnaces (Figure 8.10). The construction methods employed on all three buildings were based on the sill beam, with the superstructure mortised into the sill framework. This method of construction is not uncommon, with good examples being recorded at Castle Street and the Lanes. It is the function of these buildings, as a sequence of bronze-working workshops with associated external features such as furnaces and casting areas, that makes them unique in North-West England.

Figure 8.10. A bronze-working furnace in Caldewgate (*by courtesy of North Pennines Archaeology Ltd*)

The floor surfaces within the workshops and external working areas produced large quantities of bronze-working debris, including mould fragments for the production of cauldrons and skillets, which were common domestic wares from the thirteenth until the seventeenth centuries. The earliest timber building also contained a well-preserved internal hearth, a feature which rarely survives intact in Carlisle (Figure 8.11). Also recovered were small cast bronze fragments. These are likely to have come from bronze vessels, which had been cut up and made ready for recycling by casting the fragments into new vessels. Artefactual dating allowed the date-range for the production of bronze vessels in the sequence of three workshops to be placed between the late fourteenth century and the late fifteenth century, with an archaeomagnetic date of 1390–1475 being provided by a furnace relating to the second workshop. The eventual disuse of the third bronze workshop was defined by a build-up of homogenous silty loam soil, which contained pottery fragments of sixteenth- and seventeenth-century date, and it is tempting to assign this probable period of abandonment of the site to the last decades of the fifteenth century and the impact of the flood of 1484.

Figure 8.11. The floor surface of a fourteenth-century workshop, with intact hearth, in Caldewgate (*by courtesy of North Pennines Archaeology Ltd*)

Conclusions

From the work undertaken in Carlisle over the last 20 years it is clear that although there is little to see of the medieval city above ground, apart from the castle and the cathedral precinct, there remains a treasure-trove of archaeological features and environmental deposits beneath the streets and buildings of the modern city. Levels of preservation vary, and in many cases more recent buildings have truncated their medieval predecessors, but in others an extraordinary level of preservation is just below the pavement. The picture from the suburbs, and much of the area within the city walls, is still unfolding, although already we can see slightly different stories emerging, with a break in occupation in Caldewgate at the end of the fifteenth century, and the ultimate demise of the chapel of the Holy Trinity. Above the floodplain and within the safety of the city walls, no such breaks in occupation are discernible, but the preservation of archaeological deposits is variable. Although we have learnt a great deal about the lives of Carlisle's medieval inhabitants, there is so much still to discover on the industries, suburbs, domestic dwellings and shops that now exist only in the archaeological record.

★ ★ ★ ★ ★

Suggested Further Reading

W. Hutchinson, *The History of the County of Cumberland* (Carlisle, 1794; reprinted Wakefield, 1974)

M. R. McCarthy, *A Roman, Anglian and Medieval Site at Blackfriars Street* (CWAAS, Research Series, 4, 1990)

M. R. McCarthy, *Roman and Medieval Carlisle: The Southern Lanes* (Carlisle Archaeology Ltd, Research Report, 1, 2000)

H. Summerson, *Medieval Carlisle: The City and the Borders from the Late Eleventh to the Mid-Sixteenth Century* (CWAAS, Extra Series, 25, 1993)

Chapter 9
The Origins of the Modern City

Richard Newman

The years between 1540 and 1750 define a distinct period in the development of Carlisle (Figure 9.1). They begin with the Dissolution of the monasteries, which symbolically and to an extent practically marked the end of the medieval social order. They conclude with the beginnings of industrialisation, a process partly facilitated by the ending of the Scottish military threat. The defeat of the army of Charles Edward Stuart ('Bonnie Prince Charlie') in 1746 also defines the conclusion of Carlisle's role as a Border fortress, for until then Carlisle was distinguished primarily by its military importance as the city guarding the western route from Scotland into England.

While these broad historical processes are well known, the details of the city's development are less accessible. The documentary record is often sporadic, anecdotal and not easily interpretable. Also, as in many other towns in North-West England, Carlisle's archaeological remains from the sixteenth to eighteenth centuries are often fragmentary and more badly affected by nineteenth-century development than the remains of earlier eras. Moreover, at least in Carlisle, there are surprisingly few standing buildings from the period; while the little surviving below-ground evidence that has been found was, until recently, usually ignored and hastily removed without record in order to reach earlier, especially Roman, levels.

Fortunately, however, Carlisle is blessed with one particularly good source that helps to illuminate its developmental history, for it has a range of seemingly accurate town maps. Although these are not evenly distributed throughout the years 1540–1750, there are excellent maps dating to close to the beginning and the end of the period that provide glimpses of the city's layout and appearance. For these purposes, none is better than the map from the reign of Elizabeth I (1558–1603), now held in the British Library (Figure 9.2). The precise date of the map, like the identity of the cartographer, is unknown – though it must be after 1558 because in that year the former Franciscan friary was sold as an extant property, but on the map its location is shown as a cleared open area.

This Elizabethan map is superbly detailed. From it the city can be broken up into its principal physical components: the castle and the city walls, the religious precincts, the market place, and the urban properties. Another element – the suburbs – can be added. These areas are not depicted on the

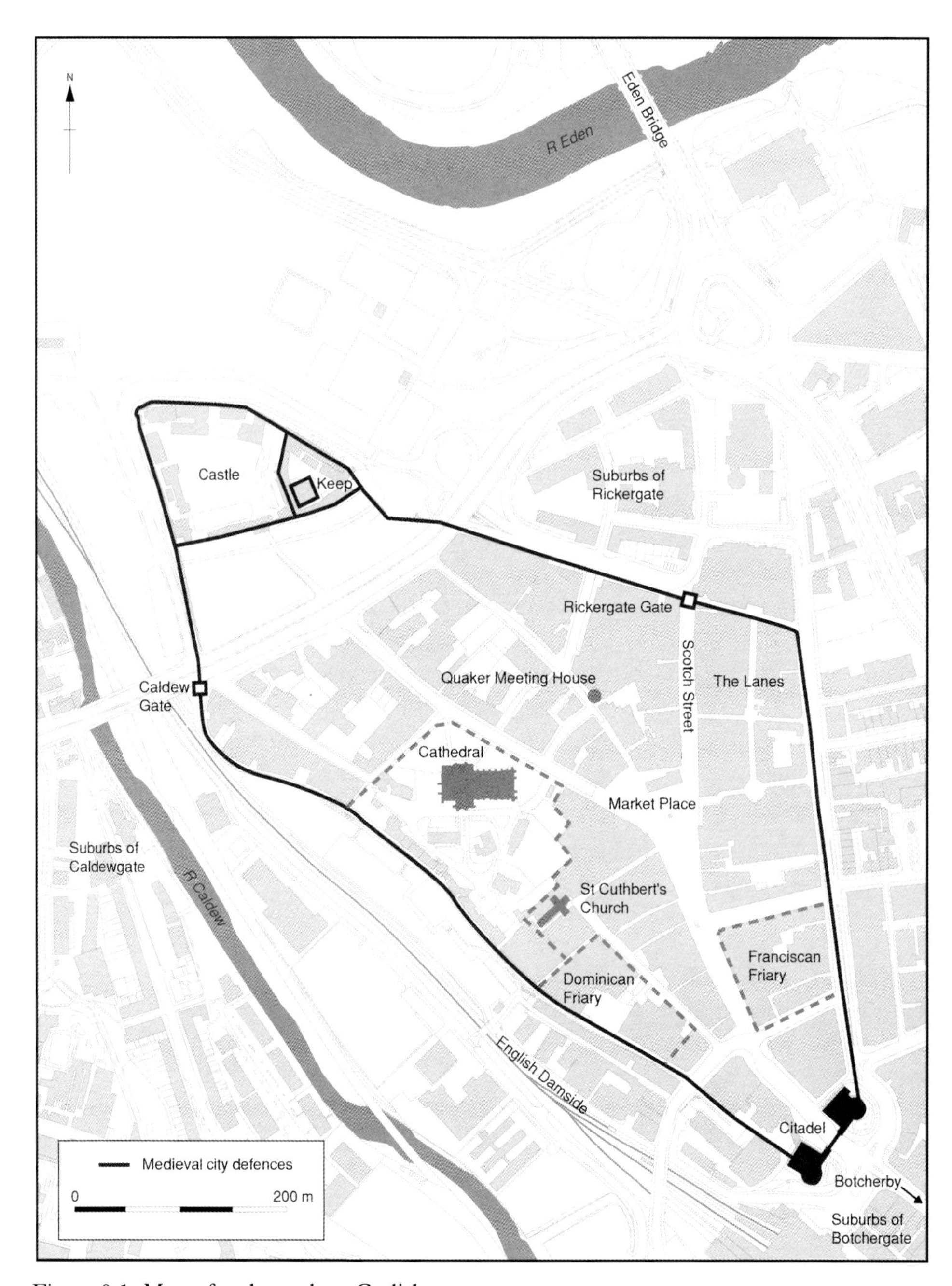

Figure 9.1. Map of early modern Carlisle

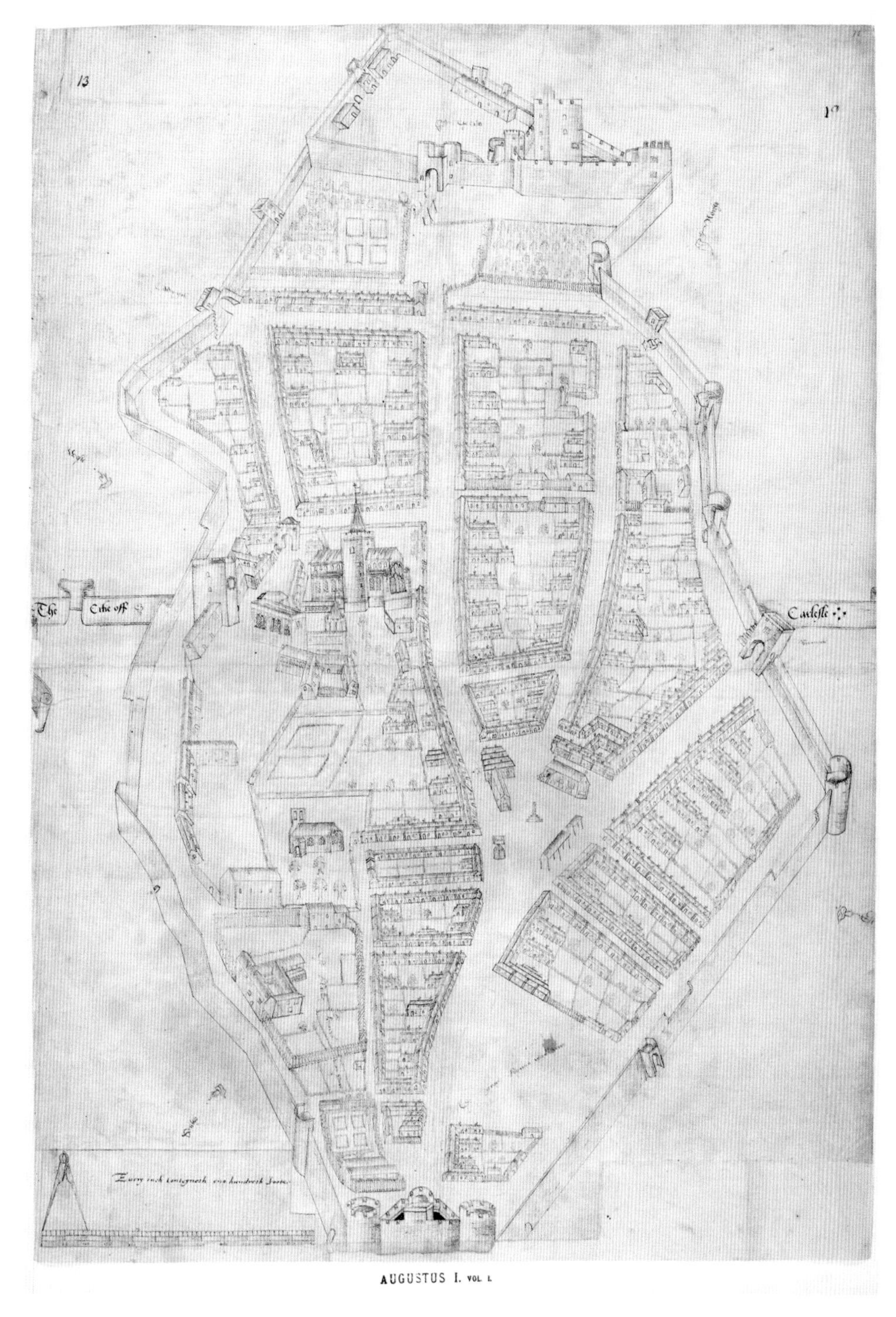

Figure 9.2. The map of the city and castle of Carlisle of *c.* 1560, British Library, MS Cotton Augustus I.i.13 (© *The British Library Board*)

Elizabethan map, but they do feature on John Speed's map of Carlisle of 1610 (see front cover). All five components form the basis for the following discussion of the physical development of the city and the changing living conditions within it.

Views of Carlisle

Comparisons between the Elizabethan map and George Smith's map of the city in 1746 suggest at first glance that the intervening 185 years or so had wrought very little change in the layout and physical character of Carlisle. The urban area remained largely contained within the city's medieval walls. There appears to have been scant intensification of urban development inside them, and the city remained dominated and defined by the castle, cathedral and market place, and by the heavily fortified Botchergate or English Gate, which later became known as the citadel. The topographical views presented in the maps can be supplemented by the impressions of contemporary visitors. John Leland wrote in the 1530s that Carlisle had a strong city wall made of squared blocks of reddish stone. More than two centuries later, Reinhold Angerstien, a Swedish traveller, noted in his diary of 1753–5 that the castle and fortifications were poorly maintained. He further observed that the town's trade was feeble and that it had no manufacturing other than the making of riding-whips and fish-hooks. John Croft, another eighteenth-century commentator, described Carlisle in 1759 as 'a small deserted dirty city, poorly built and poorly inhabited'.

These contemporary views, when combined with the map evidence, suggest a city that had stagnated. It had apparently grown little, not least in terms of industry and trade; and its principal features seem to have been its decaying medieval defences. Consequently it is not surprising that many historians have regarded seventeenth- and eighteenth-century Carlisle as a struggling city, hampered by the effects of periodic warfare and by poor communications. Sydney Towill, for example, refers to the city as having 'barely emerged from the medieval ages' by 1745. Yet this is not a complete or wholly accurate picture.

The 1801 Census records the population of the walled city and its suburbs as 10,221. This figure is sometimes used to indicate Carlisle's lack of growth and significance; and when compared with some other provincial cities, such as York, Norwich or Bristol, Carlisle does indeed seem to have been small and unimportant. When compared with other contemporary urban centres in the North-West, however, Carlisle appears to have been far more significant. True, the 1801 Census records a growing city about to break the constraints of its confining medieval walls; but the Carlisle of 1801 was not that physically distinct in urban size and development density from the mid-eighteenth-century town. Moreover, while Carlisle had expanded in the late eighteenth century, many other towns in the North-West had done so at much faster rates. Consequently mid-eighteenth-century Carlisle was still one of the largest north-western towns. It also remained along with Chester, Preston and Lancaster a key administrative centre, and with Chester it was one of only two diocesan seats within the region. It was about to be rapidly overtaken in size and economic power by the likes of Liverpool and Manchester and – within its own county – by Whitehaven; but Carlisle in the 1750s was undoubtedly a regionally prominent town.

The Garrison City

There can be little question that Carlisle's continuing military significance had some negative implications for its development. On the other hand, however, the presence of a garrison, sometimes equating to more than one-tenth of the total population, must have acted as a stimulus for some supply sectors of the local economy. A number of excavated artefacts attest to the city's active military role. Observations of sewer cuttings in the 1870s, for example, revealed a cannon ball, close to and at the same depth as a George I shilling, so perhaps it related to the siege of Carlisle during the Jacobite Rebellion in 1745, as discussed below.

On a broader front, from the 1540s the development of the city's defences, including the castle, was dominated by the need to adapt to gunpowder-based military technologies and to sporadic violence along the Anglo-Scottish frontier. Following the Pilgrimage of Grace in 1536 and the Scottish king's marriage alliance with France in the same year, there was a renewed appreciation of Carlisle's military importance. With the city walls in a ruinous condition and expensive to repair, the city's defences were re-thought, so that defence was concentrated on two strongholds: the castle at the north and the Botchergate Gate at the south. In the early 1540s, the latter was rebuilt as a fort – the citadel – and the castle was strengthened by the reinforcement of the inner ward's walls with an earthen rampart, and by the addition of the Half-Moon gun battery (Figures 9.3 and 9.4). This represented a substantial modernisation of Carlisle's defences; but with an improvement in Anglo-Scottish relations, investment was not maintained. In the 1560s the castle's walls and towers were described as 'very ruinous', and large sections of the town walls are depicted on the Elizabethan map as damaged or collapsed (Figure 9.2). For much of Queen Elizabeth's reign, with military attention focused elsewhere, very little was spent on Border defence except at Berwick-on-Tweed. Some repairs were undertaken at Carlisle in the 1550s or later in response to cross-Border raiding (Figure 9.5); but with the pacification of the Borders following the accession of the Scottish king James VI to the English throne as James I, there was even less reason to maintain Carlisle's fortifications. In the 1630s, for instance, both the citadel and the castle were

Figure 9.3. A view of the citadel shortly before its conversion into courthouses, from an engraving by Samuel Noble, *c.* 1802

Figure 9.4. The Half-Moon battery (*photograph: author*)

stripped of their 18 brass cannons, leaving only 13 pieces of iron ordnance.

Carlisle once more became of strategic importance during the English Civil Wars (1642–8). Carlisle had a garrison of 500 men from 1638, following the rising of the Covenanters in Scotland, and a royalist force remained in the city until 1645, when it fell to a Scottish army after a lengthy siege. The Scots refurbished Carlisle's defences by demolishing buildings in the cathedral precinct in order to reinforce the walls and rebuild two gun batteries in the castle's outer ward. The main additions, however, had more to do with controlling the townsfolk than with defending the city itself. Thus the Scots built guard-houses at each of the city gates, and a blockhouse in the market square that would be described in the 1770s as 'a fort with four bastions, roofed like a house, with holes for the gunners to shoot out at with small arms'.

Figure 9.5. A plaque dated 1577 in the castle's inner ward (*photograph: author*)

In 1648 Carlisle was retaken by the royalists and again garrisoned by the Scots, who were now supporting Charles I's efforts to regain power. Then, following the defeat of the Scottish army at the battle of Preston (1648), the city was re-garrisoned by Cromwell's troops; but under the Protectorate (1653–9) it received little investment in the maintenance of its defences. By the time of the Restoration of 1660, the city's fortifications were considered to be in a parlous state and, with Charles II lacking funds and with little threat from Scotland, there was no prospect of investing in military works. The various armed struggles that marked the end of Stuart rule, and the periodic attempts to re-establish it, generally did not involve Carlisle; nor did they lead to any major spending on the defences.

In 1745, however, Carlisle was occupied by Jacobite rebels, largely Scottish Highlanders, who supported Charles Edward Stuart. The duke of Cumberland besieged the city in December of that year, and pounded it with cannon obtained from Whitehaven. The surrender of the Scots on 30

December effectively ended Carlisle's role as a fortress. As might be expected, during the Napoleonic Wars (1803–15) the castle was used simply as a supply depot, and the city walls had been largely demolished by 1815.

The Cathedral City

When John Leland visited Carlisle in the 1530s, he did so as a commissioner of Henry VIII engaged in the suppression of the monasteries. He would have found a town in which about one-third of its area (excluding the castle) was occupied by buildings and property belonging to religious foundations. The town's western and southern portions were physically dominated by the religious enclave formed by St Mary's Priory, St Cuthbert's church and the Dominican and Franciscan friaries. In the 1530s one in every seven men in Carlisle was a priest, monk or friar; it was indeed, in Henry Summerson's phrase, 'a heavily clericalised city'. The priory, also the city's cathedral, was considered prosperous when it was suppressed (Figure 9.6). It was quickly re-founded as a cathedral in 1541, and retained many of its old endowments and personnel. The priory buildings were granted in their entirety to the dean and chapter of the 'new' cathedral. The choir of the priory church, and two bays of the nave, formed the cathedral church of the Holy and Undivided Trinity; while five bays of the nave formed St Mary's parish church.

Many of the old priory's buildings were destroyed during the Civil Wars, and St Mary's five bays were largely demolished during the Protectorate. In 1640 the military governor of Carlisle, fearing Scottish attack, had requisitioned some of the former priory's premises for munitions storage. The surviving fratry certainly seems to have been converted into a magazine in the early 1640s, if not before. Nevertheless, as yet no alterations appear to have been made to the cathedral itself. Traditionally the occupying Scottish army of 1645–7 is blamed for the demolition of the nave. The Scots evidently pulled down many priory buildings, including the cloisters (Figure 9.7), to repair the town's defences, but the nave was spared. In 1643 Parliament abolished church government by bishops. Consequently the cathedral church, along with the churches of St Mary and St Cuthbert, was available as a parish church, which gave Carlisle an oversupply of church buildings. Since St Cuthbert's was in a better state of repair than St Mary's, the latter was effectively redundant, and an asset to be disposed of. It appears that demolition began around 1650, but it was never completed as it was spasmodic and undertaken only when there was a need and a market for the stone. The Restoration, which saw the reintroduction of the bishop and cathedral, put an end to further demolition. By then the nave of the medieval priory had been largely removed, and a new west-end wall was built astride the nave's foundations (Figure 9.8). The cathedral and St Cuthbert's remained the only established churches in Carlisle until the 1820s. By the later seventeenth

Figure 9.6. A model showing the monastic precinct of Carlisle Priory as it might have appeared in *c.* 1540 (*photograph: author*)

Figure 9.7. The remains of the demolished monastic cloisters (*photograph: author*)

Figure 9.8. The wall stubs at Carlisle cathedral after the demolition of the nave in the mid-seventeenth century (*photograph: author*)

century, dissenter communities were based in the city, but the first bespoke meeting house was not built until the later eighteenth century.

A very different fate from that of the main churches befell Carlisle's two friaries. The former Franciscan convent was bought in 1558 and, according to Speed's map, had been redeveloped by 1610 (see front cover); but later and more accurate maps indicate that the site remained open and undeveloped until the early eighteenth century, which must suggest a lack of development pressure inside the walls of the seventeenth-century city. Even by 1746 most of the precinct behind the street frontage remained unused other than as open back plots and gardens. The former Dominican precinct became the town residence of the locally important Aglionby family and then, in 1686, the site of the county gaol.

House and Home

On the Elizabethan map of Carlisle there is some indication of social variation among the buildings shown, with a scattering of courtyard properties perhaps representing the residences of more wealthy property-owners (Figure 9.2). From the Middle Ages, major Cumbrian families such as the Cliffords and Dacres had townhouses within the city walls. Most of the sixteenth-century burgess houses, however, seem to have been single storey with limited development of the back plots.

Many of the houses depicted on the Elizabethan map were almost certainly clay dabbins. Celia Fiennes, writing in 1702, noted that the poor who lived between Carlisle and Penrith often inhabited mud-walled or dry-stoned homes. Fiennes did not record any such dwellings in Carlisle itself, which she had visited in 1698; but – except in the cathedral precinct – she saw 'no house of brick and stone' apart from the mayor's house, which (at least by 1746) lay outside the city walls in English Damside, and the chancellor's house, which also had a stone-walled garden. Other evidence suggests that brick and stone were little used in the seventeenth century. Contemporary wills and inventories indicate that the buildings fronting the east side of Scotch Street retained their medieval character; and there are suggestions that single-storey, clay-built houses were not uncommon in Botchergate. There were also wooden structures: in 1649, for example, the city's governor proposed to take down and move a timber-framed house. Furthermore, William Hutchinson's *History of the County of Cumberland* (1794) provides a description of Carlisle in about 1700 in the following unfavourable terms.

> [It] exhibited no marks of modern convenience and elegance. The buildings, mostly of wood, clay and laths, bespoke the poverty and bad taste of the inhabitants. The gables fronted the streets, the doors were generally in the centre and many of the houses had porches which projected two or three yards into the street.

Not only were houses still built of clay or wood in the sixteenth and seventeenth centuries, but turf might be used to roof them. A lease of 1589 to a house in Scotch Street refers to a slate roof over the hall, but all three rooms were covered by 'flakes', that is, turfs or sods. A nearby burgage plot had a house of five rooms, each roofed with 'flakes'. Thatch would also have been commonplace, though by the later seventeenth century ceramic roof tiles were readily available.

In fact ceramic building materials had first been used in Carlisle in the fifteenth century, for the castle's Tile Tower (Figure 6.7); and Tile Close in St Nicholas is recorded in 1610. But tiles are not known to have been made in the town until 1652. That a brick-kiln operated at Murrel Hill by 1684 also suggests a novel local demand for better built houses. Some of the earliest surviving physical evidence is a gable-end dedication dated 1700, which is of hand-made brick on a rough-cast, brick-built house in the village of Botcherby, now within Carlisle's suburbs (Figure 9.9). The date tallies with the evidence for the rebuilding and modernisation of Scotch Street, which suggests a date-range from the 1690s to about 1750. Thus 61 Scotch Street (now demolished) had cast-iron fireplaces of eighteenth-century design and a cupboard door bearing the graffito 'EA 1741'.

Figure 9.9. A brick-built house in Botcherby (*photograph: author*)

The overall conclusion is that Carlisle's ordinary domestic buildings remained clay or wooden built and traditional in character until at least the 1690s. In this respect, Carlisle was little different from many other historic towns in the North-West: Lancaster, for instance, was very similar. A major phase of rebuilding in brick then took place at Carlisle in the first half of the eighteenth century – a key indication that the city was evolving rather than stagnating at that time.

Lack of excavated evidence prevents an archaeological analysis of the intensity of the use of back plots in the post-medieval period. But the map evidence suggests that the Scotch Street backlands lacked any significant development until the mid-eighteenth century. By 1770 nine lanes existed between Scotch Street and the city walls; and by 1794 this area, soon to be known as the Lanes, was the most densely occupied part of the city, filled primarily with a combination of workers' houses and industrial workshops.

Trade and Industry

The market place lay, as now, in the centre of the city at the junction of English Street, Fisher Street, Castle Street and Scotch Street. In the late sixteenth century, it is shown as having a medieval market cross, a town hall, and some pillared roofed structures, or covered market stalls, which are marked on later maps as the Shambles. In addition, there was a booth-like structure on the site of what by the late eighteenth century was recorded as the guard house built by the Scottish occupying army in 1645–7. The booth-like structure may have been a tollbooth; the town hall itself was rebuilt in 1717 (Figure 9.10). The market seems to have been mainly for agricultural produce rather than for local manufactured goods. It was a sufficiently important grain market to attract large numbers of corn traders from Northumberland in the later seventeenth century. Plenty of meat was also for sale, and there was a busy market in cattle and horses, with the Sands area being crowded with livestock on market day. Indeed, throughout the early modern period Carlisle played a major role in the cross-Border cattle trade, which saw cattle fattened in Galloway before being sent south to market. It was presumably on the basis of this trade that Carlisle developed its noted manufacture of bullwhips.

Figure 9.10. The town hall, rebuilt in 1717, as it appeared at Queen Victoria's Diamond Jubilee in 1897, from a watercolour by Thomas Bushby (*by courtesy of Tullie House Museum and Art Gallery, Carlisle*)

The relatively localised and agricultural nature of Carlisle's trading economy is also evidenced by its activities as a port. It was appointed a head port in 1564/5, though ships did not enter the city, which used various harbours on the south Solway coast. Foreign trade was negligible, and even coastal trade was limited, and dominated from the later seventeenth century by the export of agricultural produce to Whitehaven. The city lacked manufactured goods to export, and the main trade of its merchants was not by sea but overland to Newcastle.

The lack of large-scale manufacturing in Carlisle before the later eighteenth century was stressed by William Hutchinson in 1794, and his views seem to be borne out by observers like Dr Hugh Todd, prebendary of Carlisle, who in 1687 asserted that local people lacked wealth because of 'having no manufactory or staple commodity to enrich themselves by'. Nevertheless, at this time Carlisle had guilds for butchers, merchants, shoemakers, skinners and glovers, smiths, tailors, tanners and weavers. Even if Carlisle lacked products that were special to the town, it clearly had inhabitants who, besides making bricks and tiles, processed animal hides, produced some textiles, and worked metal. Some attempts were also made to promote manufacturing, apparently with the encouragement of the city's corporation. In 1724 the Abbey Mill, a fulling-mill and dye-house, was leased to the Deulicher brothers and rebuilt at the corporation's expense; by 1740 it was referred to as a factory house with looms, and since this textile enterprise had attracted labour from outside Cumberland, it was of some significance. The business was re-let in 1743; but the corporation made no further attempts to develop industry until 1764, when permission was given to Bernard Barton to erect a water-wheel at what became the Long Island calico printing works.

Outside the City Gates

Since the map of Elizabethan Carlisle focuses entirely on the walled city, the lack of depicted suburbs does not mean that they did not exist. Speed's map of 1610 includes well-established ribbon development from outside Rickergate to the bridge over the Eden, but it does not cover a sufficient area to show whether suburbs extended from Botchergate and Caldewgate (see front cover). A map of the city's defences in 1685 reveals well-developed suburbs at Rickergate, Botchergate and Caldewgate. By 1746 suburban expansion had begun in the English Damside area; and, overall, the suburbs more than doubled in size in the 1750s and 1760s.

The medieval suburb of Caldewgate seems to have been partly abandoned by the sixteenth century. The occasional sixteenth-century artefact has been found in the area, along with the remains of a small possible agricultural building of late sixteenth- or seventeenth-century date. Significant reoccupation of the area seems to have occurred only in the seventeenth century.

By 1685 Caldewgate consisted of a small suburb immediately outside the city wall and a separate settlement to the west of the River Caldew, which had originated as a settlement of Flemish immigrants in the twelfth century. Archaeological investigations indicate that the gap between the two areas was developed only in the later eighteenth century. Rickergate seems to have continued as a functioning suburb from the fourteenth to seventeenth centuries, and the same may apply to Botchergate, but in both instances major expansion also seems to have begun only in the period 1750–70. Prior to this expansion, however, Botchergate was probably the largest of Carlisle's suburbs in the later seventeenth and early eighteenth centuries.

Post-Medieval Carlisle: A Failing Town?

There is some justification for regarding Carlisle as a stagnating town from the mid-sixteenth to mid-eighteenth centuries. The population is likely to have remained relatively static, not aided by the periodic outbreaks of plague, most notably in 1598 and during the Civil Wars. The town did not have much of a manufacturing base, and its history was relatively turbulent. Yet when placed in the context of urban development generally during the period, and in much of North-West England in particular, Carlisle compares especially unfavourably only with some of the Atlantic port towns. For much of the period, Carlisle retained its strategic significance and supported a military garrison. It was the county town, with all the attendant administrative and

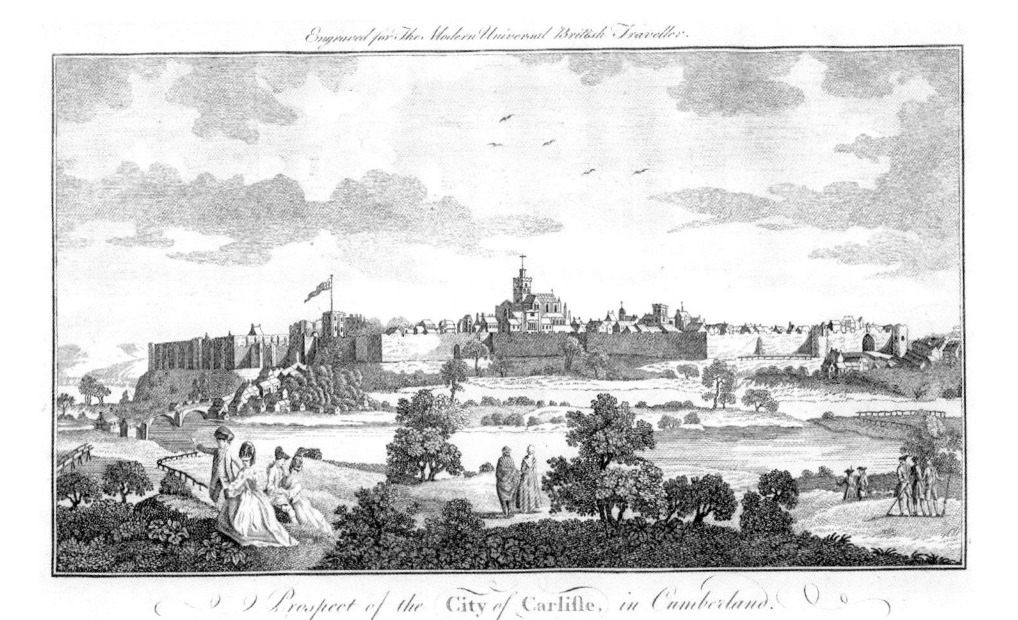

Figure 9.11. A view of Carlisle from *The Modern Universal British Traveller* (1779)

legal functions, and the seat of a bishopric. It remained a major centre for the cattle trade and a market hub within the Borders. The early eighteenth century did see a rebuilding of the town's urban fabric, some industrial development, and settlement expansion. Thus the foundations for the modern industrial city were beginning to be laid. The final removal of the threat from Scotland, and the improved communications resulting from the construction of the Military Road to Newcastle around 1750, allowed the seeds of change to germinate, and Carlisle would flourish and grow rapidly in the later eighteenth century (Figure 9.11).

* * * * *

Suggested Further Reading

B. C. Jones, 'Carlisle brickmakers and bricklayers, 1652–1752', *CW2*, 83 (1983), pp. 125–9

B. C. Jones, 'Carlisle's first factory', *CW2*, 85 (1985), pp. 187–91

M. R. McCarthy, H. Summerson and R. G. Annis, *Carlisle Castle: A Survey and Documentary History* (English Heritage Archaeological Report, 18, 1990)

D. R. Perriam, 'The demolition of the priory of St Mary, Carlisle', *CW2*, 87 (1987), pp. 127–58

M. Robinson, 'The port of Carlisle: trade and shipping in Cumberland, 1675–1735', *CW3*, 8 (2008), pp. 147–57

Chapter 10
The Industrial and Manufacturing City

Caron Newman

Carlisle's industrial rise began in the later eighteenth century and was based on water-power supplied by the medieval millraces. The first major encouragement to industrial enterprises came in the 1750s with the building of the Military Road to Newcastle, which enabled goods, previously transported by pack-horse, to be moved by large carts. Transport links to the rest of the country remained poor until the construction of a canal from Fisher's Cross (later Port Carlisle) near Bowness-on-Solway to Willowholme on the west side of the city. The Canal opened in 1823 and its influence became apparent immediately, with the development of port facilities and industries around the Canal basin at Willowholme. Bonded warehouses and coal and lime vaults were soon built, and by 1838 a timber dock and two large saw-mills were handling large quantities of imported timber.

Improved communications encouraged Carlisle's first factory-scale production in the mid-eighteenth century – initially of linen and woollen cloth, but later of cotton. Other industries also developed from the late 1700s, including brewing, bread- and biscuit-making, hat-making and engineering, all of which became characteristic features of the nineteenth- and twentieth-century city (Figure 10.1). When cotton cloth production declined from the 1850s, woollen cloth-making was reintroduced, and carpets and other fabrics were also manufactured. Following the opening of the first railway, to Newcastle in 1836, the number and types of industries increased; and the railway link (from 1837) between the Canal basin and London Road station spurred development in Denton Holme, as industries gained easy access to the railway network (Figure 10.2). The city's function as a railway hub also encouraged heavy engineering, and the manufacture of rolling-stock and cranes became a Carlisle industry of international significance.

Carlisle's industrial role continued throughout much of the twentieth century, enhanced during the First World War by the establishment of large-scale munitions works to the north of Carlisle. In the first half of that century, Carlisle was considered to be a major industrial town: even in school geography books it was described as 'a great railway centre … noted for its silesias, its biscuits, its decorated tin boxes, and its giant cranes'. Most of the heavy industries are now gone, however, and have been replaced by modern light industrial enterprises and business and retail parks.

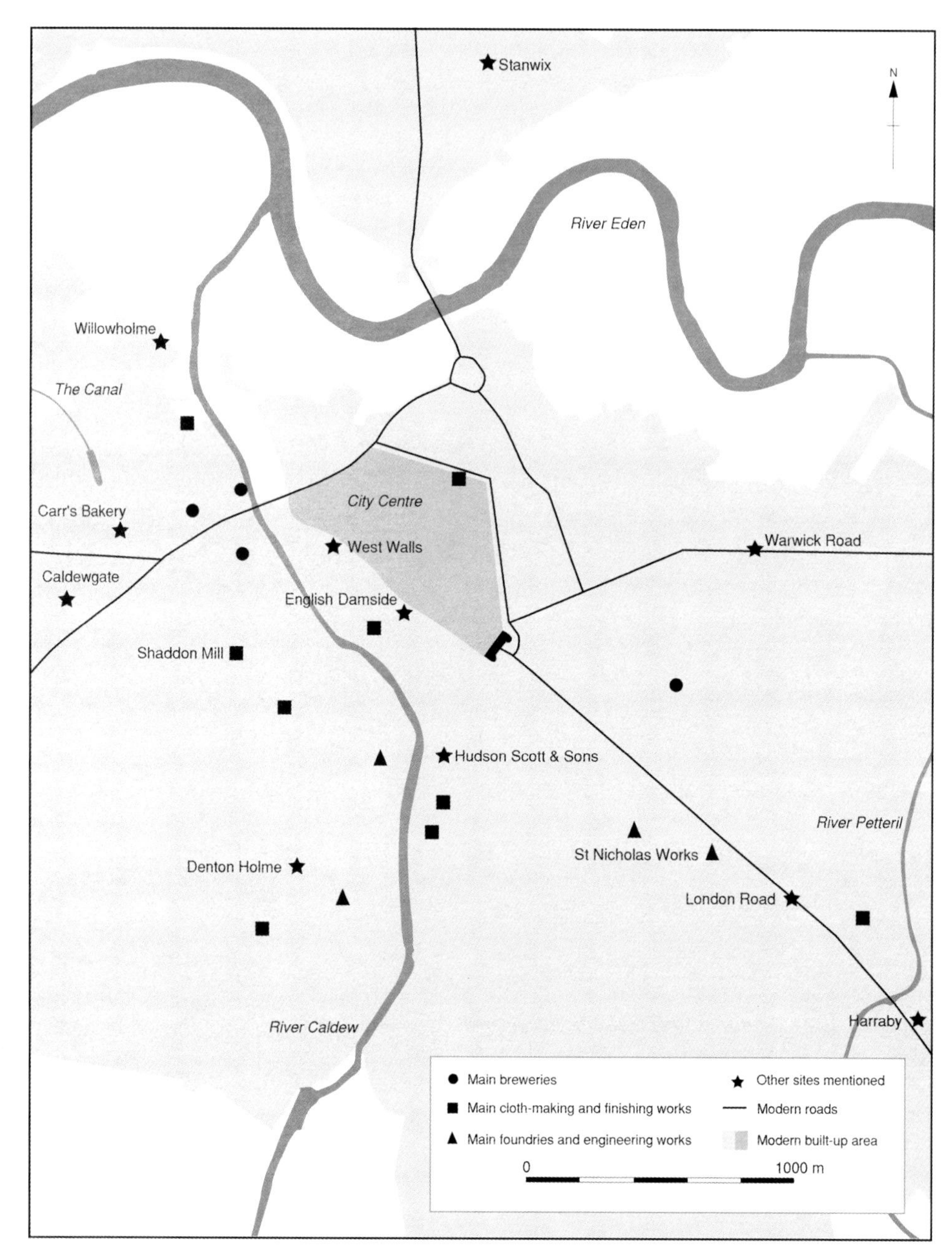

Figure 10.1. Map of industrial and manufacturing sites in nineteenth-century Carlisle

Figure 10.2. A view of Carlisle from near Denton Holme showing Shaddon Mill (left), and the rail link from London Road to the Canal terminus (foreground), from an engraving by John Archer, 1837

Cloth-Making and Finishing

Commercial cloth-making had a long history in Carlisle, with factory-based woollen cloth production beginning as early as 1724 in Abbey Mill. Carlisle's linen industry was well established by 1700, and the city became a centre for both linen and cotton cloth-finishing from the 1760s. Its printed cottons, or calicoes, were a popular substitute for highly desirable printed Indian cottons, the import of which was illegal, and the demand for which could not be satisfied by domestic production. By the 1750s there were a number of linen cloth-finishing sites, known as beetling works. One of the earliest was in a former corn-mill next to Long Island Close, which by 1780 was known as Brumwell's Stampery, indicating that printing cloth was its main purpose. It became a cotton-mill soon after, and was renamed the Long Island Works. The cotton cloth-finishing industry included dyeing, bleaching and printing works. Up to around 1800, these works dominated the south and west sides of the city, in Denton Holme and Willowholme. Carlisle was noted for the quality of its printed cottons, and in particular for the quality of the water from the rivers Caldew and Petteril for bleaching cloths prior to dyeing or printing.

By 1794 there were several major print-works in Carlisle. These included Donald's, which was founded in 1768 north of Caldewgate, and operated until 1808. Lamb Scot Forster's extensive print-works lay along the Corporation Dam, below West Walls, in the area later developed by the railways. Losh & Company established its print-works, probably by the late 1760s, along the Little Caldew millrace, between Holme Head and Denton corn-mill. Large open areas were required to dry the bleached cloth in the open air, and this acted as a brake on further industrial expansion by limiting the land available for development. The introduction of bleaching powder, however, reduced the time required to whiten the cloth from weeks to little more than a day, and removed the need for tracts of open land on which to lay out the cloth to dry. It was the small back-to-back cottages, built to house weavers in the first half of the nineteenth century, that filled the fields formerly used as bleaching grounds. Some idea of how the print-fields may have looked can be seen to the south of Carlisle, where six large and very regular fields may be the surviving drying fields for the print-works at Cummersdale (Figure 10.3).

Figure 10.3. The surviving remnants of print-fields at Cummersdale (*photograph: author*)

Cotton became the focus of factory-scale production, growing out of Carlisle's existing calico-printing and cloth-finishing industries. The earliest cloth-finishing companies had to rely on imported cloth from areas such as Lancashire, and given the difficulties of transport, it was soon apparent that it was more cost-effective to make cloth locally. One of the first spinning-mills was at Harraby, built by William Brummell in 1775. The print-works at Willowholme included a spinning-mill by 1791, and the bleaching operations at Holme Head also expanded to included spinning and weaving. The 1819 sale catalogue of the whole Denton Holme estate, including Holme Head, lists a 'newly erected and complete' mill producing cotton twist, with large warehouses, offices, manager's house and 10 cottages, as well as another cotton-mill described as 'formerly a bleaching manufactory', which appears to have been for weaving. Much of the extensive complex of buildings at Holme Head still survives, now converted into apartments (Figure 10.4). A spinning-factory built below West Walls by John Ferguson in 1825 was part of a wider range of industries owned by Ferguson, who had taken on the Denton Hill dye-works. He eventually moved all production to Denton Hill in 1877, and leased the West Walls factory to Donald's in 1862. Although parts of the factory were demolished for the Victoria Viaduct (1876) and the Grand Central Hotel (1881), some of the factory is incorporated into the rear of the hotel, and its former warehouse now forms part of a nightclub.

Figure 10.4. Holme Head Works (*photograph: author*)

Other spinning-mills included the small twist-mill on English Damside, built in 1790, and Mains Mill on London Road, built on the Botcherby millrace in 1799. At first water-powered, Mains Mill had been converted to steam by 1819, and in 1855 it was described as having 11,000 spindles. By the early nineteenth century, there were three spinning-mills in Denton Holme, including New Mill or Slater's Mill, built in 1802 by the Carlisle Cotton Twist Company. It was a large six-storey mill, steam-powered with a Boulton and Watt engine, and incorporated counting-houses, warehouses, ruling-rooms, and 24,489 mule spindles. The last purpose-built spinning-mill was Shaddon Mill of 1836 in Shaddongate, run by Peter Dixon & Sons. Its seven-storey sandstone structure, along with a brick chimney 305 feet (92.96m) tall, is one of the few mill buildings to survive intact in Carlisle (Figure 10.5). Steam-power was essential to work this substantial mill, which had a large engine-house and seven boilers. Coal for the engines was brought in from the west

Cumberland coalfield along the Carlisle Canal and then, from 1837, transferred onto the Canal branch of the Newcastle & Carlisle Railway. Weaving had been added to cotton-spinning by 1853, with the construction of a large weaving-shed to the east. Converted to woollen-spinning in 1888, the factory remained in production into the later twentieth century, and has now been converted into apartments.

Figure 10.5. The Shaddon Mill chimney, now known as Dixon's Chimney (*photograph: author*)

Most weaving in Carlisle was put out to hand-loom weavers until the mid-1840s. The numbers of hand-looms, and of those engaged in the industry, are hard to calculate. Peter Dixon & Sons was probably the biggest employer from the late 1830s, and in 1840 it was said to employ over 3,500 people in England and Scotland. The cloth they produced was taken to a warehouse on West Tower Street, where they were paid for their work. Weavers' houses sprang up around Caldewgate and also south of the city, around Water Lane and Brown's Row, to serve the nearby spinning-mills. Some houses included large loom shops, which could be considered small factories. For example, weavers' houses on Broadguards, Caldewgate, were built in 1805 with ground-floor loom shops of varying size: one had 49 looms; others had four, six or eight looms. Dwellings with loom shops were clearly common, but almost all have now been demolished, save for two rows of adjoining former loom shops in Broadguards (Figure 10.6). The earliest factory-scale weaving enterprise was begun by Stoddart Brothers, on the corner of Scotch Street and East Tower Street, in 1778. By 1794, however, Langcake, McWilliams & Company was making checks, calicoes, muslins and fancy works there. This factory continued to produce cotton and gingham cloth, probably with power-looms, but it was a woollen-mill from the 1880s to the 1950s, and then a warehouse. It stood until 1981, when it was demolished for the Lanes shopping centre development. Another textile-mill was the Lamplugh Works, built in 1865 to make cotton and woollen cloth. Its engine-house and chimney remain, but are in poor condition.

Figure 10.6. Two short rows of hand-loom weavers' cottages built on Broadguards, Caldewgate, in 1805 (*photograph: author*)

When, from the 1850s, Carlisle found it increasingly difficult to compete as a cotton cloth producing centre, especially against towns in east Lancashire with their better links to markets, many mills converted production to woollen cloth. The Raven Nook Mill, on the Botcherby millrace, was established specifically to produce woollen cloth. This steam-powered mill carried out all processes, from preparation of wool and spinning to the dyeing of the finished cloth. It had its own fulling-house, and a small gas-works for lighting. In 1872, it was bought by Robert Graham, the manager of Brampton Tweed Mill, who converted it into a tweed manufactory.

Although the major print-works had closed in Carlisle by the first quarter of the nineteenth century, cloth-finishing continued to be a significant industry for the city. Dye-works were commonly attached to existing corn-mills: for example, Denton Mill also had an indigo-mill by 1819. This was almost certainly associated with Denton Hill dye-works, tenanted by John Ferguson in 1819, which included a dye-house, a callender-house, a drying-house, and a large water-wheel for grinding indigo. Nearby was the fulling-mill where Joseph Ferguson established the Friggate Works in 1824. Ferguson pioneered new methods of finishing cotton cloth by the use of 'beetling', or the pounding of cloth with fulling hammers to produce a soft silky cotton called 'silesias', which became a renowned Carlisle product and a very successful export to the United States. In 1828 Ferguson expanded his business by moving it to the larger Holme Head Works, where he converted the spinning-mill to dyeing and finishing. A new factory was built there in 1837; it had a spinning-mill and weaving-shed by 1870, and new processes were developed. In 1901 it was described as a very large textile manufactory with integrated textile-mill, incorporating weaving, bleaching, dyeing and finishing. The last dye-works to be introduced was the Murrell Hill Colour Works, built by Alexander Morton & Company in 1918.

Hat-Making

Hat-making was important in Carlisle from the mid-eighteenth century. The oldest known business, owned by William Nelson, was probably below Caldew Bridge, where industrial-scale buildings are shown on maps of 1811 and 1821. In 1802 the business was said by the *Carlisle Journal* to have been more than 40 years old, and 'extensive and well established', with a bow shop for 20 men, two plank shops for 16 men, a dye-house, a stove and kiln for drying wool, a stiffening shop, a cutting shop, and a large hat-ware room. A second hat-works was on George Street off Rickergate, operating by 1811, but becoming a coach-works by 1865. The largest hat manufactory in the nineteenth century, on the Corporation Dam millrace, belonged to William Carrick. The business grew and, following a number of relocations, it became the South Vale hat-works. A 1901 trade directory stated that: 'A visit to their works in Norfolk Road is one of the sites of Carlisle'. It was taken over by Kangol in the 1980s, and modernised, but the site has now been redeveloped.

Brewing and Public Houses

Brewing on an industrial scale in Carlisle began in 1756 with the establishment of the Old Brewery, formed as a partnership between Richard Hodgson, a Carlisle mercer, and James Atkinson. It has stood on the north side of Caldewgate from at least 1791, though it was altered and modernised significantly on the same site in 1894, and the buildings have now been converted into student accommodation. The New Brewery, to the south side of Caldewgate, was established in 1774, next to the Little Caldew millrace, which provided water-power for grinding malt, hoisting sacks, and cranking mashing rakes. Brewing ceased on the site in 1917, though bottling continued there into the 1920s. Other eighteenth-century breweries were on West Walls: Daniel Pattinson's brewery of 1790 (Connell & Pattison's Brewery by 1821) and the High Brewery of 1794 on Water Street. The High Brewery was owned in 1840 by Joseph Iredale, under whom it flourished, and it was considered one of the most complete breweries in northern England. It was relocated to a former textile-mill, the Currock Works, in 1875 to make way for extensions to Citadel station. A small sandstone building at the east end of the site may be all that remains of Iredale's second brewery. Three new breweries opened in the nineteenth century: Meadow Brewery, Queen's Brewery and – the last to be established – Crown Brewery on Crown Street behind the Crown Hotel. The Crown Brewery opened in 1869, but it was short-lived and traded only until 1898.

The advent of the First World War brought major changes to the brewing industry in Carlisle. The munitions factory known as ROF (Royal Ordnance Factory) Gretna was the biggest in Europe, with several discrete sites between Gretna and Carlisle. It brought in a flood of workers, many of whom had to be housed in the city. This huge increase in the number of workers with disposable incomes led to a significant increase in drunkenness, and resulted in the setting up of the Central Control Board (Liquor Traffic) in 1915. It nationalised brewing and retailing in areas of important munitions production across the country, Carlisle being one of the key zones. The Carlisle Experiment, as it was known, was enacted in 1916. Carlisle's breweries were thereby nationalised, together with 400 public houses in Carlisle and Maryport districts. The New, High and Queen's Breweries were all closed down, and production was centralised at the Old Brewery. Of the 119 licensed premises and seven clubs in Carlisle, nearly half had been shut by 1918.

In 1921 the role of the Central Control Board was taken over by Carlisle & District State Management Scheme, which continued to manage brewing and public houses in Carlisle and the surrounding area until it was abolished by Act of Parliament in 1971. The Scheme built up an estate of new buildings that were specifically designed to be easily supervised, to encourage responsible consumption of alcohol, and to minimise drunkenness and anti-social behaviour. The new public houses designed by the Scheme's architect, Harry Redfern, were intended to be landmarks in the streetscape, and to provide a range of facilities that would distract customers from excessive drinking. Indeed, his work influenced public-house design right across the country. Although most of the Scheme's pubs have been severely altered since privatisation, and many have closed in recent years, good examples still survive in the Cumberland Arms on Botchergate, which was built in 1930 and has the most intact surviving interior, in the Redfern at Etterby, which was designed to commemorate Redfern's retirement by his assistant Joseph Seddon and opened in 1940, and in the former Crescent Inn on Warwick Road, which was designed in a 'Hispano-Moorish' style quite unlike anything else in Carlisle (Figure 10.7).

Figure 10.7. The Crescent Inn public house designed by Harry Redfern for the Carlisle & District State Management Scheme (*photograph: Mark Brennand*)

Food Manufacture

There were numerous small-scale manufacturers and retailers of bread, biscuits and confectionery in nineteenth-century Carlisle, with over 70 being listed in 1901. Factory-scale food production began in 1834, when Jonathan Dodgson Carr moved his bakery to a larger bread and biscuit factory in Caldewgate (Figure 10.8). The business was highly successful, and by 1865 an additional bakery had opened on the opposite side of Caldewgate, on the corner with Morton Street. In 1847 it was regarded as the most efficient of its kind in the country, with the whole process from grinding the corn to finishing the biscuit being carried out on the premises. It was also notable for introducing machinery to automate biscuit-making. Carr, a Quaker, also provided facilities for his workers, including rest rooms, a bath, a schoolroom,

Figure 10.8. Carr's bread and biscuit factory, one of Carlisle's largest businesses (*photograph: author*)

a library and a reading room. Opposite the factory, today run by McVities, his Temperance Hall (Figure 10.9) and Reading Room of 1861 still stand. Denton corn-mill, which became part of the Denton Hill dye-works, continued to grind corn. In 1837 Joseph Robinson used the mill to grind both corn and gypsum, and he later made bread and biscuits there. In 1864 production moved to William Slater's biscuit factory on James Street, though by the end of the nineteenth century it had been replaced by a large weaving-shed. Joseph Robinson & Company also ran a confectionary and biscuit manufactory at the Friggate Works by 1861, in the former dyeing and finishing works. This had become the South Vale confectionery works by the end of the century. The factory, with extensive nineteenth- and twentieth-century extensions, was based around a brick-built mill sited over the Little Caldew millrace, which may have been Joseph Ferguson's original textile-mill of the 1820s. This whole complex has

Figure 10.9. The Temperance Hall built in 1861 by Jonathan Carr for his workforce (*photograph: author*)

recently been demolished and archaeological investigations are planned ahead of redevelopment.

Printing and Tin Box Manufacture

Closely associated with food manufacture was the printing works of Hudson Scott & Sons. It was begun in 1799 by Benjamin Scott, a 'Printer, Bookseller, Stationer, and Patent Medicine Vendor', on the east side of English Street, where it meets the Market Place. Hudson Scott, Benjamin's nephew, took over management of the business in 1832, and he began printing in colour, using steam-powered presses. By the mid-nineteenth century, Hudson Scott was a well-known name in Carlisle, and in 1868 his sons took over the business, which traded as Hudson Scott & Sons. A year later, it moved to a purpose-built factory in James Street (Figure 10.10), where tin-plate decoration by transfer printing, a process first developed on the Continent around 1860, was introduced in 1876. Then, in 1877, the process was improved by the business's home-grown innovation of offset lithography. Decorated sheets were sold to customers for making their own boxes, and one of the main clients was Carr's Bakery. The firm's services were extremely popular, and by 1882 it employed 200 people.

A new phase began with the manufacture of tin boxes in 1886, which was so successful that the business took over the neighbouring Slater's Mill,

Figure 10.10. The Hudson Scott box-printing factory on James Street (*photograph: author*)

leading to extensions and rebuilding into the early twentieth century. Printing was concentrated on the original site of Hudson Scott's premises on the west side of James Street, and the manufacture of tin boxes took place on the Slater's Mill site. In 1901 it was described as 'second to none in the country and well worth a visit'; and by 1906 it had 1,200 employees and was the largest metal box manufactory in the country. The original building on James Street still stands, but the buildings on the east side have been redeveloped following archaeological investigations, which found that the original textile-mill was retained and extended.

Building Materials

The largely brick-built character of nineteenth-century Carlisle is a result of readily available raw materials close to the city (Figure 10.11). There were numerous local brickworks by the nineteenth century. Most were small quarries, but to the west of Upperby large-scale excavation has left a pond, now turned into a boating-lake known as Hammonds Pond. Much of the clay and gravel was taken to the Murrill Hill brickworks, a steam-powered business established by Thomas Nelson in 1853 to complement the marble works he had begun in 1830. Stone was brought from Cove Quarry in Scotland, and the marble works supplied many large building projects, including Silloth Harbour and the Victoria Viaduct (Figure 11.10). Following the construction in 1876–7 of the viaduct, which lay across the yard, the business moved to Junction Street. The brickworks was taken over by Thomas Nevin in 1891, and converted into a large saw-mill with associated tramway. The opening of the Canal in 1823 had quickly led to the import of large quantities of American and Baltic timber, and saw-mills were built next to the Canal basin. In Denton Holme, both the Borough saw-mill and the Denton Street saw-mill and timber-yard were established next to the railway network around the 1850s.

Figure 10.11. A terrace of brick-built houses on Blencowe Street typical of Carlisle's nineteenth-century housing (*photograph: author*)

Alabaster and plaster of Paris (gypsum) were also made in Carlisle. The two main works were at Denton Holme and Willowholme, the former established in 1837 by Joseph Robinson as an additional business to the corn-mill. Robinson made plaster of Paris alongside bread and biscuits in the same factory. The alabaster works at Willowholme seems to have been established within Donald's print-works, and John Rushton was grinding gypsum there in 1846. It later became subsumed into the Willowholme cotton-mills complex. There was also an alabaster works in Upperby by 1865, set up in Alexander Robinson's former damask and carpet manufactory.

Foundries and Engineering

Engineering was one of the largest industries in Carlisle in the second half of the nineteenth century, growing partly from foundries serving both the textile industry and the domestic and agricultural markets. The Porter brothers set up one of the earliest foundries, on West Walls. Richard, William and Robert Porter were plumbers, braziers and tin-plate workers, trading under the name of R. W. & R. Porter. Their iron and brass foundry, started in 1804, was extended in 1813 by purchasing further houses and gardens. The firm sold all kinds of cast-iron goods, including grates, bar-iron, axle-arms and sheet- and hoop-iron. Although the company went bankrupt in 1831, it was taken over by Robert's sons, George and John Francis, who set up a new company in the old foundry to make wrought-iron heel-plates. In 1834 this became Porter Hinde & Porter. The original foundry on West Walls was sold in 1881, and the sons of George Porter formed Porter Brothers & Company, which built the Victoria Ironworks on Denton Street in 1882. By 1901 the firm was described as 'engineers and iron and brass founders (brickmakers, mortar and crushing mills)'. The company continued trading until 1998, but both the original West Walls site and the Victoria Ironworks have now been redeveloped. The Waterloo Foundry, eventually based on St Nicholas Street (Figure 7.10), was an important foundry, making machinery for Carlisle's textile industry, and is the only one with surviving structures, which are now used by a variety of small businesses.

Other specialised engineering companies were set up, such as the one established by William Marsden in 1810, which was the earliest recorded manufacturer of steam-looms in Carlisle. According to the *Carlisle Journal*, Marsden had 'after many trials and considerable expense brought his much improved steam looms to what may be considered the acme of perfection. … He has also completed a steam loom for weaving woollen cloth which may be seen at work'. Nevertheless, the business does not appear to have been long-lived. The Denton Iron Works on Denton Street was started as a foundry by John Blaylock in 1848 in the former Long Island cotton works. Blaylock specialised in making ticket-dating presses and clocks, and he had gone into partnership with William Pratchitt by 1861, when they were listed as boiler-makers and engineers. The lease to the Long Island Works expired in 1863, and the business moved to Denton Holme, where the Denton Iron

Works, an iron and brass foundry, was established. By 1884 the company was listed as Pratchitt Brothers, engineers and millwrights. In the 1960s the works became part of L. A. Mitchell, suppliers of equipment to the chemical industry, and the foundry buildings appear to have been amalgamated within a larger industrial complex.

Carlisle's largest engineering works was the St Nicholas Engineering Works on London Road (Figure 7.10). A foundry, saw-mills and timber merchants were first established on this site in 1848 by George Davy Richardson. He went bankrupt in 1857 and the business was sold off at auction, with its fixtures and fittings. It appears to have been more than a small engineering works, and the fixtures included a number of cranes, both completed and under construction. The works was also substantially equipped with stationary steam-engines for working the machinery, and with internal railway sidings linked to the Newcastle & Carlisle Railway. Of particular value would have been the many foundry patterns, including items for railways. The business was bought by Cowan Sheldon & Company, which made parts for railway wagons and carriages as well as other railway equipment. It soon outgrew its site at Woodbank: the forging work moved to Darlington in 1852 and the rest to the St Nicholas site in 1857, though Woodbank continued to operate until 1869. With the acquisition of Richardson's works, Cowan Sheldon & Company added crane-making to its business, and its first crane was produced in 1858 (Figure 10.12). The St Nicholas Works also specialised in the manufacture of wooden railway turntables, in which it likewise became a world leader. The success of the company meant that the complex continued to grow, with the addition in 1875–7 of new stables, fitting shops, turntable shops, machine shops, a foundry, smithying equipment and a weighing machine. In the 1880s, the firm expanded into heavy marine and dock cranes, and its railway equipment was exported all over the world. In the second half of the twentieth century, the firm merged with other companies, and in 1982 they became Cowan Boyd. The decline of heavy industries eventually led to the closure of the St Nicholas Works in 1987, with production being transferred to other factories away from Carlisle. The works was demolished,

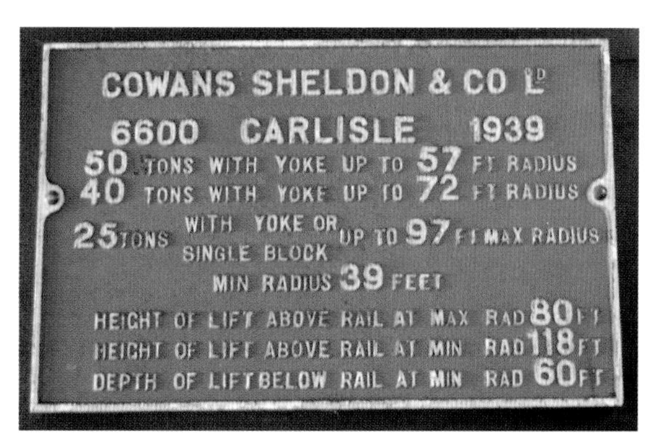

Figure 10.12. The plaque from a crane built by Cowan Sheldon & Company now displayed in the underpass beneath Castle Way, and one of the few physical remains of this nationally important engineering works (*photograph: author*)

sadly without any archaeological recording, and the site has now been redeveloped for retail, with no visible reminder of one of Carlisle's greatest industrial enterprises.

Other Industries

Carlisle had a number of smaller industries in the nineteenth century, many linked to or supporting other trades and industries, including the traditional trades of whip-making and fish-hook manufacture. Whip-making was associated with Carlisle's important livestock market, which was described in Jackson's *Postal Directory* of 1880 as 'the great northern centre for live stock exchange in England'. Animal hides supplied the long-established tanning industry, which in turn supplied leather to the whip-making industry. Tanning dominated the Willowholme and Irish Damside area, known locally as the 'Barky' (so-called after the oak-bark used in the tanning process), where there was an extensive area of tan-pits between the west wall of the castle and the River Caldew. The livestock market also supplied bones for the production of bone manure, or artificial fertiliser, which was considered to be a business of 'large dimensions' in 1901. There were two main production sites, at Willowholme and in Blackwell Road to the south of the city. The Willowholme works, known in the later nineteenth century as the National Guaranteed Manure Company Works, was in operation by 1839, and the Blackwell Road works was established in 1861 on the site of a pottery. The soap works run by Messrs Barker & Langcake in Kings Arms Lane would have supplied the textile-finishing works. In 1794 it was paying about £1,500 duty annually, a sum appropriate to a substantial business, and in 1801 it was described as 'an extensive building with the ware rooms, yard, and other conveniences lately occupied by Barnes, Langcake & Co. … soap boilers and tallow chandlers containing every convenience for carrying on these trades'.

Other industries, such as pottery and clay tobacco pipe manufacture, developed to serve the city's growing population. Some clay tobacco pipe works were substantial: Samuel Hamilton's works on South John Street was described by the *Carlisle Journal* in 1885 as 'a large tobacco pipe manufactory [with] moulding and trimming shops, commodious warehouse, kiln, 65ft chimney, storehouse for clay and a large yard'. John Pringle and his son James ran a factory on John Street in the second half of the nineteenth century. Recent archaeological work in John Street uncovered a large number of clay pipes, one marked with the name Pringle, which suggests that the kiln where they had been made was nearby. By the end of the nineteenth century, most sizeable towns had commercial laundries serving the growing urban populations. Carlisle had two large-scale businesses: at Upperby, a laundry and wadding works occupied the former alabaster works; and, on Warwick Road, the Carlisle Steam Laundry and Carpet Beating Company, known as

Petteril View Laundry, was a large industrial complex. This was only recently demolished, following a programme of archaeological recording.

Other Amenities

Civic amenities developed as industrialisation led to population growth. During the nineteenth century, the city acquired 14 new chapels, 13 new churches, and 21 schools, counting in the rebuilding of the Grammar School. As well as building houses for their workers, many factory owners provided services and facilities for them, including schools, clubs, coffee-houses and reading rooms. Amongst these were the Temperance Hall (Figure 10.9) and Reading Room on Wigton Road built by Carr's for its employees in 1861, and the Holme Head coffee tavern provided by the Fergusons for their workers in 1882. A Mechanics' Institute opened in Fisher Street in 1824, with a library and reading rooms, and from 1846 other reading rooms were established by working men through subscriptions in Shaddongate, John Street, South John Street, Lord Street, Parham Beck and Trinity Buildings. Behind the Mechanics' Institute was the Carlisle School of Art, and in Finkle Street there was a small museum of antiquities, maintained largely by working men. The first public library, however, did not open until 1893, following the purchase of Tullie House and other Castle Street properties by the Corporation. The Corporation was also responsible for the opening of the Public Baths in 1883–4, to which was added a Turkish baths in 1910 (Figure 10.13). Carlisle gained its first gas-works, on Brown's Row, in 1819, a piped water-supply in 1847, a sewerage disposal system by the mid-1860s, and its first electricity station, on James Street, in 1899. Following the installation of an electricity supply, a tram service opened to link the city centre with Stanwix and Harraby, with a tram depot on London Road. Although the tram system was closed down in 1931, the tram depot still survives (Figure A.8).

Figure 10.13. The Public Baths on James Street (*photograph: author*)

The city also had to deal with the poor and the sick. The workhouses of St Mary's, built next to the castle in 1785, and St Cuthbert's, built at Harraby

Hill in 1809, were soon found to be inadequate. They were replaced by the Fusehill Union Workhouse, built in 1863 in the Italianate style, though the workhouse at Harraby Hill continued to be used for children. The Union Workhouse later became the City General Hospital. Carlisle's first provision for the sick was the Dispensary, established in 1782, though rebuilt in 1857. It was followed by the House of Recovery, established on Collier Lane in 1820, and by the Cumberland Infirmary, built at Willowholme in 1830. This grew to incorporate the Crozier Fever Hospital, established near the Infirmary in the late nineteenth century to replace the old House of Recovery. In 1877 Strathclyde House was built as a hospital for incurables of the Border counties, that is, for 'persons who are hopelessly disqualified from fulfilling the ordinary active duties of life'.

The Industrial City

In the nineteenth century, the core of the city retained the form of a planned medieval town and, though the city walls had been largely demolished by 1815, their line can still be traced in modern streets. Industrial development was shaped to a great extent by the location of the medieval mills and their mill-streams, concentrated in the south-west of the city to take advantage of water-power from the River Caldew. Even with the introduction of steam-power, water was still in demand for many industrial processes, and the area west of the city, at Willowholme, Caldewgate, Denton Holme and West Walls, filled up with factories and homes for industrial workers. The early workers' houses were crammed into the available spaces, lacked sanitation, and were mainly back-to-backs and crowded courts. The concentration of industrial activity immediately south and west of the walled city can still be seen in the distribution of commercial and light industrial premises, even though many of the factories and almost all the early workers' houses have now been demolished.

The advent of the railways spread development south of the town, particularly on either side of London Road, and it extended westwards along the Canal branch railway. In the late nineteenth century, there were large-scale housing developments on a grid-iron plan at Denton Holme, between the railway lines and Holme Head, and to the east of London Road up to Warwick Road. This later housing, in the form of brick-built terraces, was very different from the early industrial cottages, as the terraces were built to minimum legal standards. The expansion east of the city was limited naturally by the River Petteril, which was itself the focus of some industrial development. The east side of Carlisle, particularly along Warwick Road, was the main area of middle-class housing. Away from the densest industrial areas, it grew as ribbon development along the main road, with larger terraced housing and public green spaces, including squares and bowling-greens. Detached and semi-detached Victorian and Edwardian villas were built along Dalston

Road and Wigton Road to the south-west, where the municipal cemetery and Morton Park acted as a barrier to further development. Stanwix, too, had developed as a middle-class suburb by the end of the century, with large terraced houses and detached villas fronting the river, as well as a number of large-scale market gardens for supplying the town with food. The middle-class suburbs were encouraged by the opening of the tram system in 1900, the north end of which terminated in Stanwix, and whose branches served Warwick Road, Newtown, Upperby and Holme Head.

The development of Carlisle in the early nineteenth century had much in common with many of Lancashire's industrial towns, particularly older towns such as Preston and Lancaster which, like Carlisle, were also key administrative and market centres. Carlisle could not compete with the largest industrial towns of east Lancashire. It lacked the kind of access to markets, and to capital for investment, enjoyed by towns closer to Manchester and Liverpool; and by the end of the nineteenth century, Carlisle's population was less than half Burnley's and just over one-third of Blackburn's. Even so, Carlisle benefited from having a wide range of industries, so that economic downturns in one industry did not necessarily lead to a terminal decline in the city's industrial capacity. The city also benefited from the development of nearby ROF Gretna, and the continued importance of railway transport in the inter-war years. Consequently, while Carlisle never attained the later nineteenth-century, mushroom-like expansion of the largest Lancashire mill towns, it did not decline like them after the First World War.

Since the 1970s, many of Carlisle's traditional industries have either shrunk dramatically or ceased altogether, and many former industrial sites have been cleared and redeveloped, a process that has been particularly active from the 1990s. Both Shaddon Mill and the Old Brewery, for example, have been converted into accommodation. The St Nicholas Works and Carnaud Metal Box Works (Hudson Scott) were cleared in the 1990s, and redeveloped into retail outlets. More recently, Mains Mill, the South Vale hat-works and the Penguin confectionery works (South Vale confectionery works) have been demolished. Such developments have resulted in the loss of most of Carlisle's industrial heritage, though archaeological work has routinely been undertaken since the 1990s to record buildings and below-ground remains.

In the 1950s, Carlisle was still a heavily industrialised city. Thus, according to Hunter Davies:

> [It] seemed to be full of factories, belching smoke. You had to time it carefully going up street … or, when the hooters and horns blew, you would be knocked over by the human tide, pouring out of all the textile, engineering, metal, railway works and biscuit factories. There were no pretty bits, no trees, no green places in the town itself.

Figure 10.14. The gas-holder erected on Rome Street in 1879 (*photograph: author*)

This view is inevitably impressionistic, and gives no idea of the extensive parks and squares around the city. Its point, however, is that Carlisle was then a very different city from that of today. Some important and iconic monuments to Carlisle's industrial past do survive, however, and these should be celebrated. They include the ornamental metal framework to one of Carlisle's gas-holders (Figure 10.14), the surviving chimney of Shaddon Mill (Figure 10.5), and Citadel station (Figure 11.3). All these sites are listed and so have a level of protection. Other, less obvious monuments include the still-used Public Baths on James Street (Figure 10.13), the Lamplugh Works engine-house and chimney, Carr's offices of 1929, and the much-altered loom shops on Broadguards (Figure 10.6). All have the potential to contribute to the city's character and its sense of place in the future, and they deserve to be better known.

★ ★ ★ ★ ★

Suggested Further Reading

S. Davidson, *Carlisle Breweries and Public Houses, 1894–1914* (Carlisle, 2004)

M. K. Dickens, *A Suburb of Carlisle: Linton Holme* (Carlisle, 1999)

A. Earnshaw, *Carlisle's Crane Makers: The Cowan Sheldon Story* (Kendal, 2004)

K. A. Rafferty, *The Story of Hudson Scott and Sons: Metal Box, James Street, Carlisle* (Carlisle, 1998)

O. Seabury, *The Carlisle State Management Scheme: Its Ethos and Architecture* (Carlisle, 2007)

Chapter 11
The Railway City

Peter Robinson

During the late nineteenth and early twentieth centuries Carlisle, thanks to its frontier position between England and Scotland, was one of the great centres of railway operation in Britain. The development of the railway system in and around Carlisle therefore had a major impact on the city's topography, economy and population. At its 'railway' peak, the city was the hub of eight radiating routes operated by seven independent railway companies, and very few of Carlisle's inhabitants would not have had some family or business connection with one or more of these companies and the employment they provided.

The degree of this impact was demonstrated in the 1921 Census. Compared with almost any other substantial urban centre in England, Carlisle then had one of the highest proportions of workers engaged in railway operation, with 3,736 men – or 22.5 per cent of the total male employment – working in the transport and communication industry, and with more undertaking related servicing and engineering occupations. In turn, this greatly affected the provision and distribution of workers' housing in the city in relation to the main centres of railway employment, namely the multiple engine sheds, goods stations and marshalling yards. Unusually, however, the railway companies played only a small part in the provision of housing in Carlisle for their workers, leaving a large rented housing market to be provided for by local builders and developers. A survey undertaken for the City Council in 1917 showed that 1,714 households were headed by railway workers (14.4 per cent of all households), and that only 114 of these (6.7 per cent) lived in railway-owned dwellings.

The Carlisle Canal

The unique character of modern Carlisle was created by the rapid development of the national railway network from the mid-1840s; but the local story begins much earlier, with the Carlisle Canal. This venture was born of a degree of frustration about the lack of progress on a much larger project from the 1790s for a canal between the Irish and the North Seas. With William Chapman as its engineer, this scheme was intended to link Newcastle and Maryport, with its proposed route skirting south of Carlisle, but though it was promoted several times, there was never enough support to finance it.

However, with the growth of Carlisle's industries the need for efficient transport was becoming ever more urgent. Small coasting vessels were, with some difficulty, able to sail up the River Eden to a wharf at Sandsfield, but there still remained some four miles (6km) by a poor road into the city. A public meeting on 21 May 1807 resulted in the formation of a committee to promote a canal from Carlisle to the sea, and William Chapman was engaged as its engineer. His report was reviewed by Thomas Telford with a recommendation for an outlet on the coast at Fisher's Cross, one mile (1.6km) east of Bowness-on-Solway. Ten years later, with no progress having been made, another public meeting led to another committee, which again appointed Chapman, and his report was published in September 1817. This time financial support was forthcoming from the leading industrialists of the city, local landowners and the City Council, and an Act of Parliament providing the necessary powers received Royal Assent on 6 April 1819. Capital totalling £73,750 was raised, and the Canal's completion was marked by a lavish opening ceremony, including a procession of vessels from Port Carlisle, on 12 March 1823.

Eleven miles (18km) long, the Canal was capable of accommodating small sea-going vessels, which entered a sea-lock at Port Carlisle and negotiated seven more locks before reaching the basin in Carlisle (Figure 11.1), which

Figure 11.1. The Canal basin looking south-east, from a drawing by James Carmichael, c. 1835 (*by courtesy of Tullie House Museum and Art Gallery, Carlisle*)

measured 450 by 120 feet (137 by 37m). The siting of the basin on the higher land to the west of the River Caldew was to have a major influence on subsequent railway development, and hence on the nineteenth-century morphology of the city. Goods carried by the Canal in about 1830 included locomotives for the Liverpool & Manchester Railway, dragged overland from Robert Stephenson's engine works in Newcastle, and loaded onto vessels at Carlisle for shipment to Liverpool.

Yet, though the Canal was modestly profitable in its operations for a few years, especially after the completion of the Newcastle & Carlisle Railway in 1836, it had begun to run into problems by the later 1840s, partly from silting of the Solway around Port Carlisle, and mainly from the effects of competition from the new railways connecting Carlisle directly with larger ports, first Whitehaven and later Liverpool.

The Newcastle & Carlisle Railway (N&CR)

Despite the building of the Carlisle Canal, the need for a link across England had not been fulfilled. Such a task was, however, now made considerably easier to achieve with an eastern terminus at Carlisle, saving nearly 30 miles (48km) of construction through to Maryport. Re-examining his canal scheme in 1824, William Chapman concluded that it would be more economic to build a railway instead, and that his proposed route would be equally suitable. A committee was formed following a meeting called by the High Sheriff of Northumberland, and on 26 March 1825 it resolved unanimously in favour of a railway with immediate subscriptions being taken. Completion on the ground would, however, take another eleven years.

Undertaking surveys, refining the route to appease major landowners, and obtaining parliamentary powers, were to take up the first four years, so that the Act incorporating the company, authorising the raising of the initial capital of £300,000, and giving it powers for constructing the railway, was not passed until 22 May 1829. Sections at each end of the route were built first in order to develop revenue from the eastern lead traffic and the western coal traffic. In the west, a formal start was made on 25 March 1830 when Henry Howard of Corby Castle laid the foundation stone for the Eden Viaduct at Wetheral. This section was to open on 20 July 1836, with completion through from Blaydon to Carlisle being achieved on 18 June 1838.

The railway approached Carlisle some distance south of the then urban area, crossing the River Petteril on a stone-arched bridge. The station was on the east side of London Road, about one mile (1.6km) from the city centre (Figure 11.2). A branch continued under the road, curved gradually towards the north-west to cross the River Caldew, climbed towards a level crossing on Dalston Road, bridged Wigton and Port Roads, and then reached the Canal basin, where a substantial traffic for shipment in coal from the

Brampton coalfield was soon to develop. The merger of the N&CR with the North Eastern Railway was authorised on 17 July 1862, and the latter immediately negotiated entry to Citadel station, its services being transferred from London Road on 1 January 1863.

Figure 11.2. London Road station looking east, after its closure to passengers in 1863 and conversion to a goods station (*by courtesy of Tullie House Museum and Art Gallery, Carlisle*)

The Maryport & Carlisle Railway (M&CR)

During the eighteenth and early nineteenth centuries, the harbour and town at Maryport had been developed by the Senhouse family of Netherhall to provide an outlet for coal extracted from the northern part of the west Cumberland coalfield. With the approaching completion of the N&CR's line, a proposal to extend the route of railway communication westwards from Carlisle was put to Humphrey Senhouse in 1835. It had the potential not only to carry coals from the local collieries, but also to enable Maryport to compete with Port Carlisle for traffic for shipment, both from Carlisle itself and from the N&CR. With enthusiastic support from local landowners and coal owners, the M&CR obtained its Act of Parliament in 1837 and appointed George Stephenson as its engineer.

Like the Newcastle–Carlisle line, the M&CR was built in sections. The west section, linking the collieries with Maryport, opened in 1840, and the Wigton–Carlisle section was built in 1843–5. The route approached Carlisle down the Caldew valley, curving eastwards as it neared the N&CR's line to make a junction near what is now Currock Road, with a small station at Bogfield. Trains continued eastwards onto the Newcastle line before reversing into London Road station, performing the same manoeuvre in reverse on departure. However, the Maryport & Carlisle company was determined to establish a station nearer to the city, and acquired land and powers for a site on Crown Street behind Botchergate. This station opened on 30 December 1844 with a temporary wooden building providing passenger facilities, but still with only an east-facing link, so that trains had to use the same procedure as formerly used at London Road.

The Lancaster & Carlisle Railway (L&CR) and the Caledonian Railway

By the mid-1830s, with railways having already been completed or planned from London to Lancaster, railway communication between England and Scotland was the obvious next step. One of the first advocates of the route northwards via Carlisle was John Steel, editor of the *Carlisle Journal*, who on 22 August 1835 published an editorial proposing such a line. Only three months later, the Grand Junction Railway, which operated between Birmingham and south Lancashire, commissioned its engineer, Joseph Locke, to report on possible routes northwards from Lancaster into Scotland, and Locke reported back to his board on 27 January 1836.

Progress, however, was to be seriously delayed by intense lobbying and counter-proposals on behalf of communities and other interests, which felt that they had much to lose if the railway did not serve them directly. There was also a parallel proposal for an East Coast route to Scotland, and the government intervened to appoint a Royal Commission to report on the best route for this vital Anglo-Scottish link.

Finally, two separate companies were promoted to construct and build the L&CR and the Caledonian Railway. Securing its Act of Parliament on 6 June 1844, the Lancaster & Carlisle company obtained powers for a compromise route directly serving Lancaster and skirting the fell to the east of Kendal as it climbed to cross the ridge between the Kent and the Lune valleys, before making a direct assault on Shap Fell. Some 69 miles (111km) of railway, completed through to Carlisle in an amazing 30 months, were opened on 17 December 1846 and brought London within 12 hours of Carlisle. The L&CR approached Carlisle down the Petteril valley and, like the Maryport–Carlisle route, made an east-facing connection with the Newcastle line, initially using London Road station. In 1859 the Lancaster & Carlisle company was leased to the London & North Western Railway, which consequently controlled the whole route between Carlisle and London Euston.

As for the Caledonian Railway, its promoters had experienced a long contest with rival interests before their Act received Royal Assent on 31 July 1845. The single contract for the construction of 122 miles (196km) of railway was one of the largest ever in Britain, with the line from Carlisle to Beattock summit near Moffat opening on 10 September 1847, and completion to Glasgow and Edinburgh coming five months later.

As partners in the West Coast route, the Lancaster & Carlisle and the Caledonian companies had jointly to explore the best potential route round or through Carlisle, and a location for what would become a major station. Options were considered to the east of the city with a station around Portland Square, as well as to the west with a station in Caldewgate. The situation was made more complex by the Maryport & Carlisle company's Crown Street proposal, powers for this being obtained on the same day that the L&CR's Act of 1844 was passed – despite pleas from the L&CR that both the M&CR and the N&CR should enter discussions about a joint station to serve all local railway companies. When the L&CR finally decided on a route through Carlisle close under West Walls, with the station sited near the Courts, this became an acute embarrassment as the L&CR's line to the new station crossed the M&CR's line twice in a very short distance.

Citadel station (Figure 11.3) was opened with the completion of the southern section of the Caledonian Railway in 1847. Designed by the eminent architect Sir William Tite, the long elegant façade hid a train shed supported by two intermediate rows of cast-iron columns. Running northwards the Caledonian Railway crossed the rivers Caldew and Eden (Figure 11.4), and cut through the bluff at Etterby to break out onto the estuarial flats and mosses with a long straight racing stretch to Gretna. From 1850 a junction was formed at Gretna with the Glasgow & South Western Railway, constructed by the promoters of the Nithsdale route, though its services were to use the Caledonian line into Carlisle.

The Port Carlisle & Silloth Railways

The opening of the L&CR was not good news for the Carlisle Canal. One of its best trading years was in 1846, but receipts had more than halved by 1850. Two years later instructions were given to prepare plans to convert the Canal into a railway, with the intention of extending to a new town and dock at Silloth, further down the Solway from Port Carlisle. The first stage was achieved very quickly, with an Act of Parliament for the conversion being obtained on 3 August 1853 and the Port Carlisle Railway opening on 22 May in the following year, to make an end-on junction with the N&CR's Canal branch. Trains to Port Carlisle ran from a new Canal station just south of the former Canal basin, which was converted into a goods station.

By contrast, there was delay in obtaining powers for the Carlisle & Silloth Bay Railway & Dock company because of strong opposition by the M&CR; but the railway on from Drumburgh to Silloth was finally ready to open on 28 August 1856. The remaining stub of line to Port Carlisle was then worked for the next 58 years by a horse-drawn dandy carriage. However, the

Figure 11.3. Citadel station, *c.* 1930, its façade remaining little altered today (*by courtesy of Carlisle Library*)

Figure 11.4. A Caledonian Railway train approaching Carlisle from Scotland across the Eden bridge at Etterby, from a drawing by Matthew Nutter, *c.* 1850 (*by courtesy of Tullie House Museum and Art Gallery, Carlisle*)

Marshall Dock at Silloth was not opened until August 1859, by which time the company was in dire straits, for it had lost much of its shipment traffic between the North-East and Liverpool.

The North British Railway (NBR)

Rescue for the Port Carlisle & Silloth Railways was to come with the arrival of the NBR in Carlisle. Overtures had already been made to the formers' hard-pressed companies by the Caledonian Railway, which went as far as building a short connecting line from Port Carlisle Branch Junction, near the castle, to Canal, which opened on 30 June 1860. Fearing the motives of the Caledonian, however, the companies resisted this potential take-over.

The NBR had completed a line from Edinburgh to Hawick in 1849. A possible partnership with the Midland Railway encouraged it, from the mid-1850s, to seek a line southwards to Carlisle via Liddesdale, but it met with strong opposition from the Caledonian Railway, which was determined to keep an intruder out of its 'territory'. A further aim of the NBR was the development of Silloth docks to handle its traffic with Liverpool. Authorisation for the Border Union Railway was eventually gained on 21 July 1859. It crossed the Solway Plain from Longtown and bridged the Caledonian main line at Kingmoor, two miles (3.2km) north of Carlisle, to make a temporary terminus at Canal station. Reaching Citadel station still posed a problem as the Caledonian was asking a very high rate for travelling the short distance over its tracks from Canal. After arbitration, the first North British trains ran into Citadel on 29 October 1861, with services through to Edinburgh commencing on 1 July 1862. The NBR assumed control of the Port Carlisle and Silloth lines at the same time, though trains from those lines were not to transfer to Citadel until 1 July 1864.

The Problems of the 1860s

By the mid-1860s Carlisle was already a very congested railway centre (Figure 11.5). Since it was a terminus for all the companies operating into the city, no passenger trains ran through without changing locomotives from one company's to another's, and goods trains were disassembled on arrival for working forward to the marshalling yard of the onward company, where re-marshalling of wagons would take place. Each company had its own locomotive sheds, and the larger ones were major centres of employment. These were established at West Walls (Figure 11.6), Upperby, London Road, Canal (off Newtown Road), and Currock; and by 1870 the companies concerned were the Caledonian Railway, the London & North Western Railway, the North Eastern Railway, the NBR and the M&CR, respectively. Goods stations and marshalling yards were close by these sheds – with more to come.

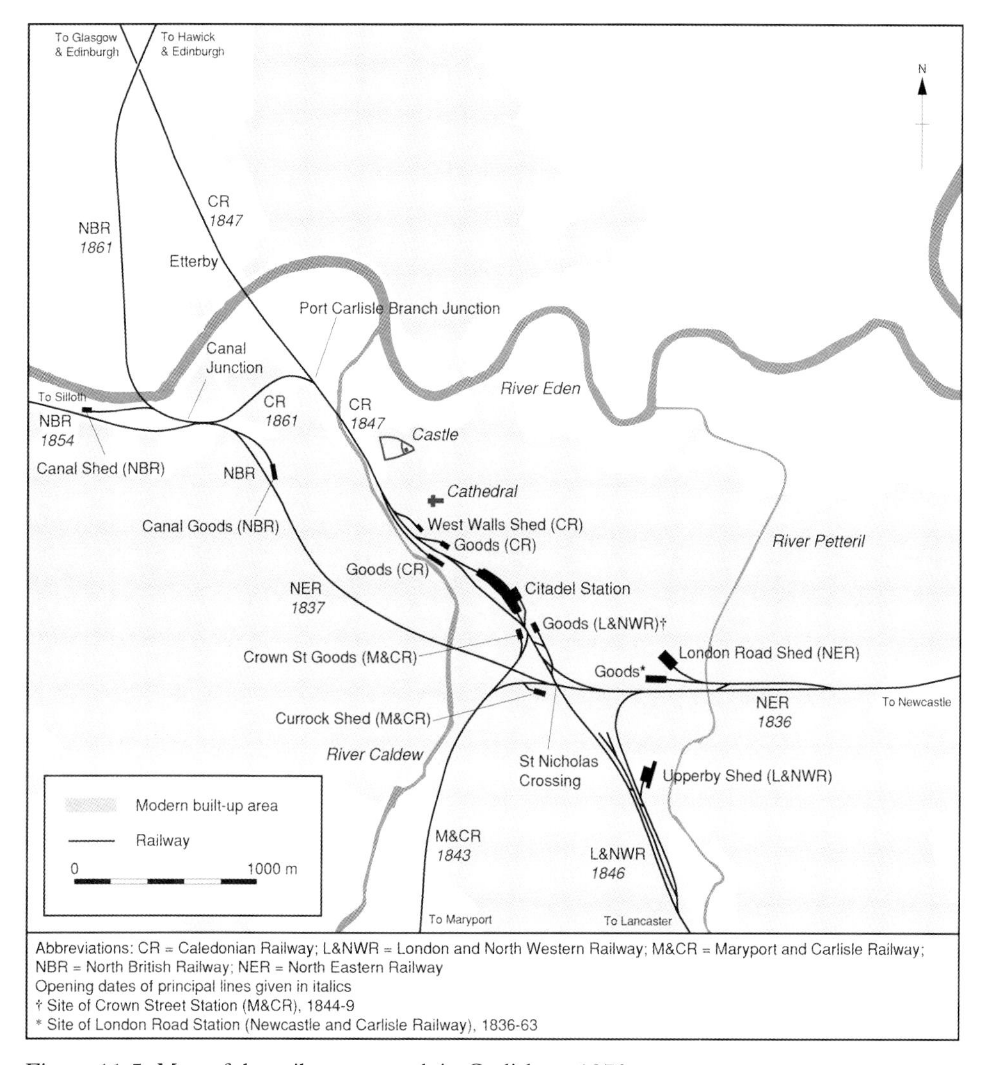

Figure 11.5. Map of the railway network in Carlisle, *c.* 1870

A number of major factors then came together to force a radical redevelopment of the railway system in Carlisle. First there was the problem that the NBR encountered in getting a fair and efficient exchange of its traffic to and from England. The two West Coast partners, the Caledonian and the London & North Western Railways, adopted an obstructionist stance with regard to the NBR, which in its frustration was forced to ask its engineer, Thomas Bouch, to undertake surveys for possible new lines in the city to facilitate the exchange of traffic. The second factor was the impending arrival of the Midland Railway with its Settle & Carlisle line, while the third arose from the tragedy of a major railway accident just south of Citadel station in 1870.

Figure 11.6. A Caledonian Railway 2-2-2 express locomotive (No. 78) with its crew in the yard of West Walls shed prior to its relocation to Kingmoor in the 1870s (*photograph: author's collection*)

The circumstances that led to this accident had their roots 20 years earlier. After the M&CR had opened its Crown Street station in 1844, the company, along with the N&CR, had for a short time become part of the business empire of George Hudson, the so-called 'Railway King', but only after the company had come to an agreement with the L&CR about the transfer of the station's land. Hudson repudiated this agreement, and the L&CR eventually obtained a court judgement in its favour. It was implemented on 17 March 1849, when a large workforce invaded Crown Street to dismantle the station and remove the tracks, forcing the next train from Maryport to proceed to London Road station instead. Back in local control again by 1850, the M&CR negotiated entry to Citadel station as a tenant, obtaining powers to build a direct line which opened on 1 July 1851, and created a second crossing of the Canal branch on the level within a quarter of a mile (0.4km). As traffic grew, these crossings were not only a growing cause of congestion but a growing hazard.

The inevitable happened on the night of 9–10 July 1870. An empty coal train from Canal ran into a southbound express at St Nicholas crossing: six passengers died and 30 were injured (Figure 11.7). The immediate cause was the negligence of the driver who, somewhat the worse for drink, failed to stop at the signals; but the crossings had proved their inherent danger and had to go. The opportunity was provided by the coming of the Midland

Figure 11.7. St Nicholas crossing looking south-east, *c.* 1878, the site of the fateful collision in July 1870 (*by courtesy of Carlisle Library*)

Railway's Settle & Carlisle line – and by the chance to oblige the Midland to pay the largest share of the cost. The resulting scheme would also resolve the problems of traffic interchange between the various railway companies in Carlisle.

The Settle & Carlisle Line

The Midland Railway (MR) originated from the amalgamation of a number of smaller companies in the industrial east Midlands in 1844. Rapidly growing prosperous and powerful, it developed ambitions to become a national operator, and would extend its main lines to London St Pancras (1868), Manchester (1866) and Liverpool (1873). It also took over other railway companies, so that by 1852 it controlled the lines as far north as Lancaster and Ingleton, and at both locations it aimed to exchange its Scottish traffic with the L&CR – but it encountered an obstructionist response.

Reluctantly the MR had therefore to examine a potential route of its own to Carlisle. Since the obvious and easier routes had already being taken, its surveyors were sent into the Yorkshire Dales to find a route through to the Eden valley. Thus was born the Settle & Carlisle line, for which powers were obtained on 16 July 1866. However, the determination of the MR brought the London & North Western Railway, in control of the L&CR's route over Shap since 1859, back to the negotiating table, and an agreement was reached in 1868 for the joint management and operation of the line over Shap. The MR now had to go back to Parliament for powers to abandon its Settle & Carlisle Act; but in face of determined opposition from its allied companies, both north and south of Carlisle, and from local interests, the Abandonment Bill was thrown out in 1869. The MR faced up to the challenge to build this 72-mile (116-km) railway – through extreme difficulties and at an ultimate cost of over £3 million.

The new line approached Carlisle from the east to make a junction with the Newcastle line just before it crossed the River Petteril. Opening to passengers on 1 May 1876, the line immediately carried through services to Glasgow and Edinburgh in conjunction with the Glasgow & South Western Railway and the NBR respectively.

The New Lines in Carlisle

To accommodate the MR, and to overcome the operational and capacity problems of the 1860s, a massive programme of new railway construction got underway in Carlisle, and powers were granted in 1873 for twelve new lines (Figure 11.8). Not only would the London & North Western Railway and the M&CR have new approach lines to Citadel station, bridging over the Canal branch, but a whole new series of goods lines would remove this traffic from the environs of Citadel. One enormous benefit to the city was the removal of the Caledonian engine sheds from below West Walls to Etterby, north of the River Eden. The main new jointly managed goods line extended from St Nicholas in the south, and crossed the Canal branch at Rome Street Junction. It then closely followed the River Caldew, made a junction with the Caledonian main line north of Caldewgate, and turned west to terminate at Willowholme Junction with the Caledonian's Port Carlisle Branch, just short of Canal Junction. This new network was completed on 6 August 1877, and was supplemented by the Denton Holme Joint Goods Lines, the common property of the Midland, North British and Glasgow & South Western Railways, with a large new goods station adjoining Charlotte Street, which opened on 1 October 1883.

Also an urgent necessity was the enlargement of Citadel station (Figure 11.9), which operated with one long platform for all through traffic. A new island was therefore built to provide two additional platforms for Anglo-Scottish traffic, with all platforms being enclosed under a glass roof extending to almost six acres (2.4 hectares). The island platform, though still without its roof, was opened on 4 July 1880, just in time to handle the traffic for the Royal Agricultural Show being held in Carlisle during that month. The

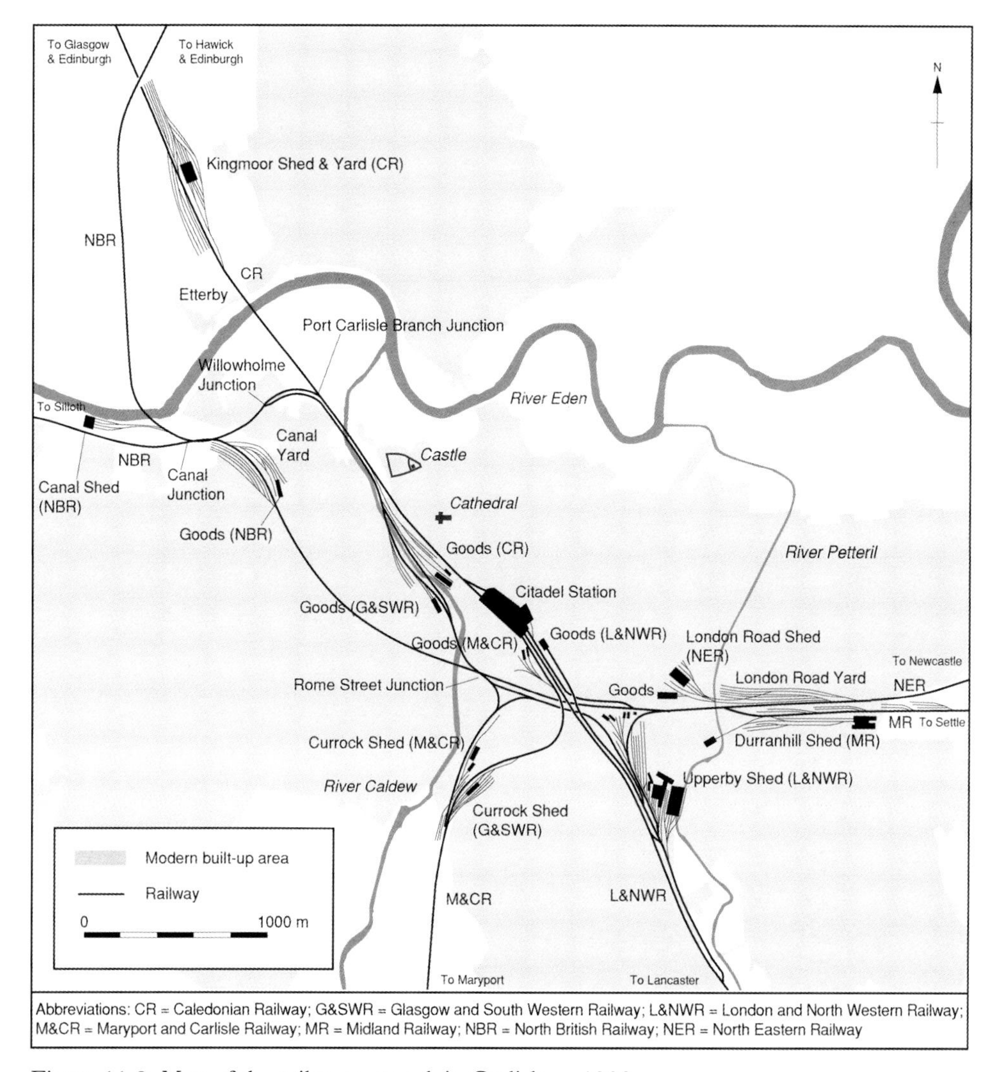

Figure 11.8. Map of the railway network in Carlisle, *c.* 1900

proposed extension of the station forced the City Council to confront the problem of access between the city centre and the suburb of Denton Holme, hitherto reached via a tunnel under the station from English Damside. The Victoria Viaduct (Figure 11.10) over the north end of the station overcame this problem, providing access directly onto English Street; it was opened by Princess Louise on 20 September 1877.

Decline

The railways of Carlisle had almost reached their maximum extent. Amalgamation in 1923 under the Railways Act (1921) reduced the number

Figure 11.9. A Glasgow & South Western Railway 4-4-0 locomotive (No. 77) at Citadel station, *c.* 1892; above is the Tudor-style timber and glass end-screen to the station's roof dating from the early 1880s, and removed in 1956 (*photograph: author's collection*)

Figure 11.10. The new viaduct for the Caledonian Railway looking south-east to the Victoria Viaduct and the County Gaol, *c.* 1878 (*by courtesy of Carlisle Library*)

of railway companies from seven to two, but little rationalisation was achieved before nationalisation of the railways in 1948, other than the closure of some locomotive depots. Wartime saw a minor addition to the system with the construction of a new goods line crossing the River Eden on a concrete bridge, thus removing the bottleneck over the river at Etterby.

Figure 11.11. The 'City of Carlisle' (No. 46238) standing at Citadel station on 17 July 1961, and epitomising the peak of steam traction over the West Coast main line; one of its nameplates is now in Tullie House Museum and Art Gallery (*by courtesy of Cumbrian Railways Association Photo Library*)

Despite earlier schemes, real rationalisation of the railways of Carlisle was to await the proposals that emerged from the British Railways Modernisation Plan (1955), and the great changes in rail transport that resulted from the massive growth of road haulage and the motorway system from the 1960s (Figure 11.11). The opening of Kingmoor Marshalling Yard in 1963, enabling the closure of yards and depots round the city, and the electrification of the West Coast main line in 1974, were further factors. The Yard itself was already obsolescent when it opened and contraction occurred rapidly in the 1970s and 1980s. With all these changes came a drastic reduction of railway employment in the city and a consequent decline of the significance of the railway industry in the local economy. By a strange irony, the goods avoiding lines, born out the accident of July 1870, were closed by another derailment, fortunately without injury or fatality, when a runaway goods train demolished the Caldew bridge at Denton Holme on 1 May 1984.

★ ★ ★ ★ ★

Suggested Further Reading

P. E. Baughan, *North of Leeds: The Leeds–Settle–Carlisle Line and Its Branches* (Hatch End, 1966)

Carlisle: 150 Years of Railways (Cumbrian Railways Association, Barrow-in-Furness, 1986)

B. Fawcett, *A History of the Newcastle & Carlisle Railway, 1824 to 1870* (North Eastern Railway Association, Manchester, 2008)

D. Joy, *A Regional History of the Railways of Great Britain. Volume 14: The Lake Counties* (Newton Abbot, 1986)

D. Perriam and D. Ramshaw, *Carlisle Citadel Station: 150 Years a Railway Centre* (Carlisle, 1998)

D. Ramshaw, *The Carlisle Navigation Canal, 1821–1853* (Carlisle, 1997)

B. Reed, *Crewe to Carlisle* (London, 1969)

P. W. Robinson, *Rail Centres: Carlisle* (London, 1986)

J. Thomas, *The North British Railway* (Newton Abbot, 1969–75)

J. Thomas, revised by A. J. S. Paterson, *A Regional History of the Railways of Great Britain. Volume 6: Scotland: The Lowlands and Borders* (Newton Abbot, 1984)

Appendix: Main Places to Visit in Carlisle

Tim Padley

People have been living in Carlisle for nearly 2,000 years. Some of its long history can be seen in the buildings that survive, but most of the archaeology of the city remains below ground or exhibited in its museums. As you walk around Carlisle you may be walking the same routes as Roman roads and lanes, or over medieval houses, buried metres beneath your feet. If you descend into the subterranean Cathedral Treasury, you will be standing at the former Roman ground level, for a series of Roman road surfaces and buildings were excavated in order to construct the Treasury.

Roman Carlisle

The fort, which remained in use from around AD 72–3 to the end of the Roman occupation in the fifth century, was located between the castle

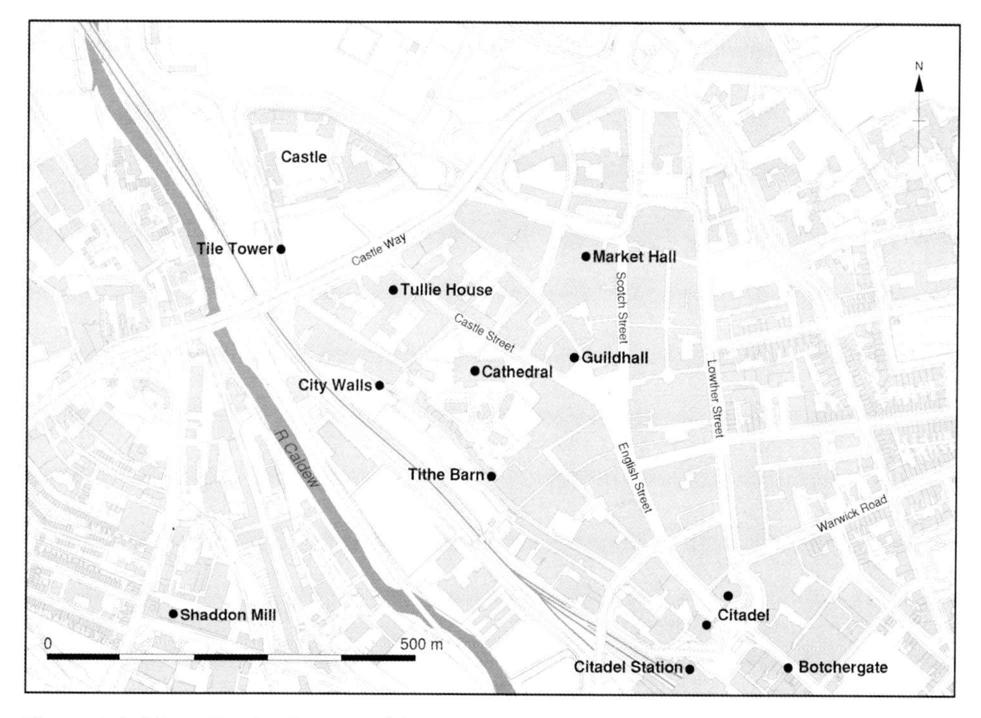

Figure A.1. Map of main places to visit

and Tullie House, straddling the area now divided by the Castle Way dual carriageway (Figure 3.1). The central range of the fort was approximately at the top of the steps that go up from the pedestrian underpass to the castle. Excavations have shown that the annexe to the fort extended down Castle Street.

The civil settlement has been most extensively examined in the area now occupied by the Lanes shopping centre (Figure A.2). This had a military beginning, but later came under civilian control. The area under the Victorian market hall housed the main bath-house for the town.

Figure A.2. The Lanes shopping centre constructed in the 1980s on the former site of the Roman and medieval town (*photograph: author*)

Further evidence of the Roman town can be seen in the fabric of the castle and the cathedral, both of which contain re-used Roman building stones. The most obvious example is in the gatehouse of the castle. Here the lintel of the doorway between the solar and the prison rooms below has been made from a Roman altar, which was turned on its side, and had the lettering turned in towards the wall (Figure 1.1).

As with all Roman towns, the cemeteries were outside the inhabited area. They have been located along the main roads coming in from the east, west and south. The largest occupied the area on either side of London Road and Botchergate, from the cutting just past the Swallow Hilltop Hotel to the traffic lights by the railway station. Many of the finds as well as the major gravestones and tombstones can be viewed in Tullie House Museum and Art Gallery (see below).

VIKING CARLISLE

The only Viking item, apart from exhibits in Tullie House and the Cathedral Treasury, is an inscription written in runes in the cathedral (Figure A.3). This is low down on the inside west wall of the south transept. When translated the inscription is a simple graffito: 'Dolfin wrote these runes on this stone'. The position suggests that the runes were written after the stone had been laid in place during the building of the church, and therefore presumably date after 1122.

Figure A.3. A runic inscription within the cathedral (*photograph: author*)

THE CATHEDRAL AND AUGUSTINIAN PRIORY

The cathedral (admission free) was founded as a house of Augustinian canons in 1122 and became a cathedral in 1133 (Figure A.4). The church is built of two different colours of sandstone. The early Norman work displays grey sandstone, which came from the Roman buildings in the area, while the later Early English and Decorated elements are red sandstone. The nave, which has the surviving Norman work, was largely demolished in the seventeenth century because it was unstable. This truncation gives Carlisle the second smallest cathedral in England after Oxford. It also gives it the only cathedral where the nave is shorter than the chancel. The uneven ground on which

Figure A.4. The cathedral as it stands today (*photograph: author*)

the church was built has led to subsidence that has distorted the surviving Norman arches in the nave. As the clerestory (upper level of the church, pierced by windows) is not affected, the subsidence must have occurred by the time it had been built in the fourteenth century.

The wooden roof of the choir is medieval, and was erected after the fire of 1292 (Figure 7.3). This has been confirmed by a dendrochronological (tree-ring) date of 1355. The projecting beams have led some scholars to suggest that the roof was Tudor and had hammer-beams, but this is incorrect. The vault and decoration were restored in the nineteenth century with much new woodwork.

The Cathedral Treasury houses a small collection relating to the excavations carried out in the grounds as well as to the history of the building.

Admission is free, with a voluntary donation requested. There is also a display of cathedral and diocesan plate.

Although the Augustinian priory buildings survived the Dissolution in 1540 (Figures 7.4 and 9.6), much was destroyed by a century of neglect. The fratry or refectory (now a restaurant) was built in the early fourteenth century and redesigned in the fifteenth century and later. The Deanery and Prior's Tower date to 1510–20, while the gatehouse onto Abbey Street has an inscription dating it to 1527. The ceiling in the upper room of the Prior's Tower retains its original timber roof and painted design.

The priory held the right to tithes (one-tenth of produce) from a number of parishes, including St Mary's and St Cuthbert's. These were stored in the fifteenth-century tithe barn (Figure A.5), which is now the parish hall of St Cuthbert's church. The interior, including the original timber roof, can be seen through the large windows on the side facing St Cuthbert's church.

The Chapel of St Alban

A Civic Trust plaque on the wall above the Bon Appetit French restaurant on Scotch Street commemorates the chapel of St Alban (Figure 7.6), which

Figure A.5. The fifteenth-century tithe barn, now St Cuthbert's parish hall (*photograph: Mark Brennand*)

was dissolved along with other chantries in 1549. The origins of this chapel remain unclear. Although St Alban is the only English saint to have been worshipped from Roman times onwards, the dedication does not prove an ancient foundation. Excavation in 1988 found that the foundations cut through some medieval graves, which suggests at least re-building, and the chapel may have been a re-foundation. Certainly in its later history the chapel functioned as a chantry, that is, a chapel founded for the saying of masses for the salvation of the founder's soul.

The Castle

The castle, now managed by English Heritage (admission charge), originated with King William II in 1092, but none of its original structure survives. It has been occupied continuously since then, and the surviving buildings date from many different periods.

The oldest part of the castle is the keep (Figure 6.5). It started life as a palace of King David I of Scots (1124–53), but as time went on the residential function declined and it was used as a prison, barracks and armoury. The small rooms and stairs in the thickness of the walls enabled the keep to work as a residence. There was access to the castle's well, which provided a good water-supply in case of siege, and a small kitchen can be identified by a fireplace on the second floor and a chimney rising through the wall. Also in the thickness of the walls is a room with carvings made by prisoners around 1480 (Figure A.6), as well as the small chapel where David I died in 1153.

The gatehouse of the castle was built in the twelfth century, but modified in the fourteenth century (Figure 6.8). The upper floor, which contains a hall, solar, kitchen and service area, was used as the March warden's apartments.

The main defensive feature of the inner ward or bailey is the Half-Moon battery, whose row of gun ports would have enabled the outer ward to receive covering fire (Figure 9.4). This is a Tudor addition built in 1542 by Stefan von Haschenperg, a Moravian engineer employed by King Henry VIII both here and at the citadel. Other evidence of modernising the castle to provide for artillery can be seen on the roof of the keep, which was strengthened in the sixteenth century in order to take cannon. Once past the battery, attackers would have come up against the inner gatehouse, or Captain's Tower, with its portcullis and double gates to get through.

None of the apartments that were originally in the inner ward now survives. These lost structures included the tower where Queen Mary of Scots was held captive in 1568, as well as the royal apartments and the governor's apartments.

The outer ward contains many structures that testify to the castle's continued military importance into modern times, notably a parade ground (now partly grassed over), late Georgian barrack blocks, and a former

Figure A.6. Fifteenth-century carvings made by prisoners held in the castle (*photograph: Mark Brennand*)

officers' mess (1876), now the county headquarters of the Duke of Lancaster's Regiment. The histories of the various regiments associated with the castle are commemorated on site in the Museum of the Border and King's Own Royal Border Regiments (separate admission charge).

The Citadel

Stefan von Haschenperg built the citadel, which marks the southern end of the medieval city, in 1542 (Figure 9.3). It was erected as part of a national defence system commissioned by King Henry VIII. As originally planned, it had a central rectangular bastion or tower and two smaller round towers, each protected at the front by artillery emplacements. After helping to defend the city in two sieges, the central bastion was removed to make a new entrance into the city centre. In 1807 conversion of the lesser towers into courthouses for the Cumberland assizes began under the direction of Thomas Telford and Sir Robert Smirke, and the new courts opened in 1823. Extensive renovation work then and since means that little early stonework survives, but the original Tudor gun ports of the east tower can still be seen at ground level. The west tower is open to tour groups (admission charge).

The City Walls

Most of the city walls have disappeared. They were in ruins at the beginning of the nineteenth century, and so were largely demolished between 1811 and 1815. However, some stretches of the west wall, overlooking the railway, a car park on English Damside and the River Caldew, do survive, though they are in part obscured by buildings. A walk along the street behind them (West Walls) gives a good impression of how the city sits above the flood plain on the river cliff. Two shorter lengths of the city wall can also be viewed near the castle. One runs close to the modern footbridge over the dual carriageway (Castle Way), and includes the fourteenth-century Tile Tower (Figure 6.7); the other runs between the road and the other end of the castle.

The Guildhall

This timber-framed building, facing the Greenmarket, was erected by Richard de Redness in 1407 (Figure 8.2), a date that has been confirmed by dendrochronology. It was built as four medieval tenements, with shops on the ground floor and living quarters above. This can be appreciated from the inside where parts of the partitions between the tenements survive. Also visible are the carpenters' marks, which show how the building was prefabricated and then re-erected on site. The main entrance to de Redness's dwelling, which lay behind the tenements, was on Fisher Street, and now forms the way into an Italian restaurant. The Guildhall is the only domestic medieval building in Carlisle, and its interior can be visited. Admission is free, but access is by a steep staircase. The Guildhall Museum also houses artefacts connected with the political, civic and retail history of the city, as well as information about the building itself.

The Mills

The original mills in Carlisle were water-powered and the Denton Holme millrace can still be seen running along Shaddongate. It exits from the River Caldew at Denton Holme and rejoins it at Willowholme.

One of the most impressive mills was Shaddon Mill, founded in 1836 on Shaddongate (Figures 10.2 and 10.5). It was built to run on steam, using water from the millrace. It was designed by Robert Tattersall and engineered by William Fairbairn, both from Manchester. The chimney, one of the few that now survive, is 305 feet (92.96m) high even though the stone topping has been removed. When opened Shaddon was the largest cotton mill in the country. It is now a series of luxury flats.

The Citadel Railway Station

In Carlisle's heyday as a railway city, seven companies ran into Citadel station, which was opened in 1847 (Figure 11.3). The mock Tudor design was by Sir William Tite, designer of the Royal Exchange in London. As rail traffic increased the station was expanded in 1862 and 1880, when the iron and glass roof was put in. In the 1950s some of this roof was replaced with steel and cut back to the roof that survives today. New end screens and low canopies over the platforms were installed during this refurbishment.

The Market Hall

The purpose-built covered market was erected in 1889 (Figure A.7). The local crane-makers, Cowan Sheldon & Company, made the roof. Originally the market included what is now TK Maxx and Wilkinsons, and today the roof can best be viewed from the TK Maxx store. Evidence of the different markets and their building-dates can be seen from the collection of inscribed commemorative tablets placed above the entrance in Fisher Street.

Figure A.7. The market hall (*photograph: author*)

The Tram Depot

At the bottom of London Road where it is joined by St Cuthbert Street, opposite Halfords, is the original tram depot (Figure A.8). The building has a Dutch gable and is built on a curve, with an open area at the front where the trams emerged. Originally the building had a coat of arms on the front, but this has been removed. The building is next to the Newcastle–Carlisle railway line and may have been connected to London Road station, which was alongside (Figure 11.2).

Figure A.8. The former tram depot on London Road (*photograph: author*)

Tullie House Museum and Art Gallery

This is the main archaeological and local history museum in the city (admission charge), and its collections cover all the chief periods. There is an important assemblage of Roman material, including inscribed and sculptured stones from the city and the western end of Hadrian's Wall. The Viking burials from High Hesket (between Carlisle and Penrith) and Great Ormside (near Appleby) are on display, as well as a wide range of material spanning the last 400 years, including the English Civil Wars and the 1745 Jacobite Rebellion. There is also a collection of railway memorabilia.